MW01629378

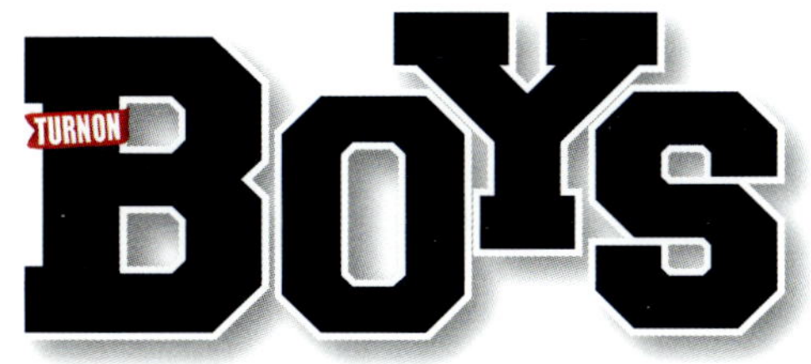

BRUNO GMÜNDER

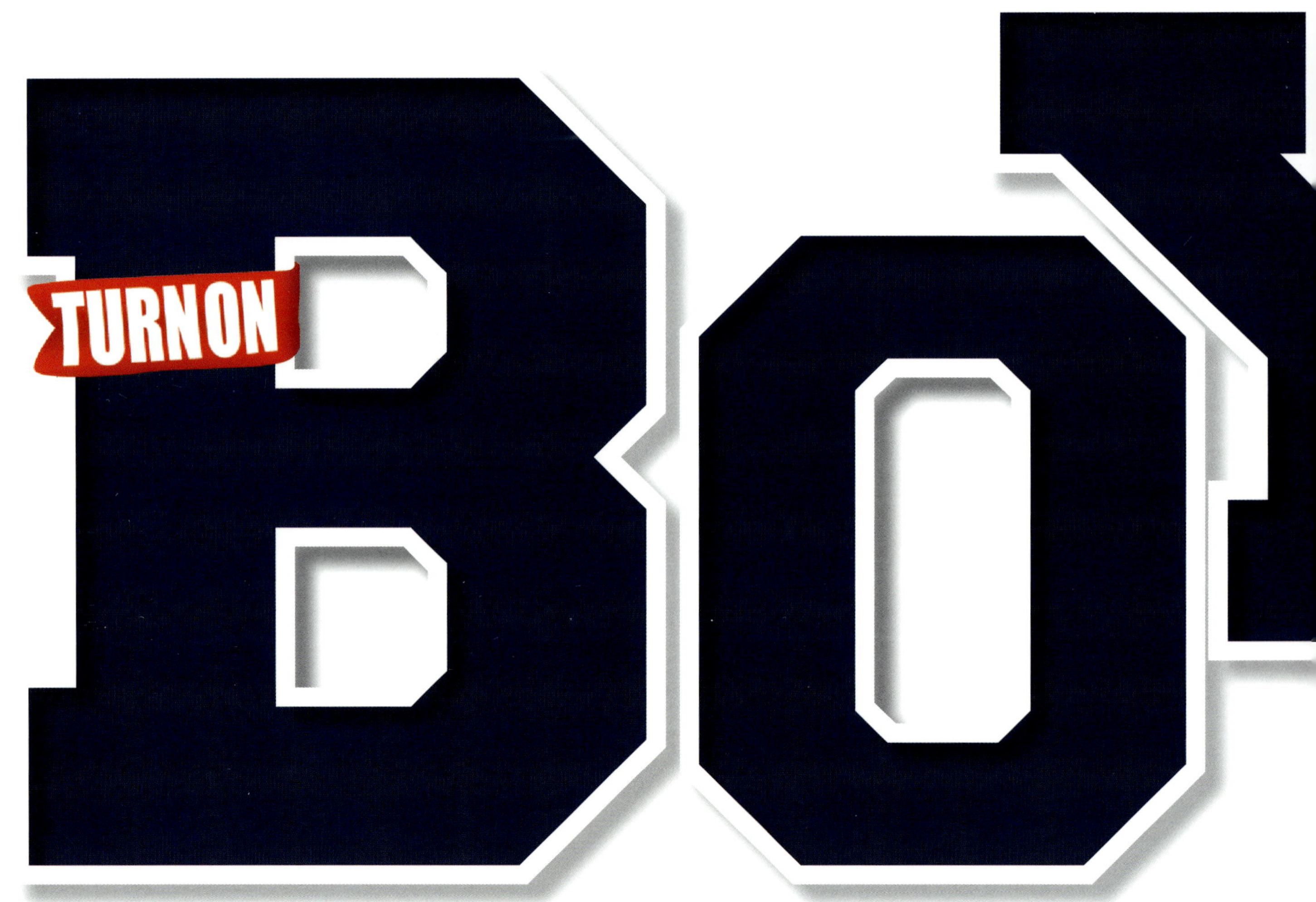

TURNON
BO

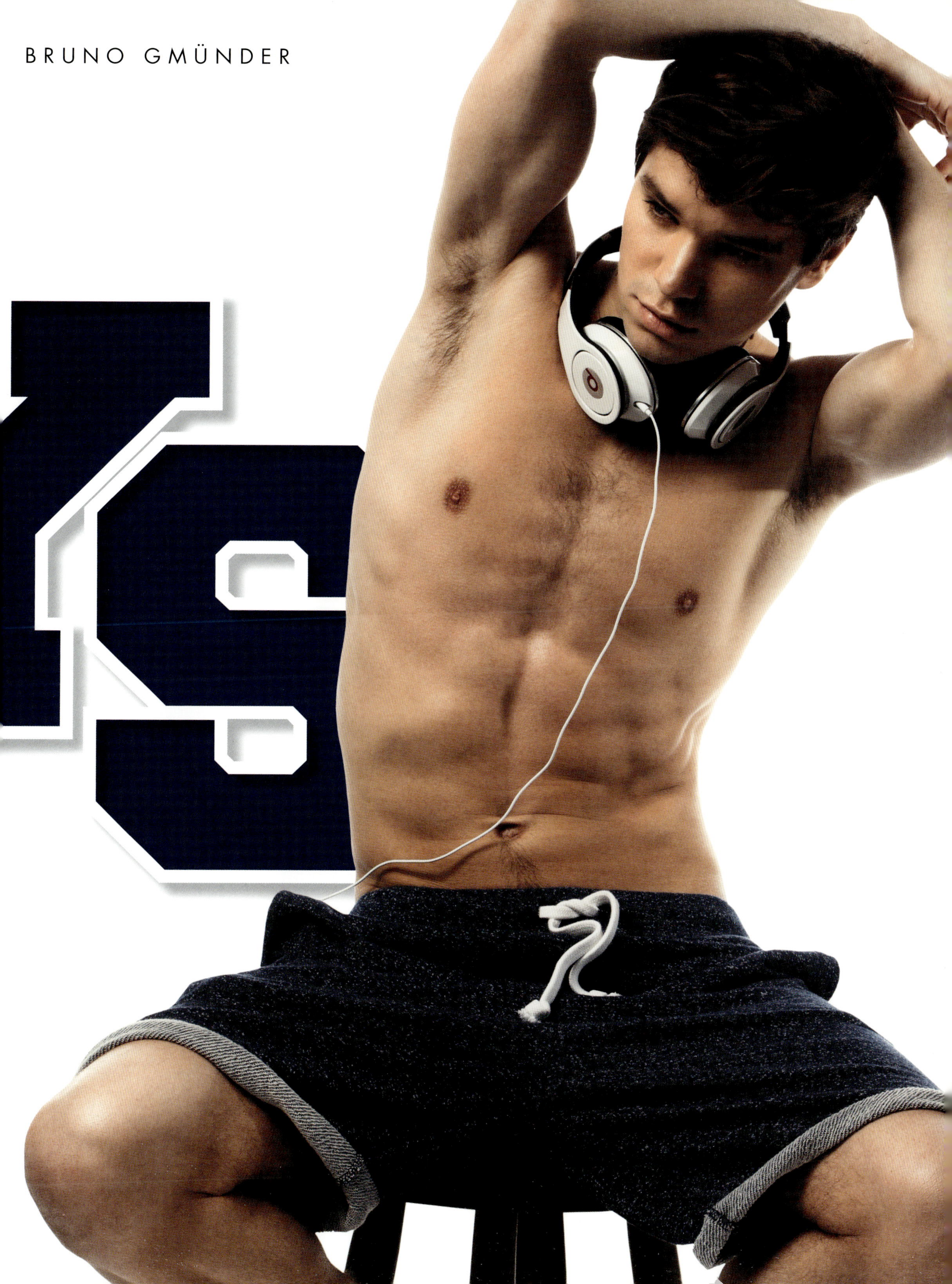

BRUNO GMÜNDER

THIS BOOK
IS ABOUT BOYS,
THEIR YOUTH,
THEIR BEAUTY.

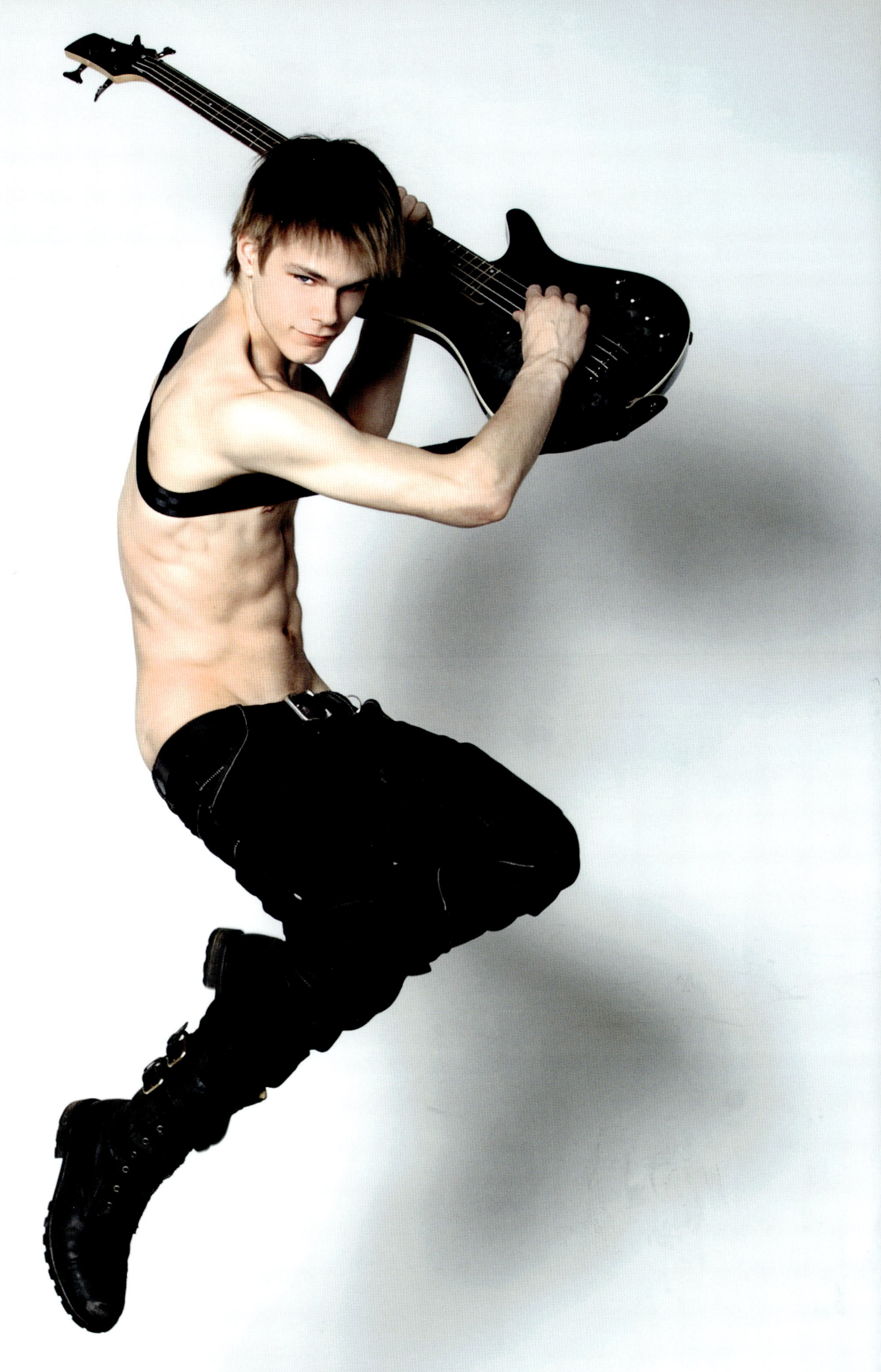

Michael Andrew

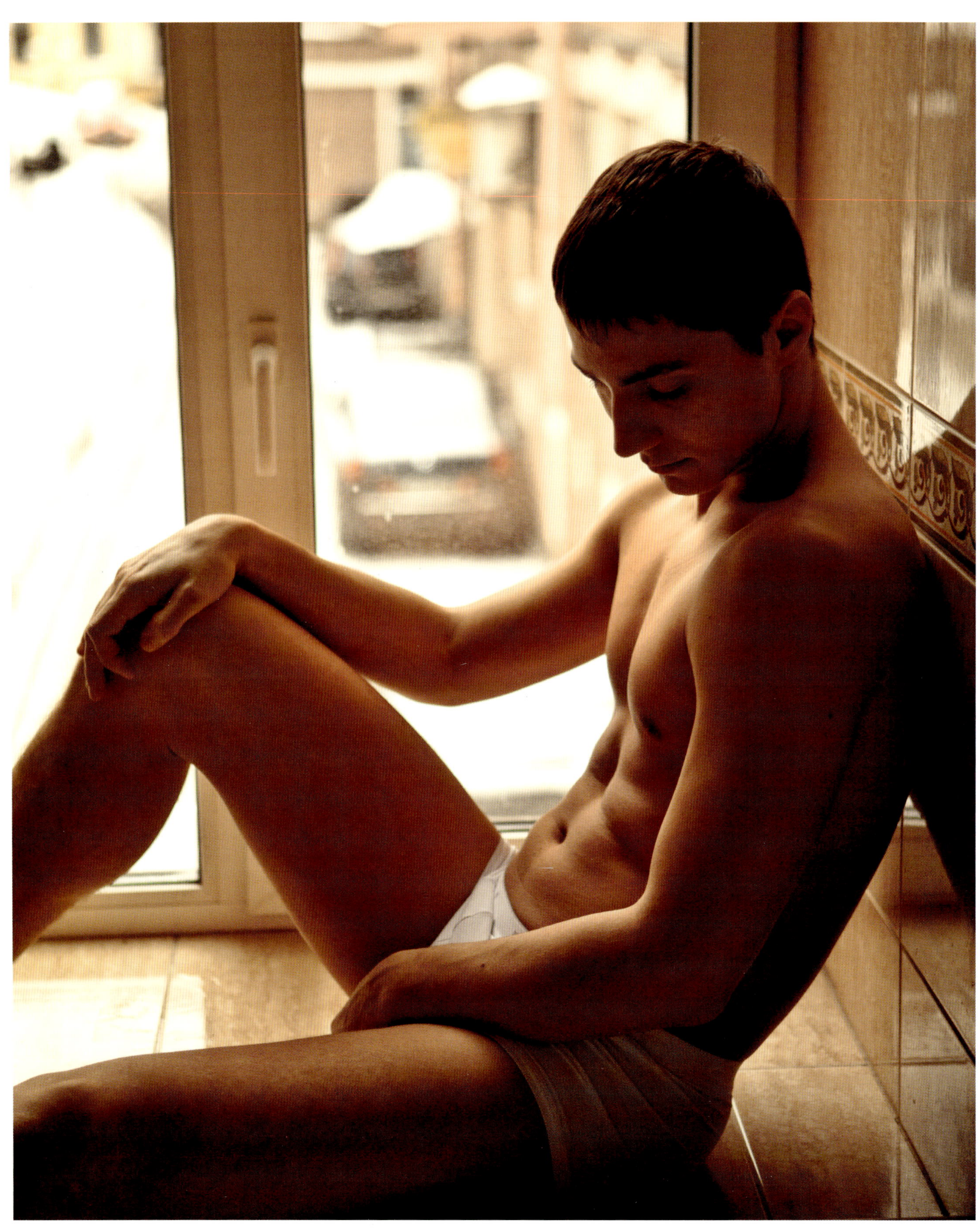

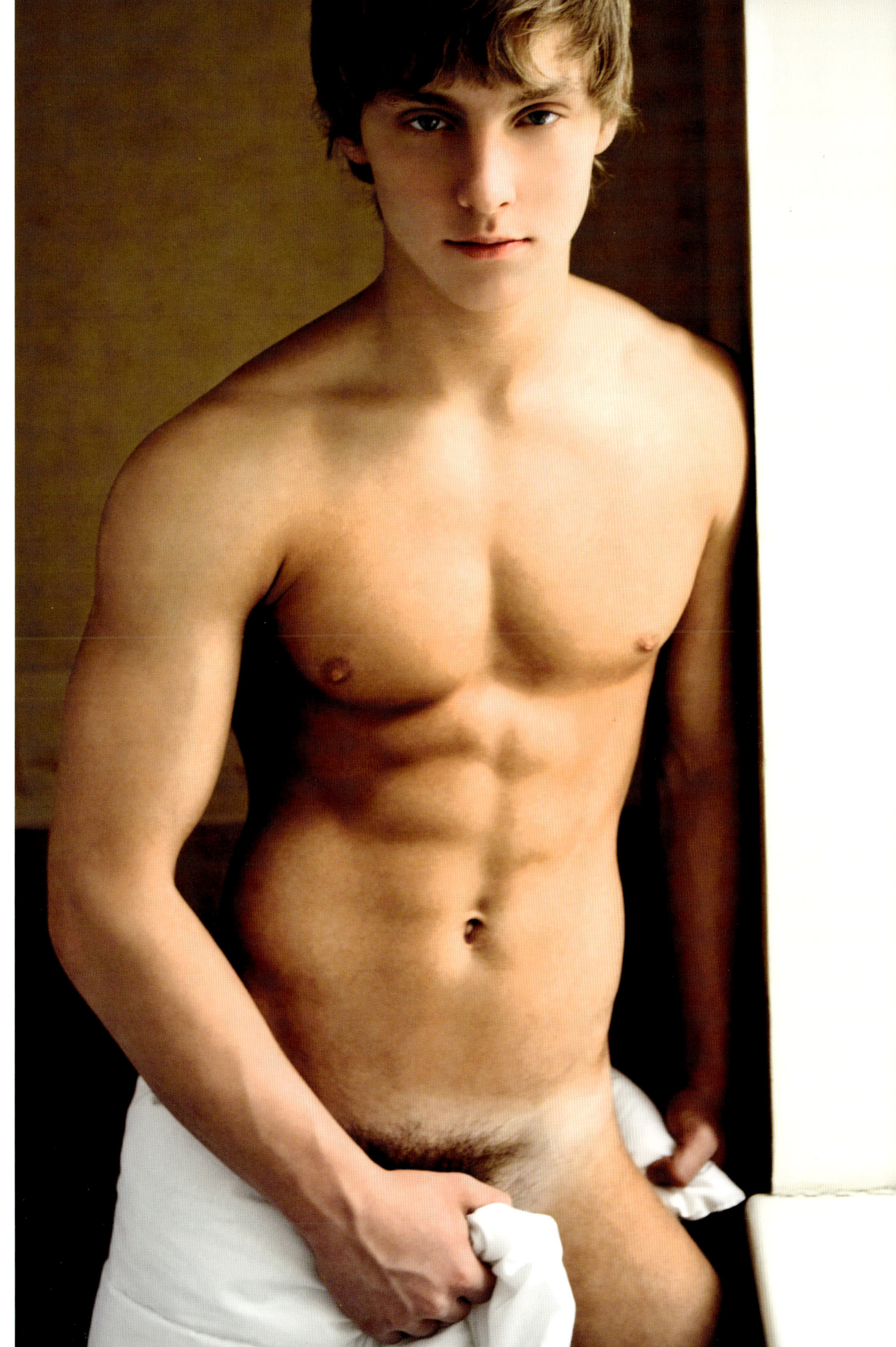

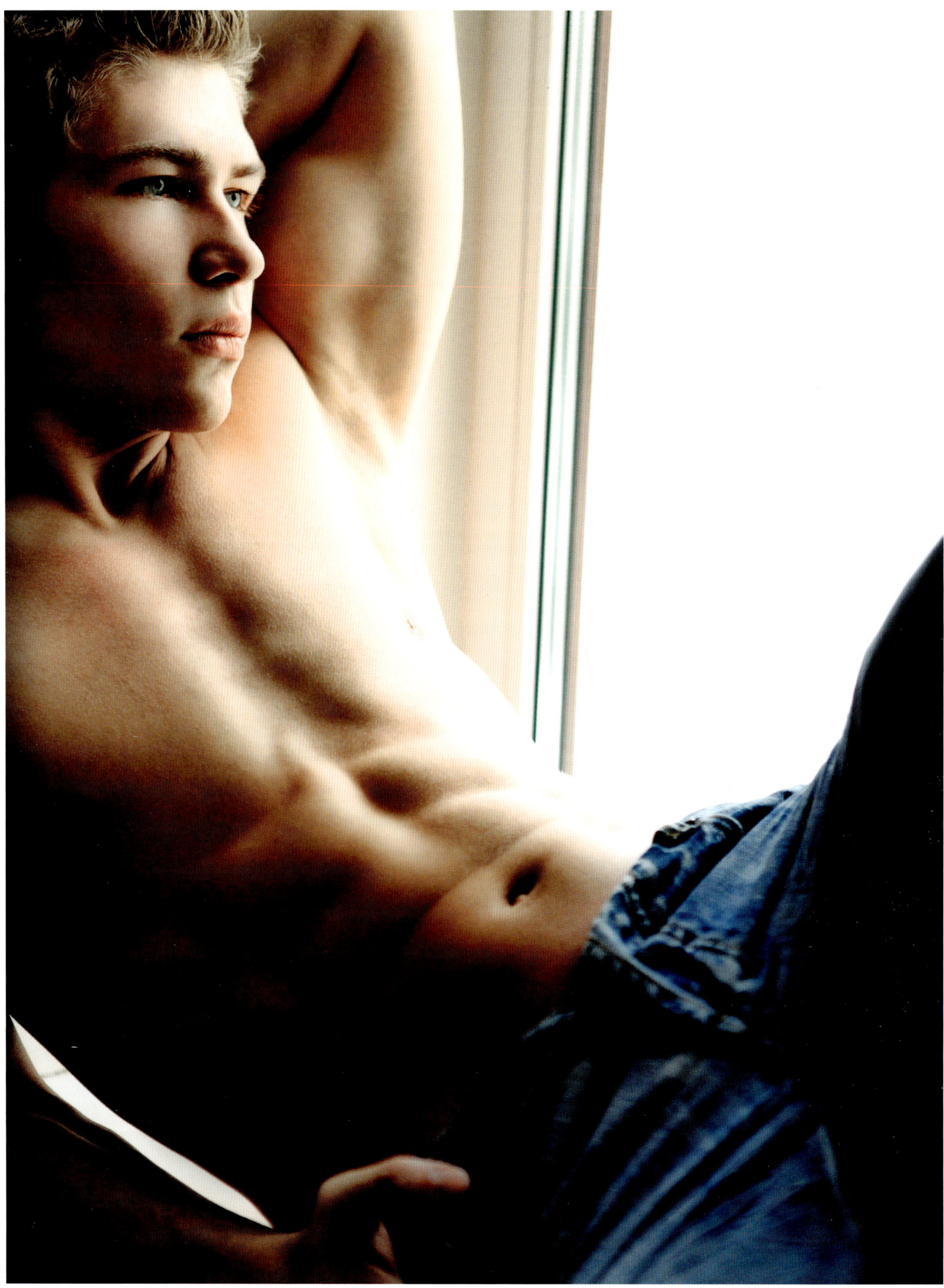

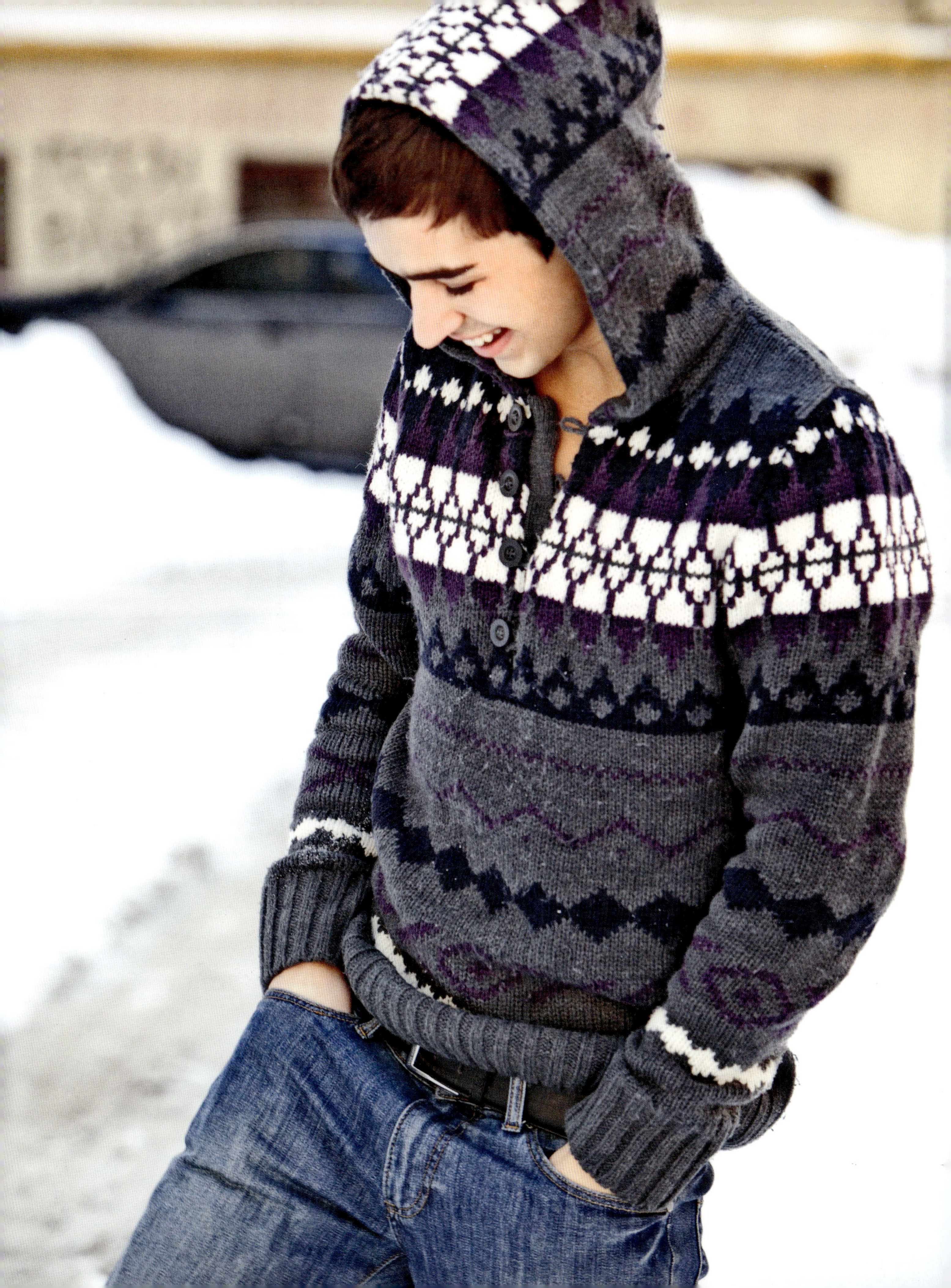

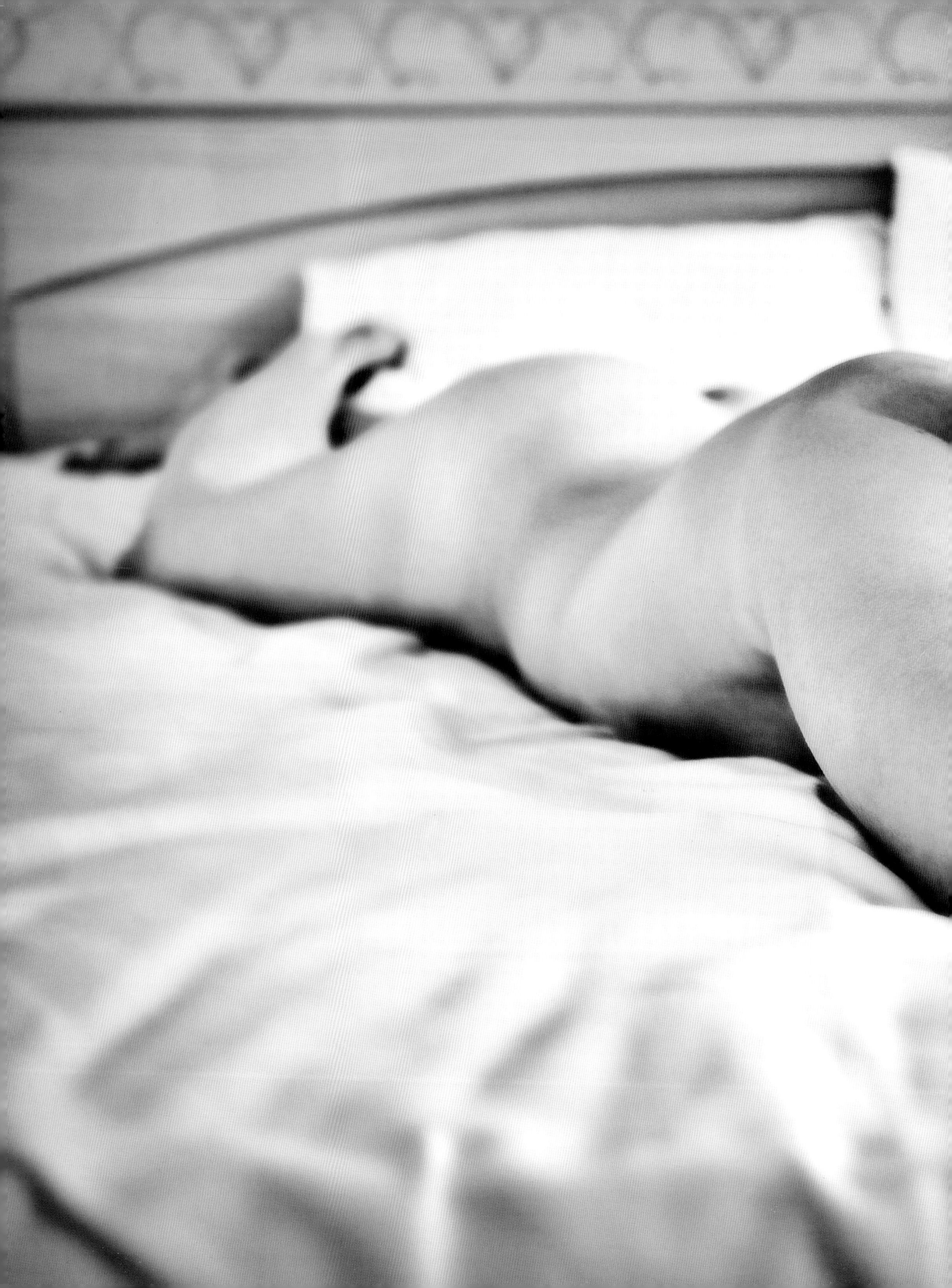

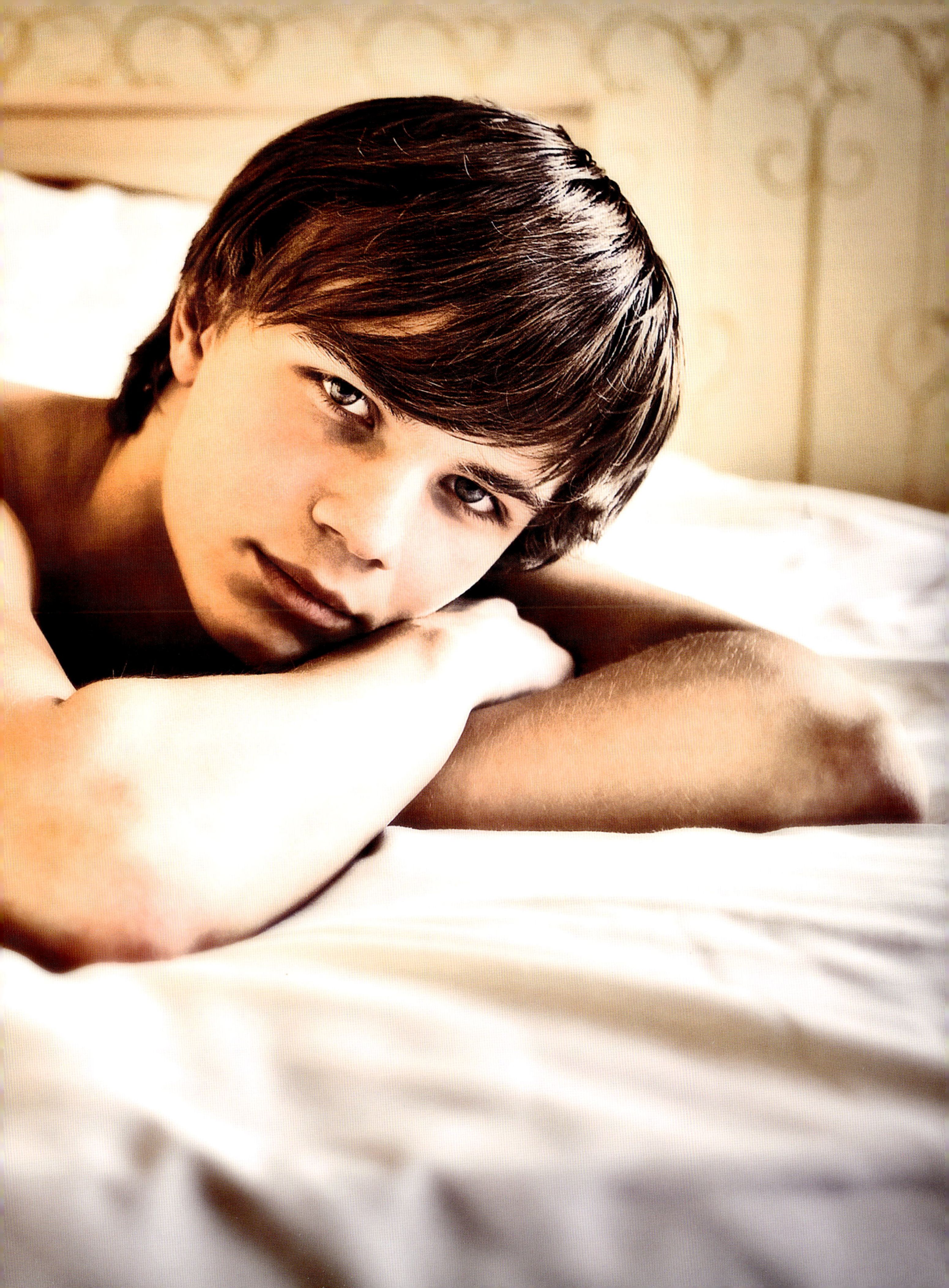

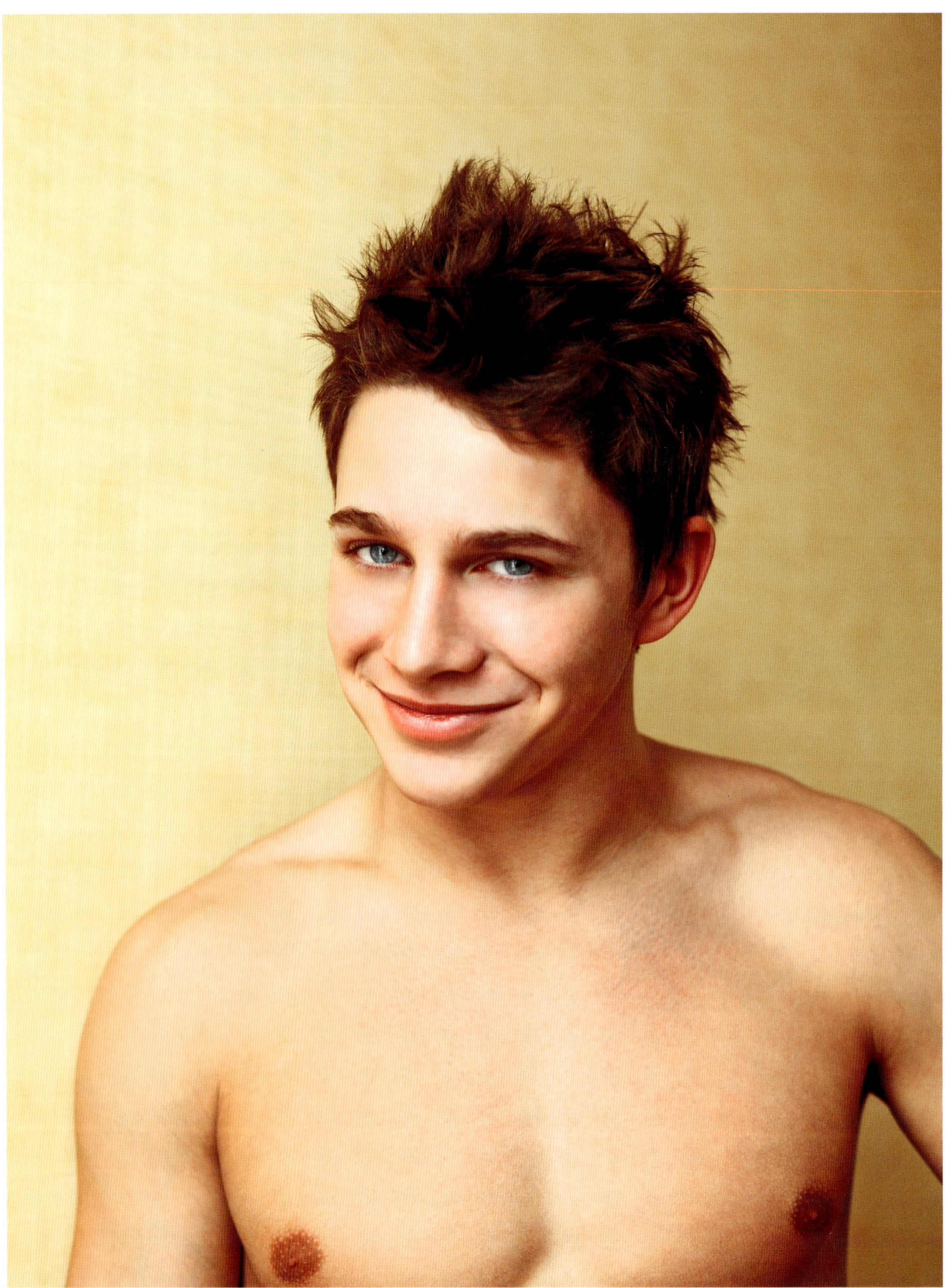

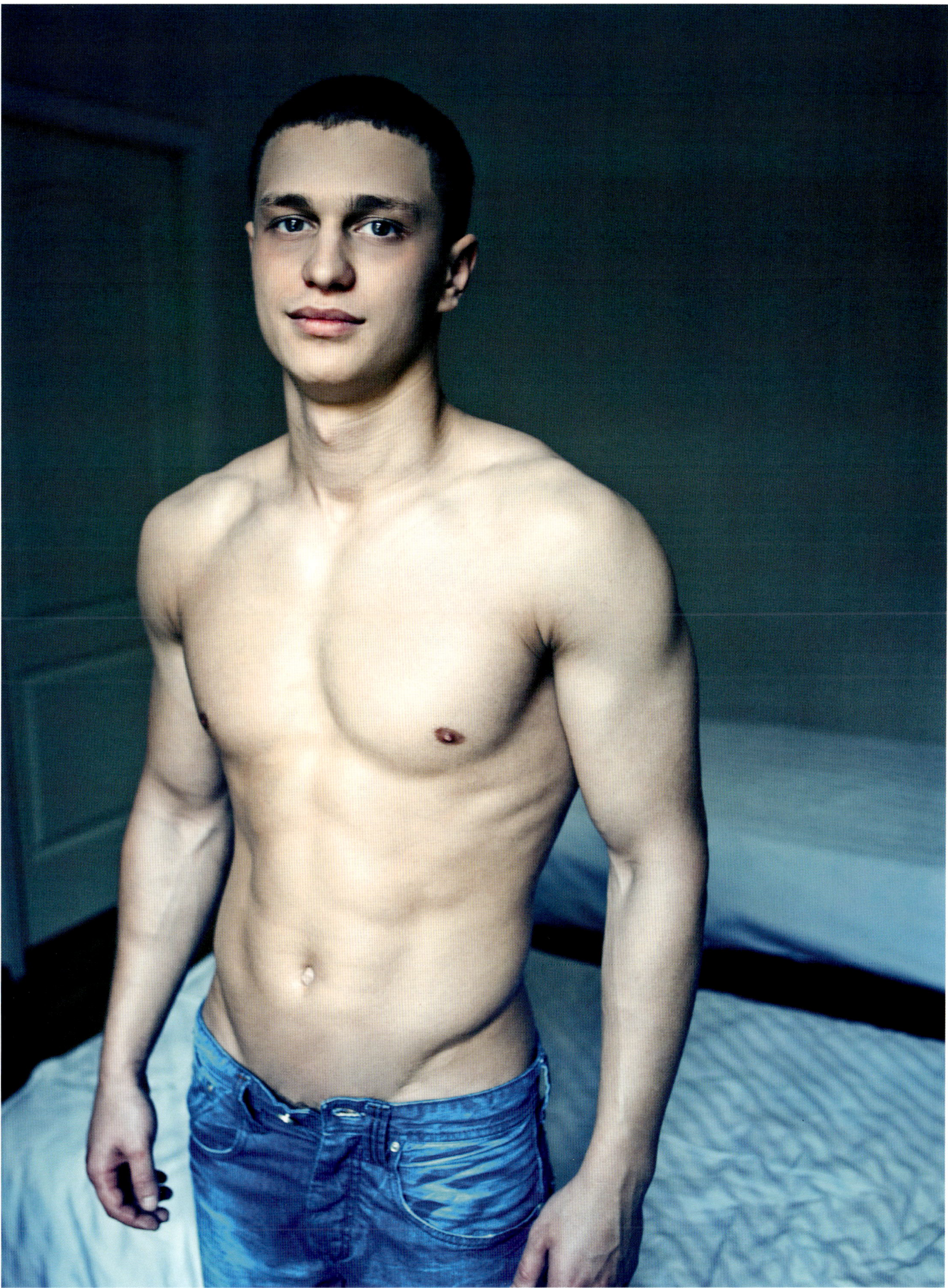

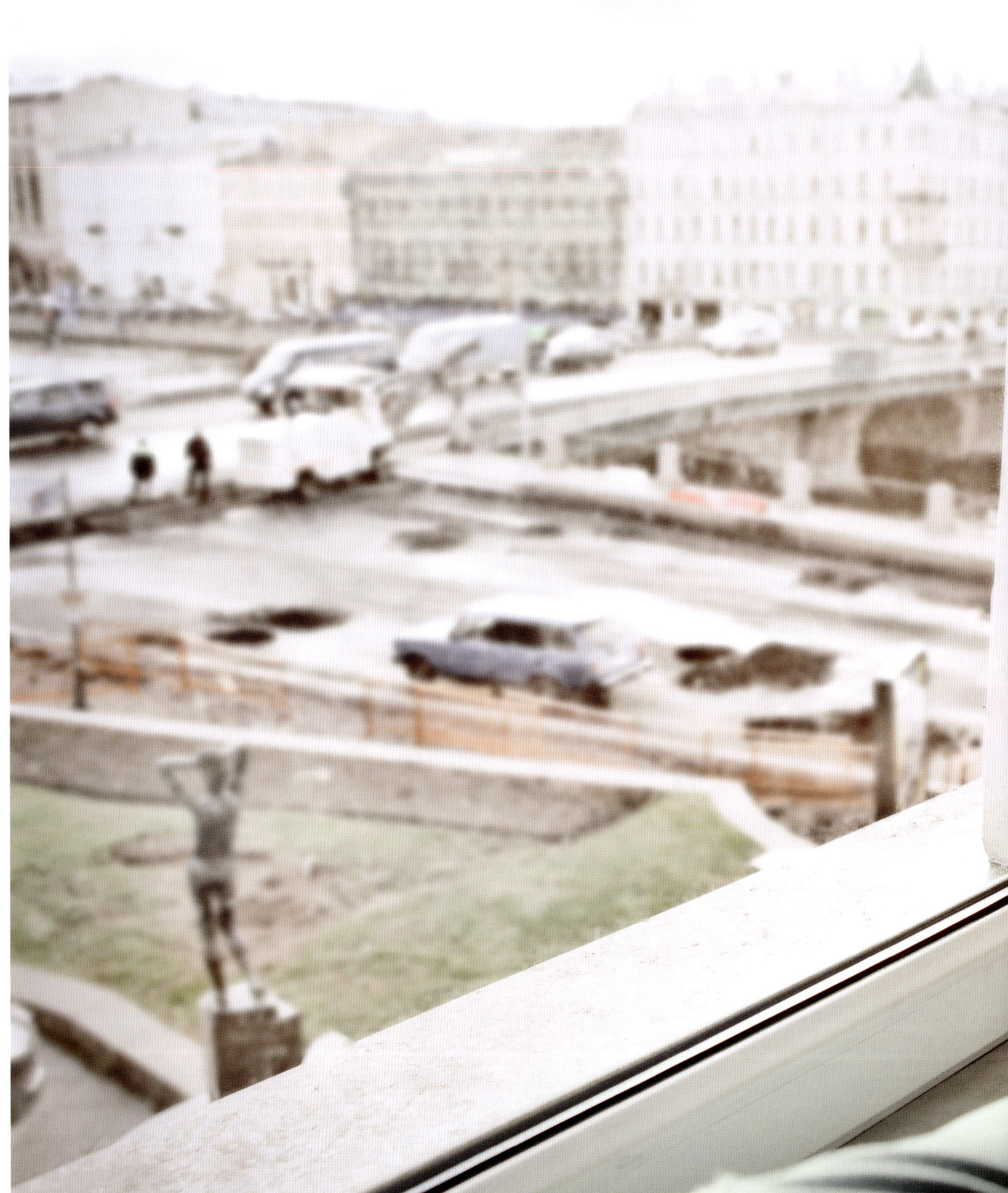

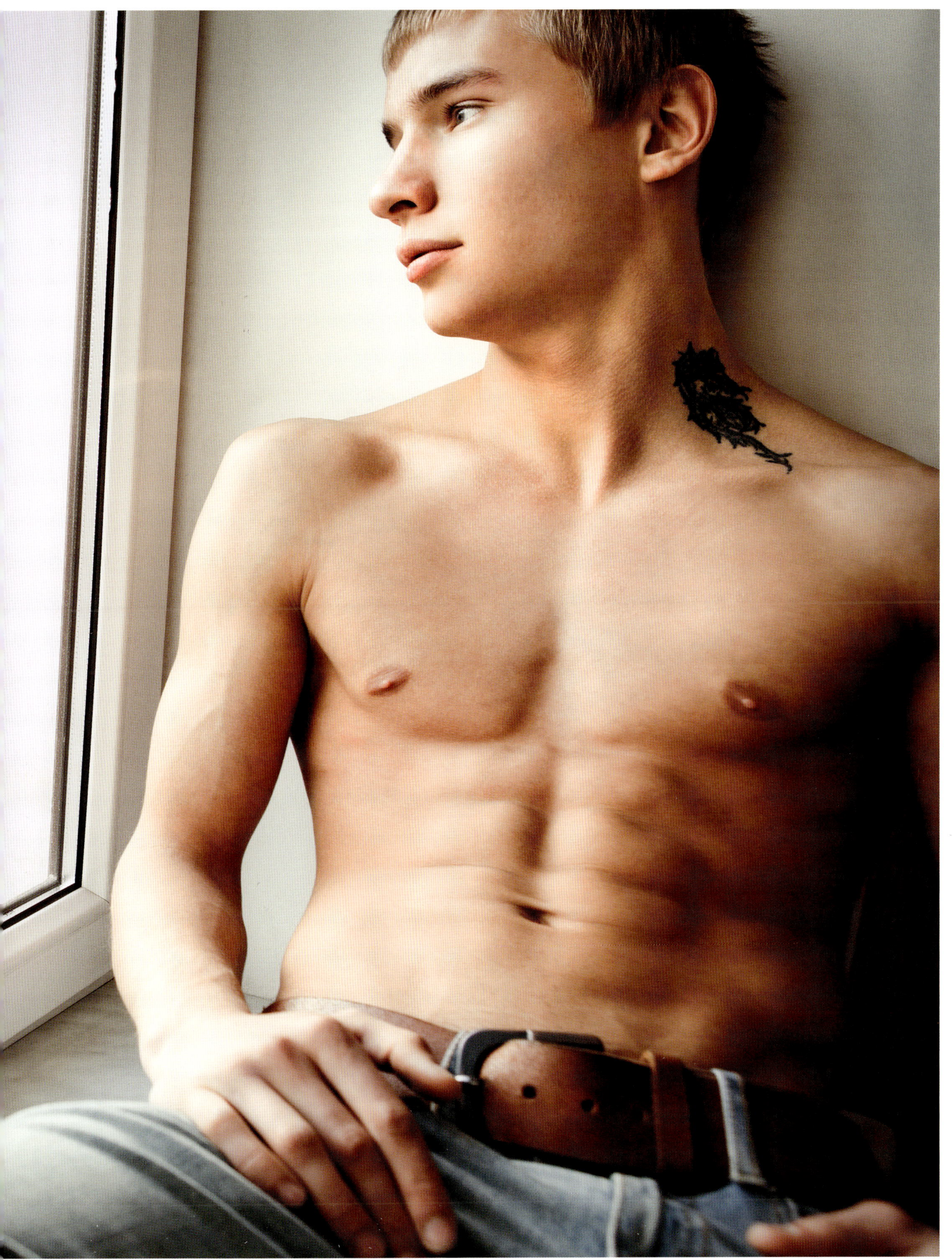

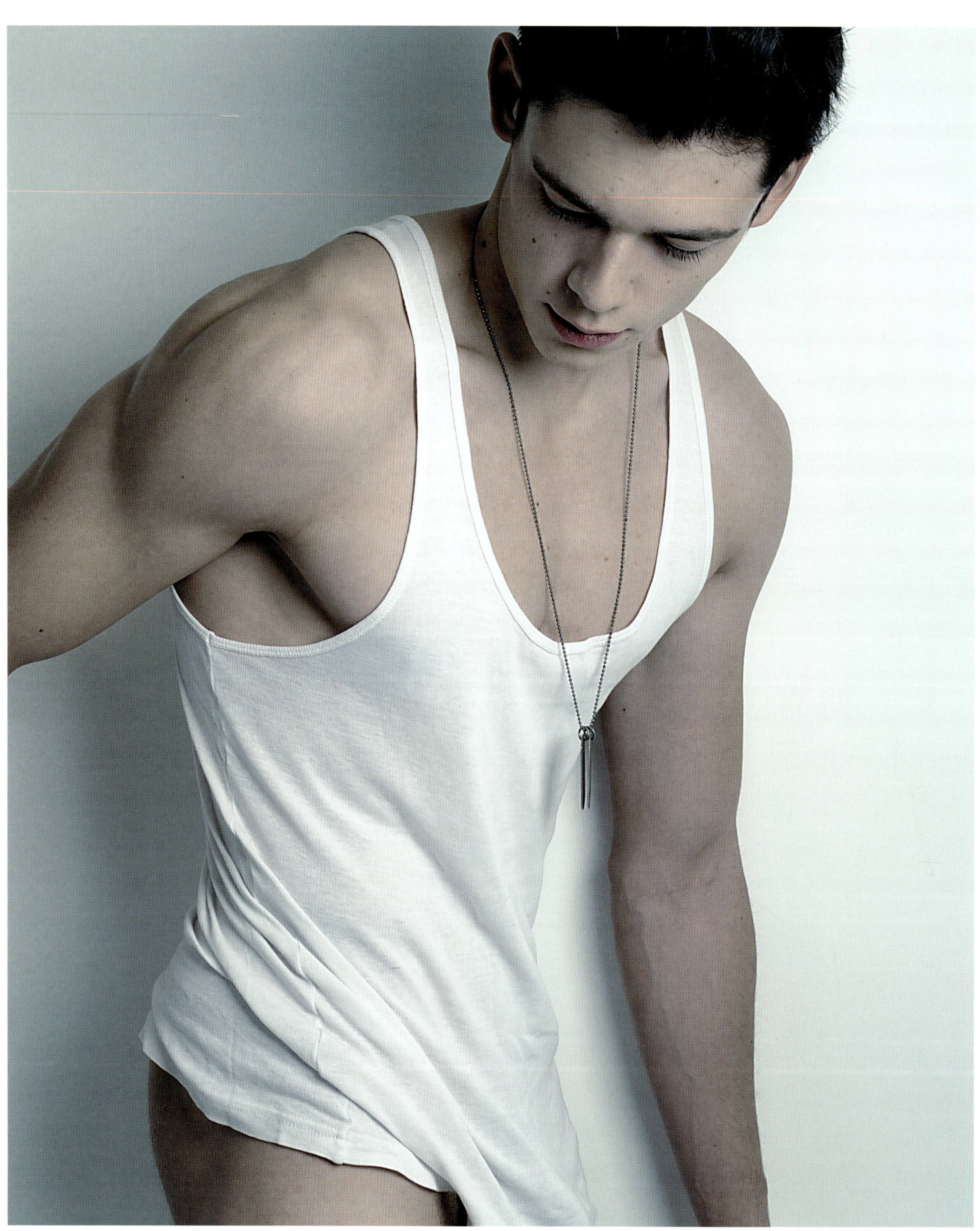

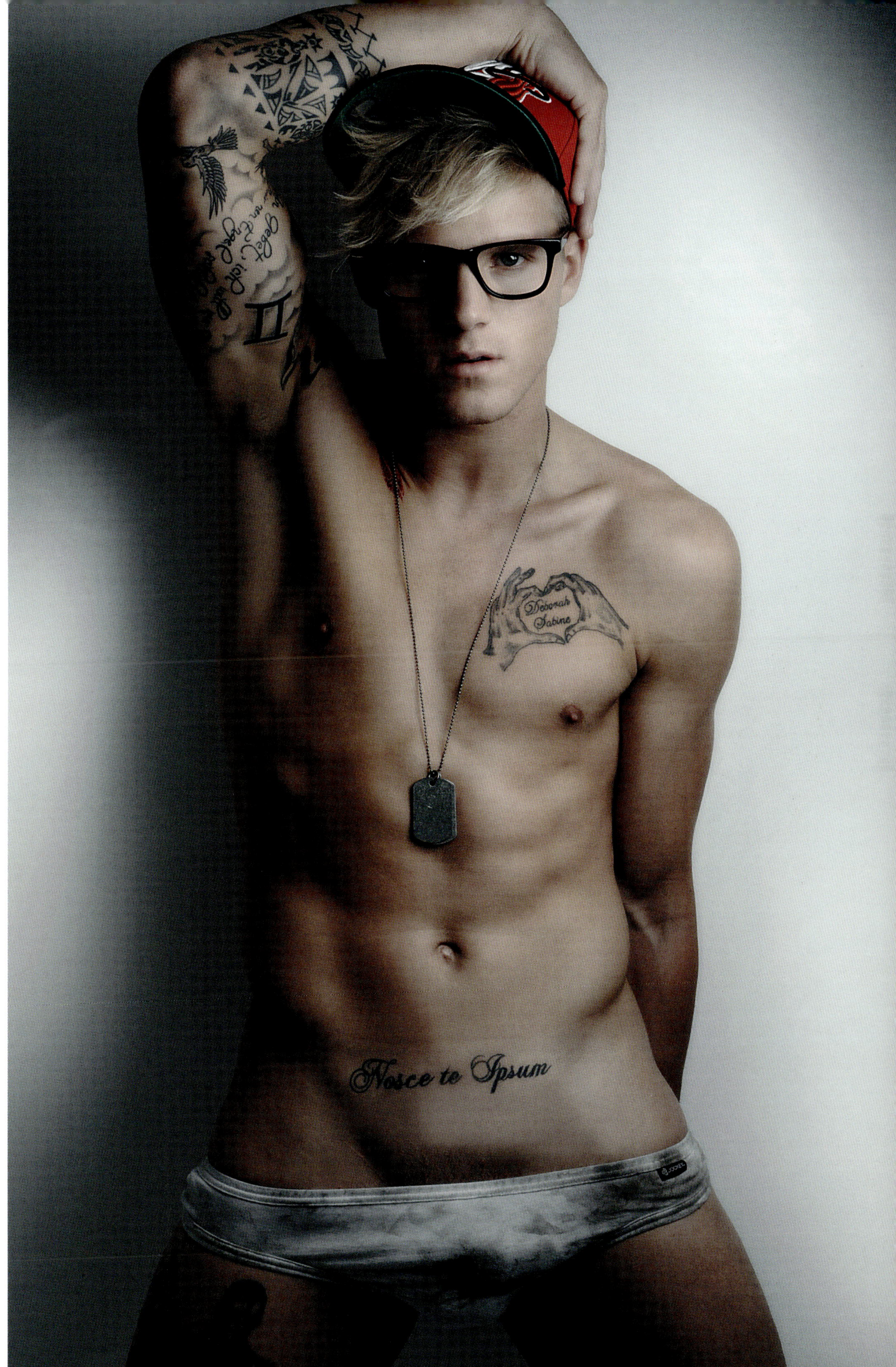
Deborah
Sabine
Nosce te Ipsum

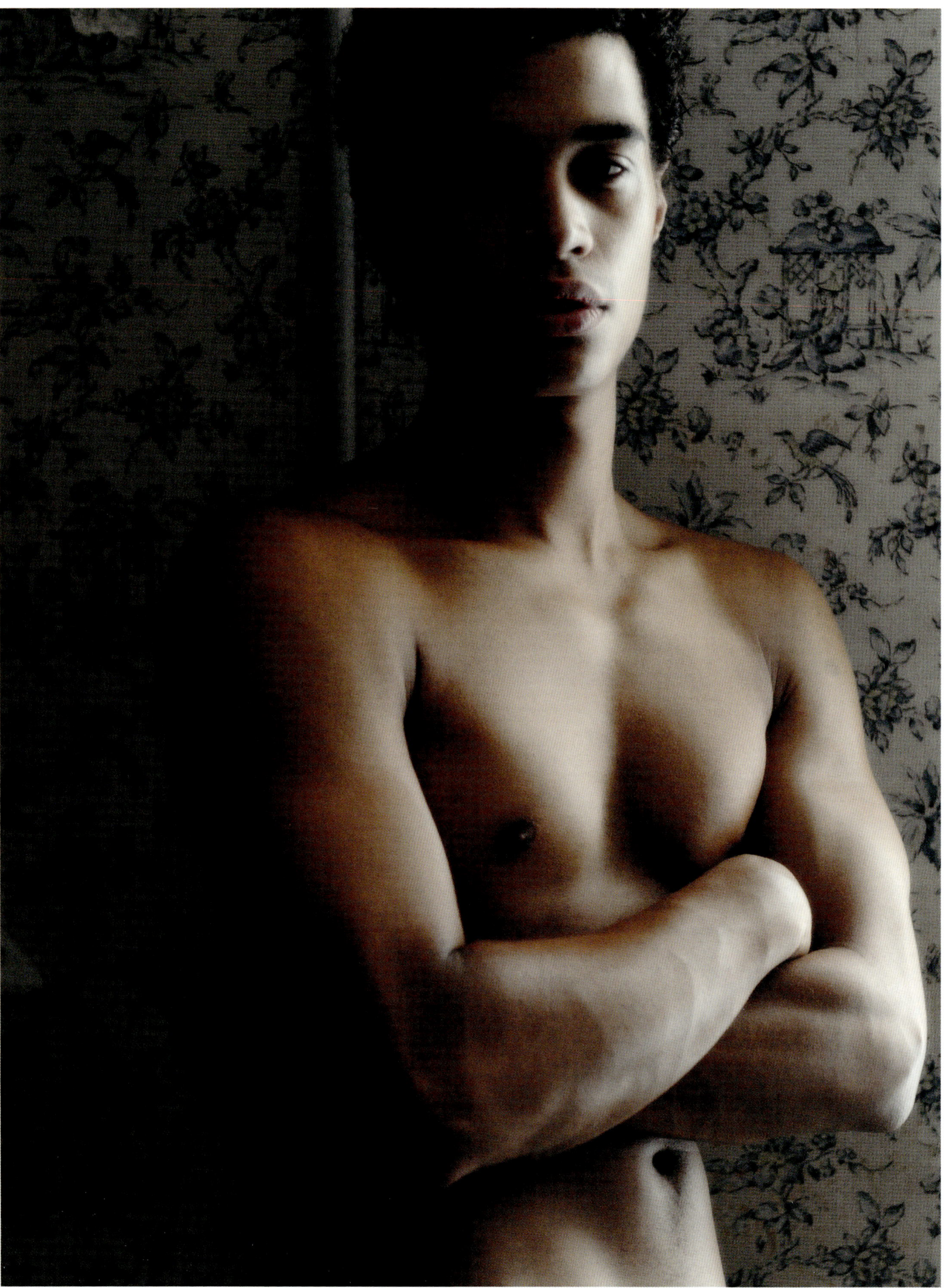

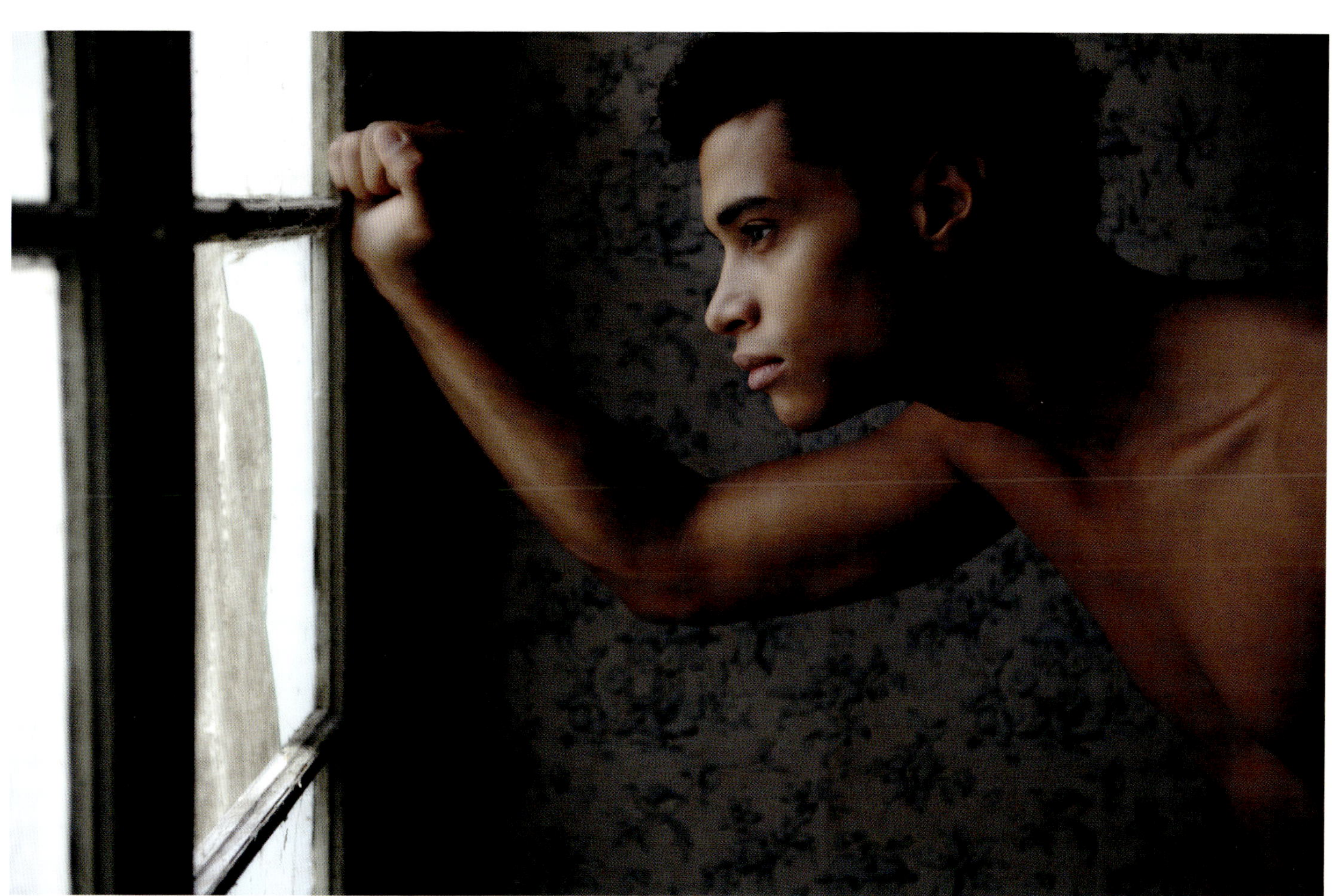

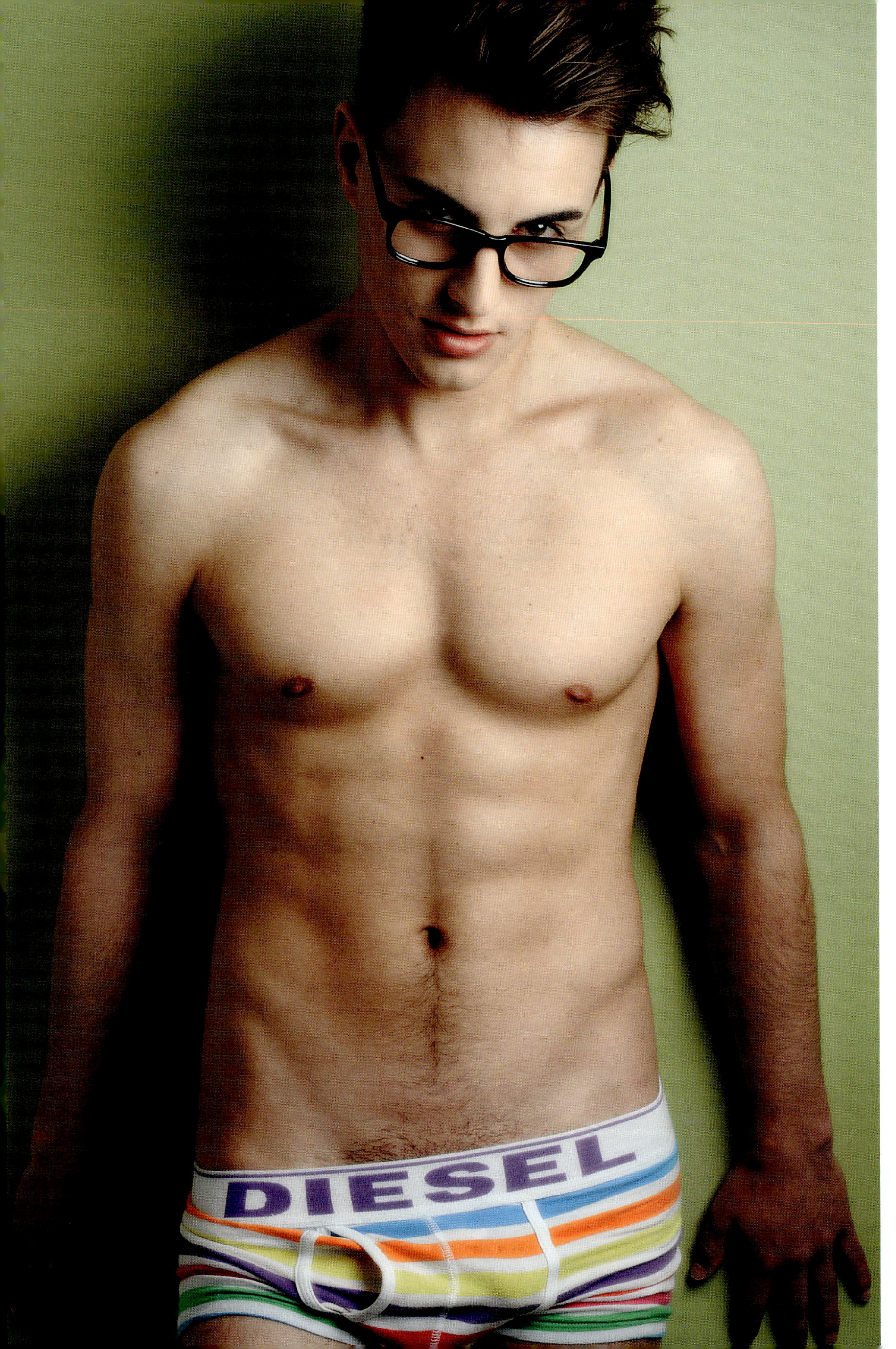
DIESEL

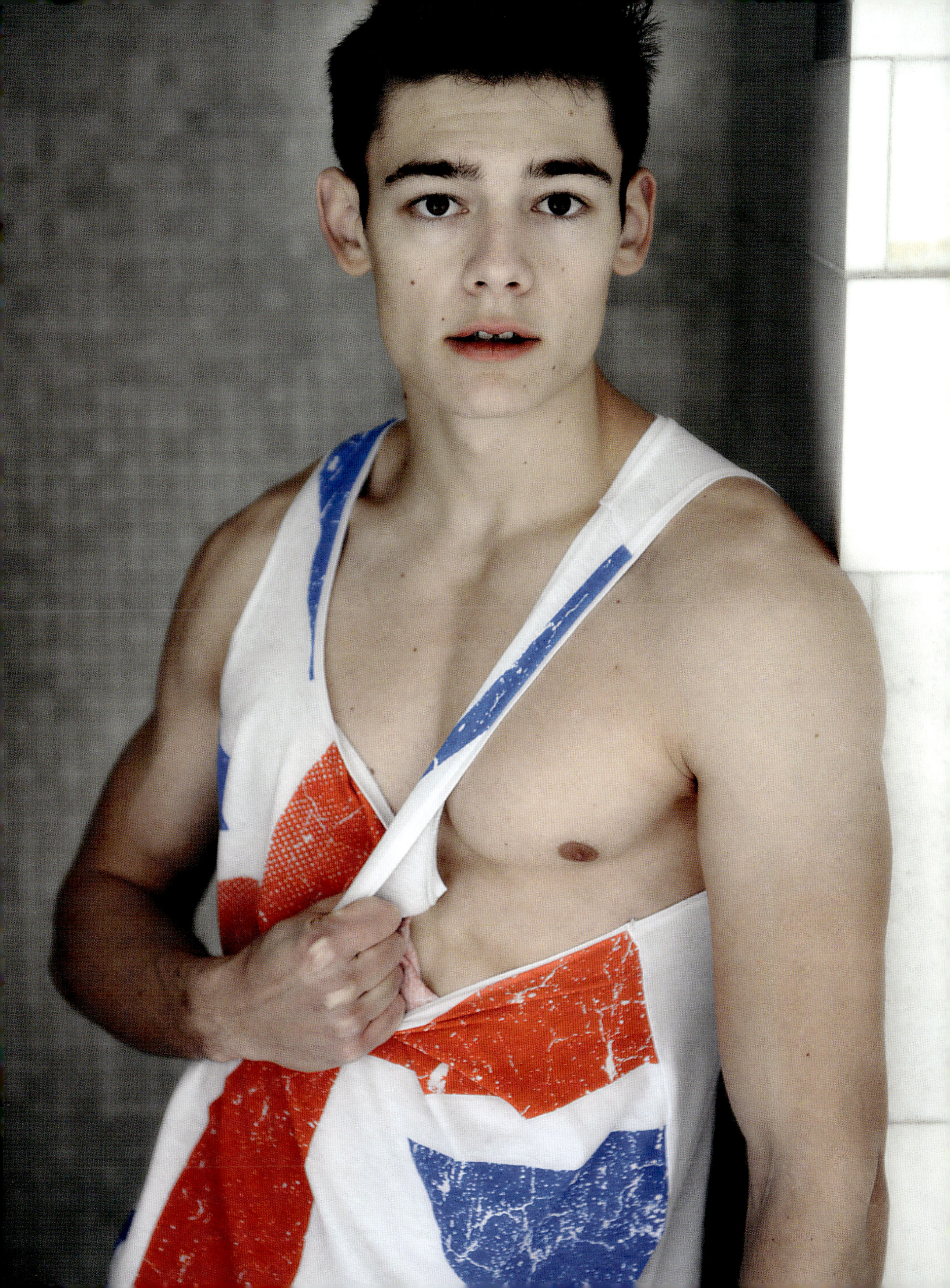

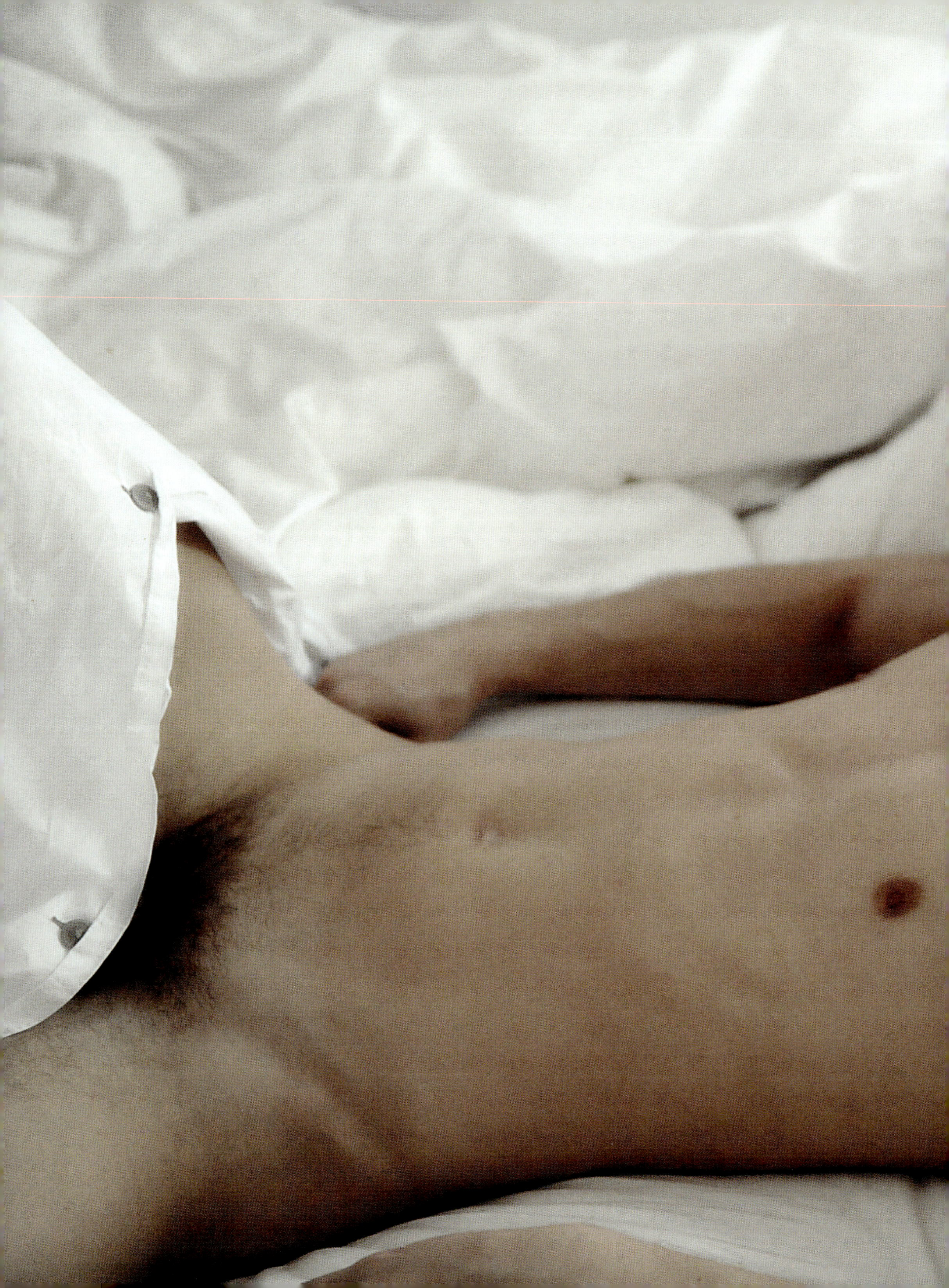

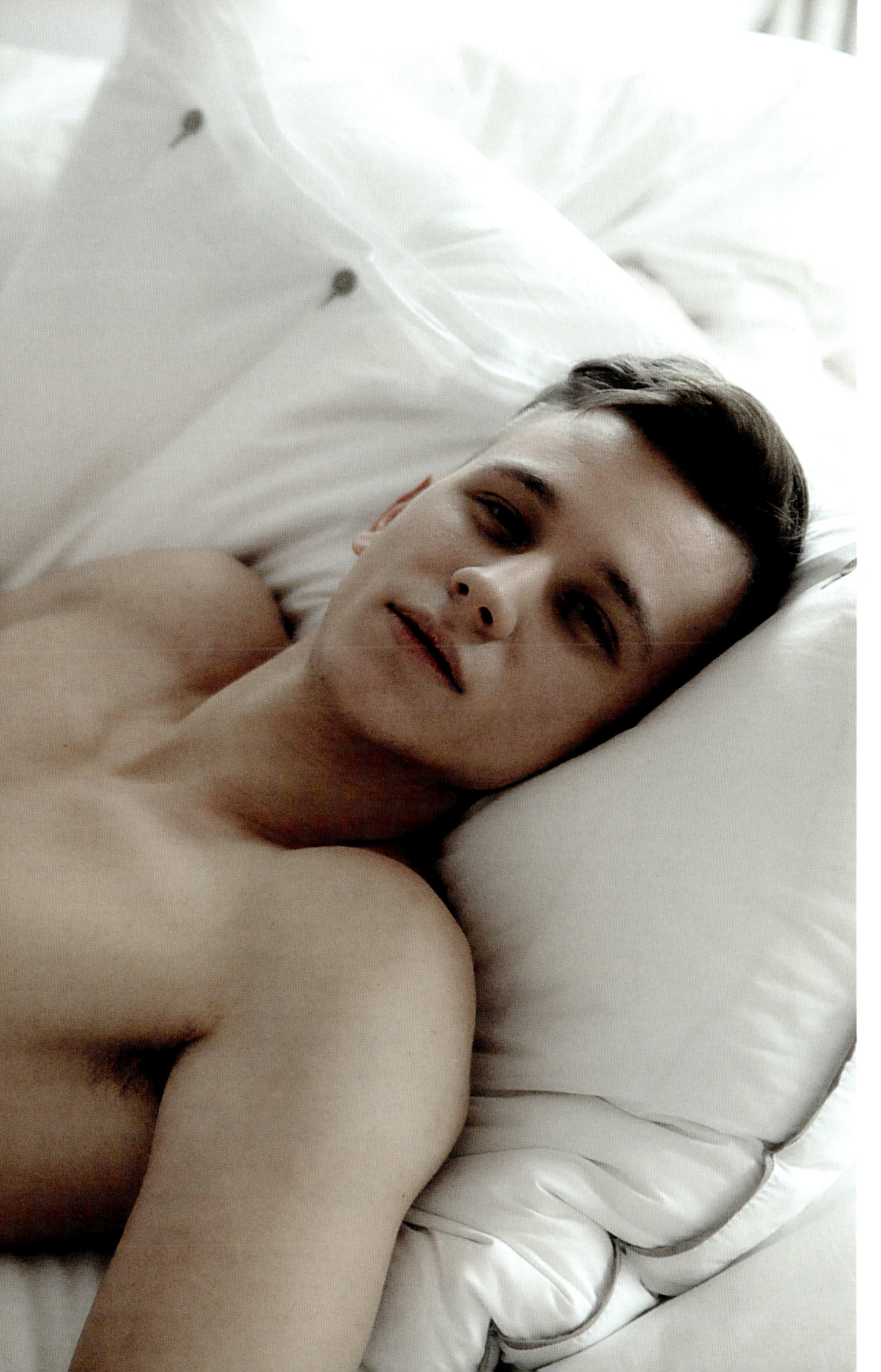

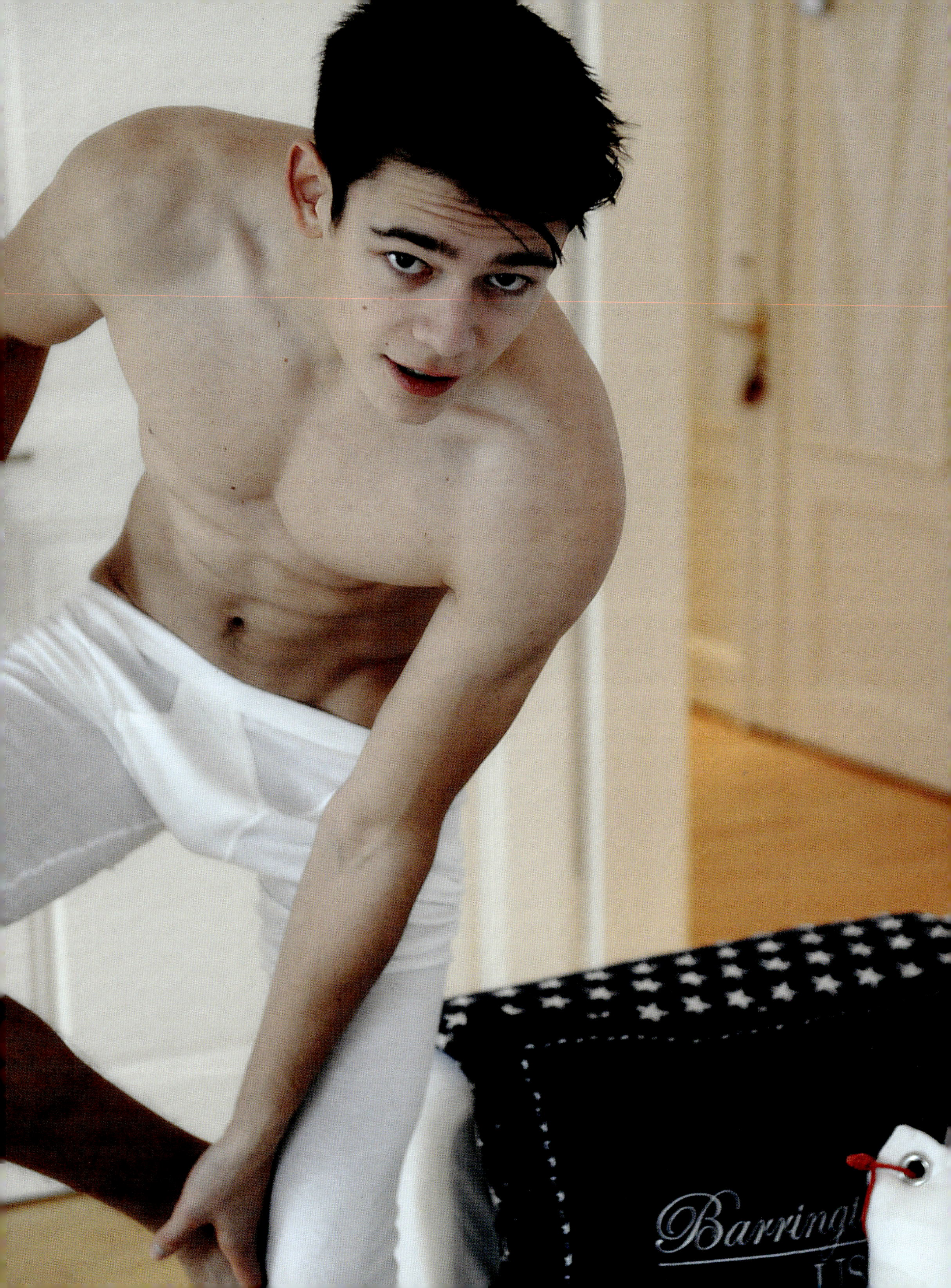

Barringt
US

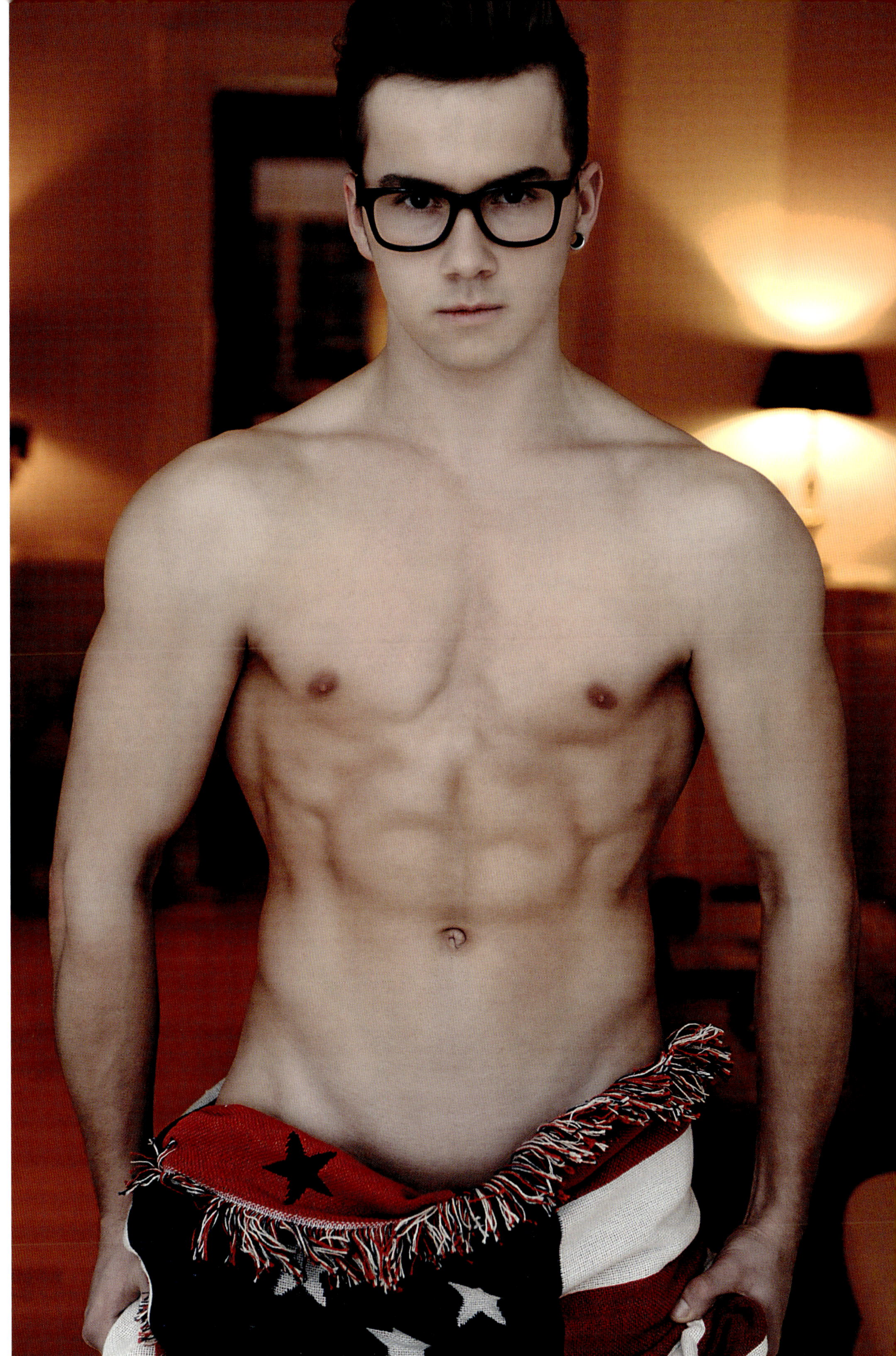

BARTLOMIEJ CHABALOWSKI

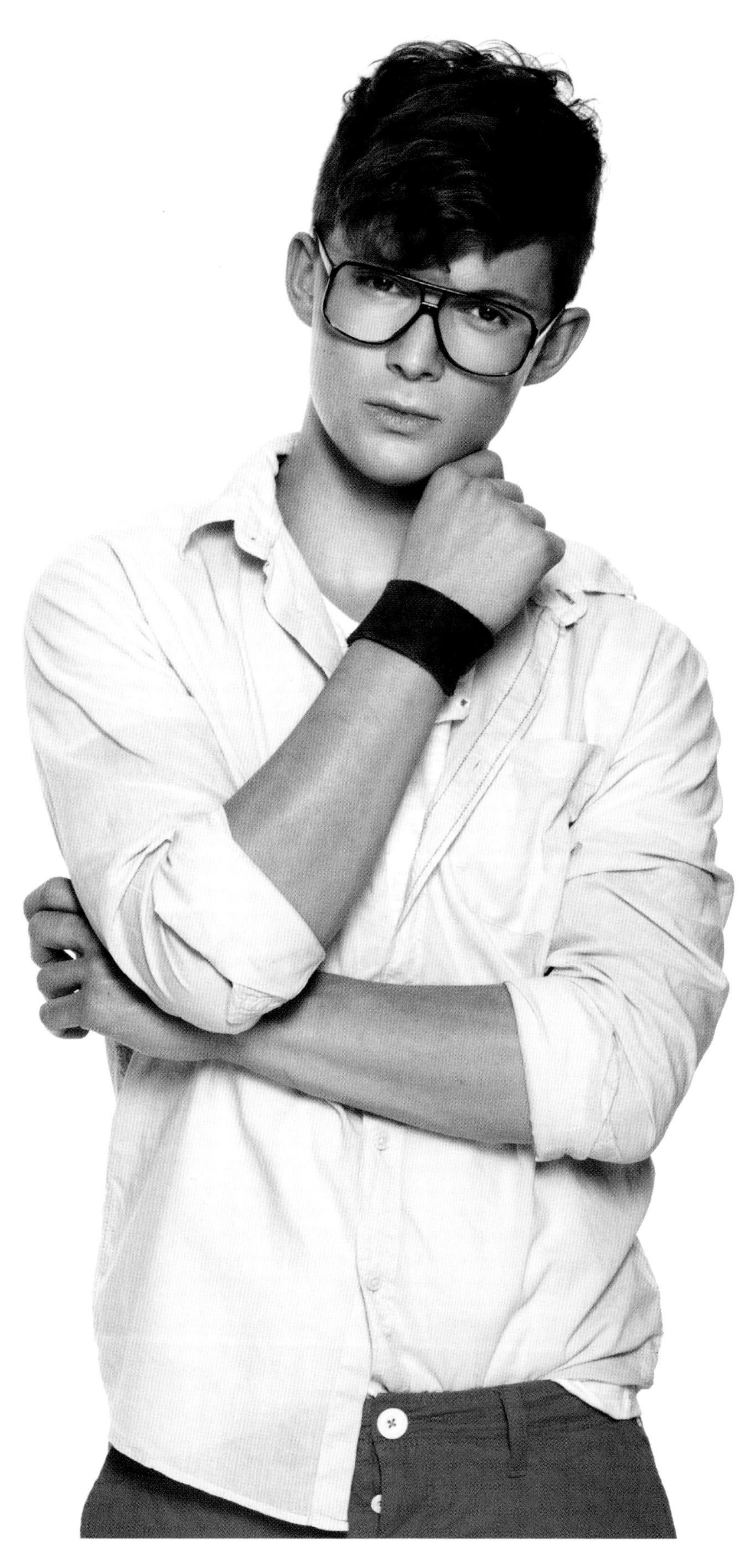

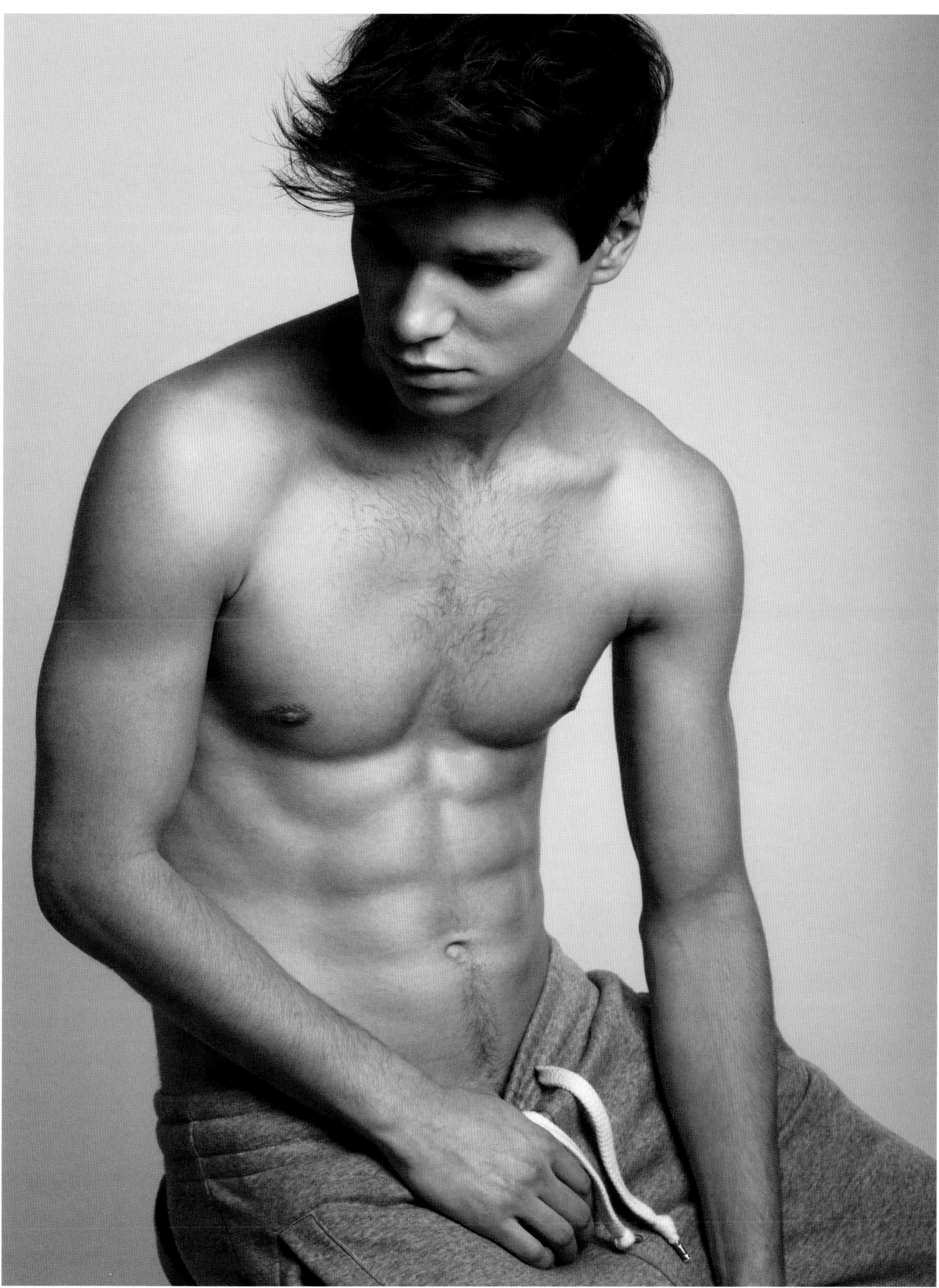

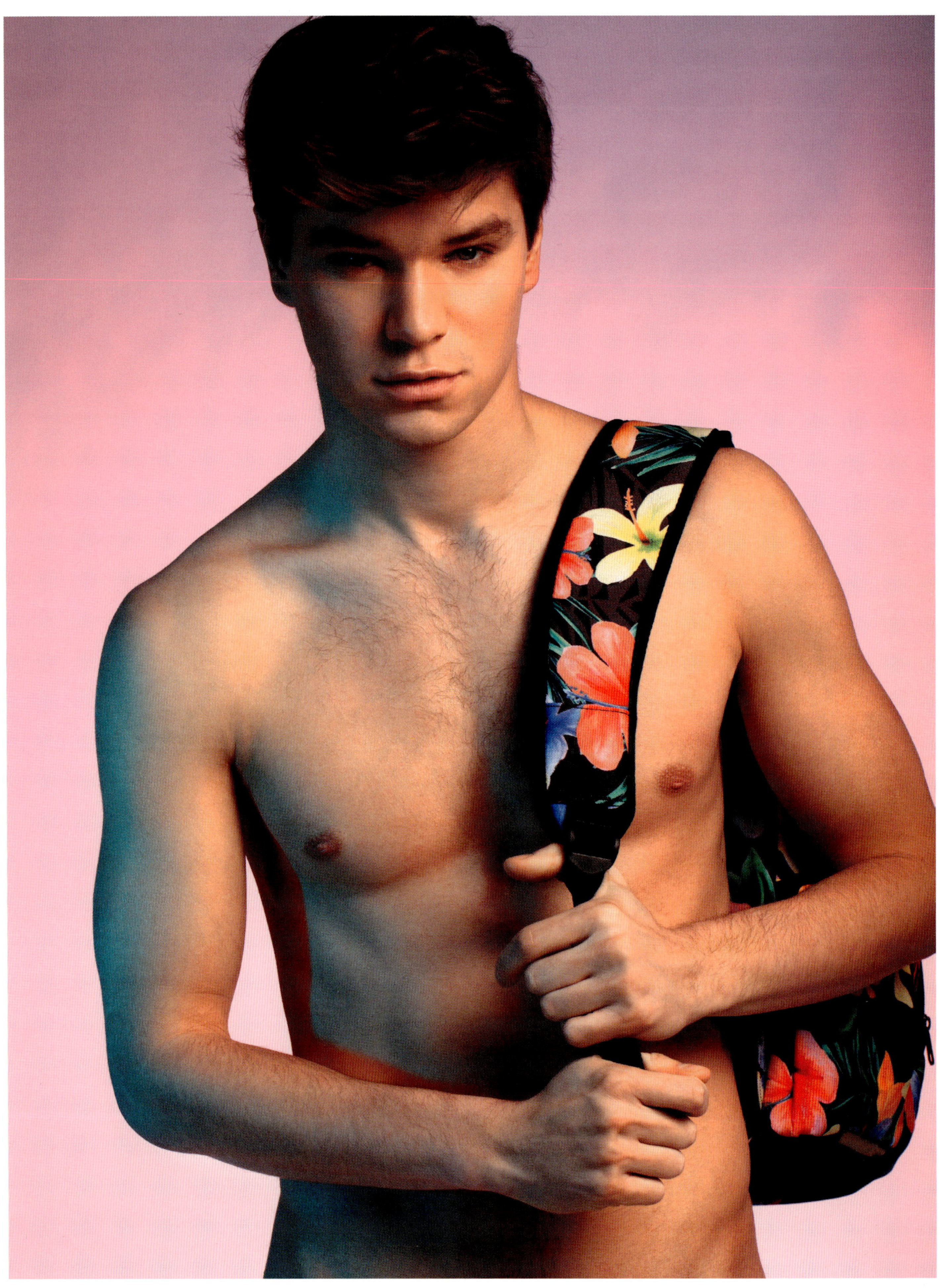

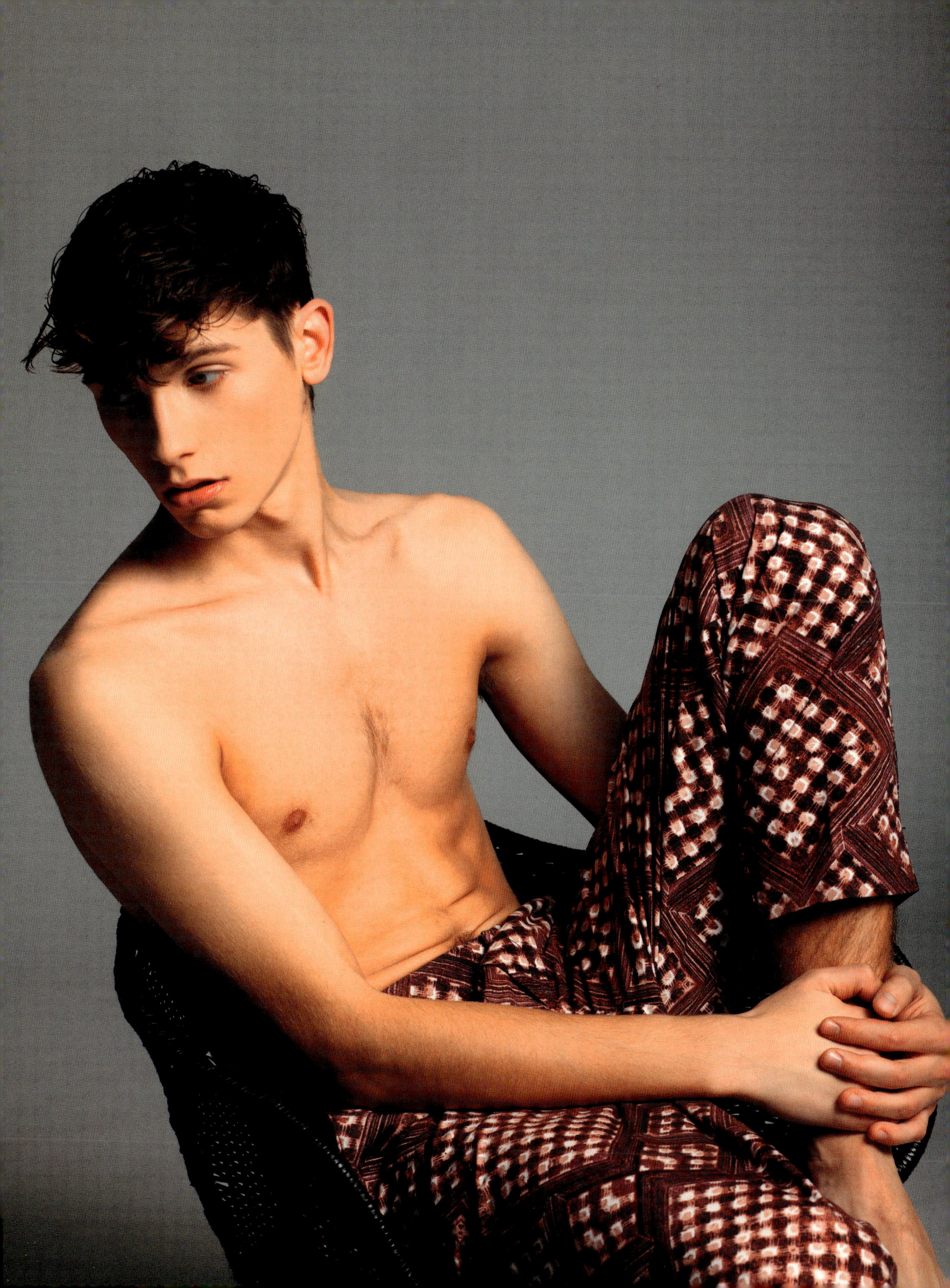

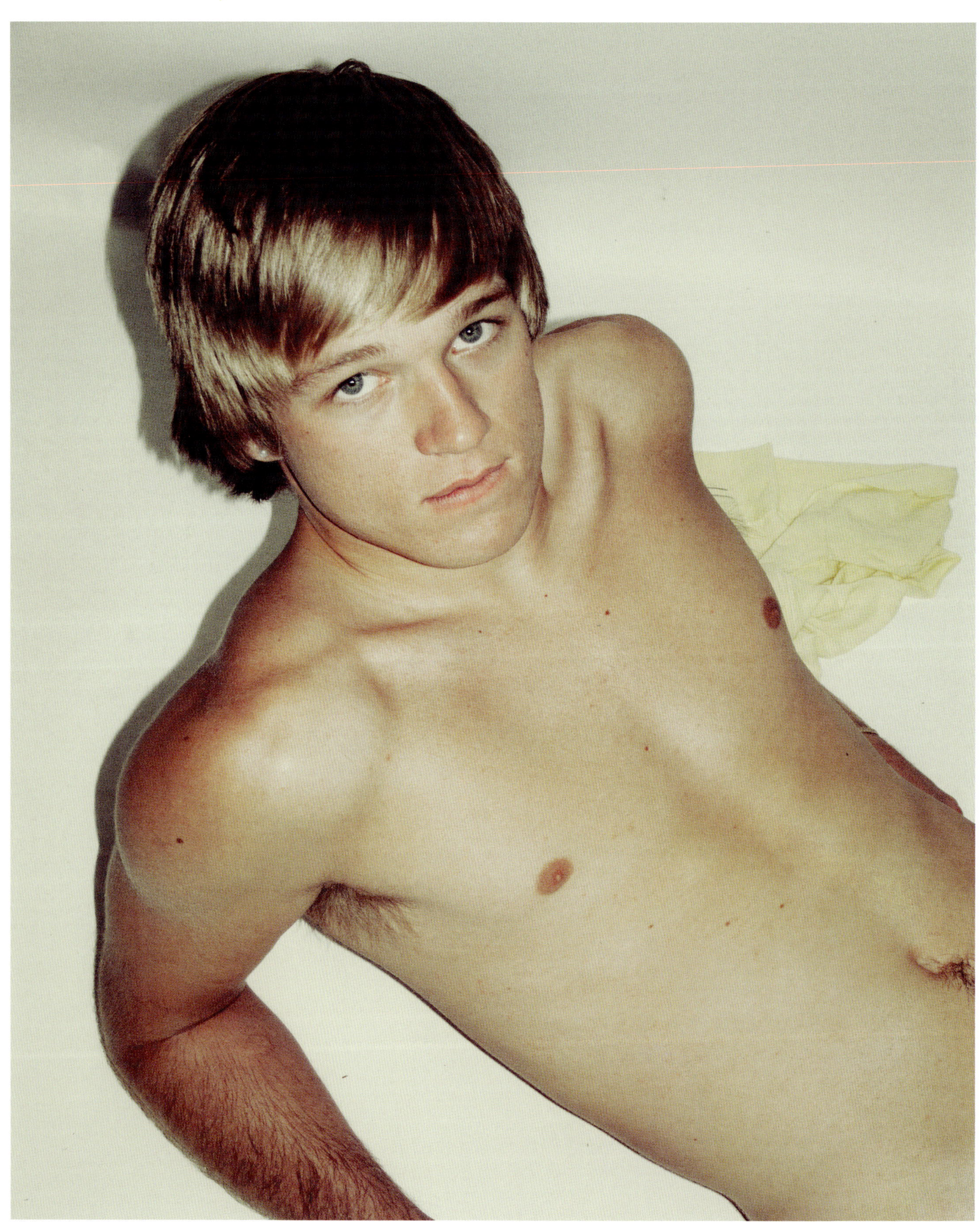

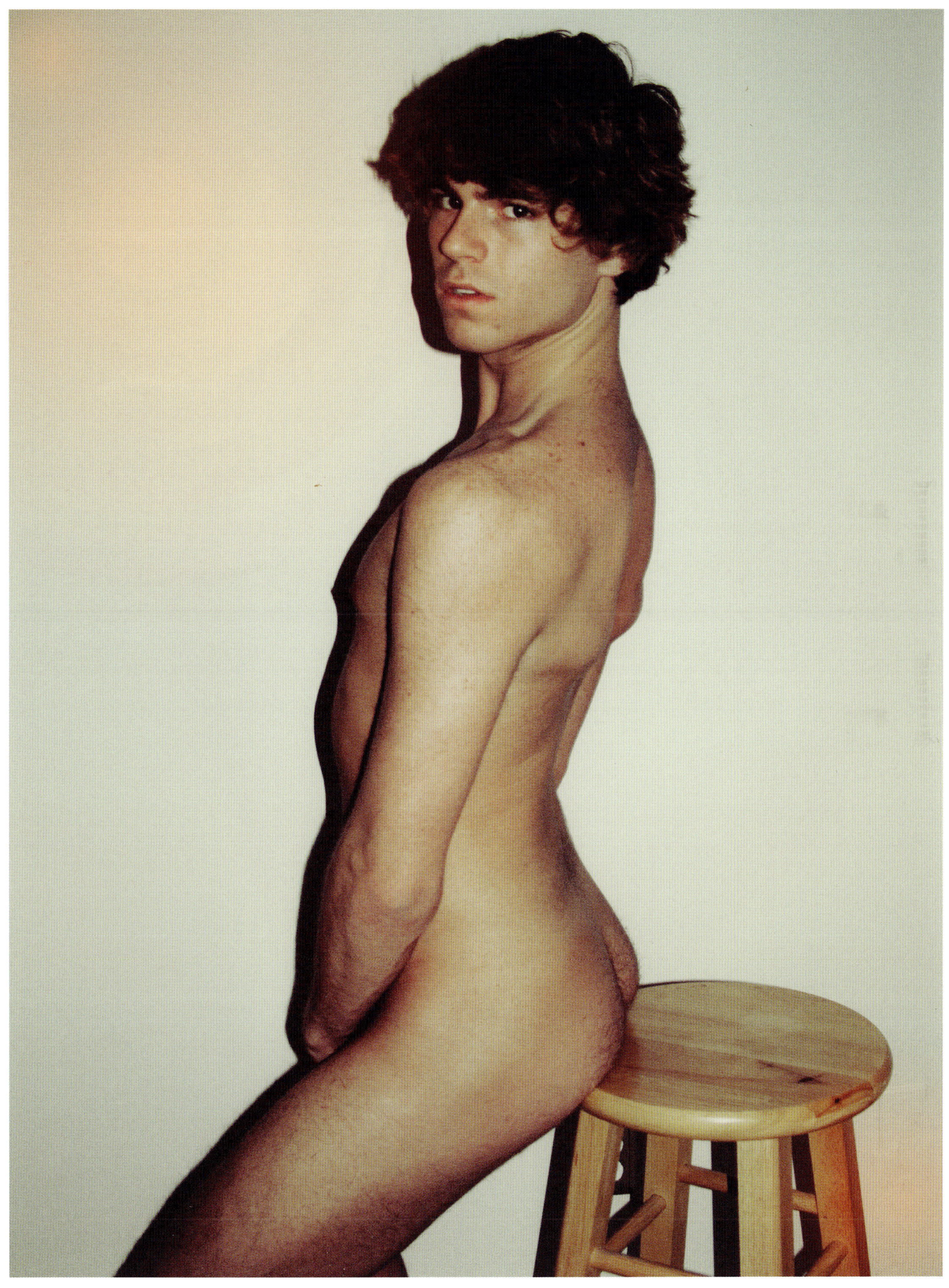

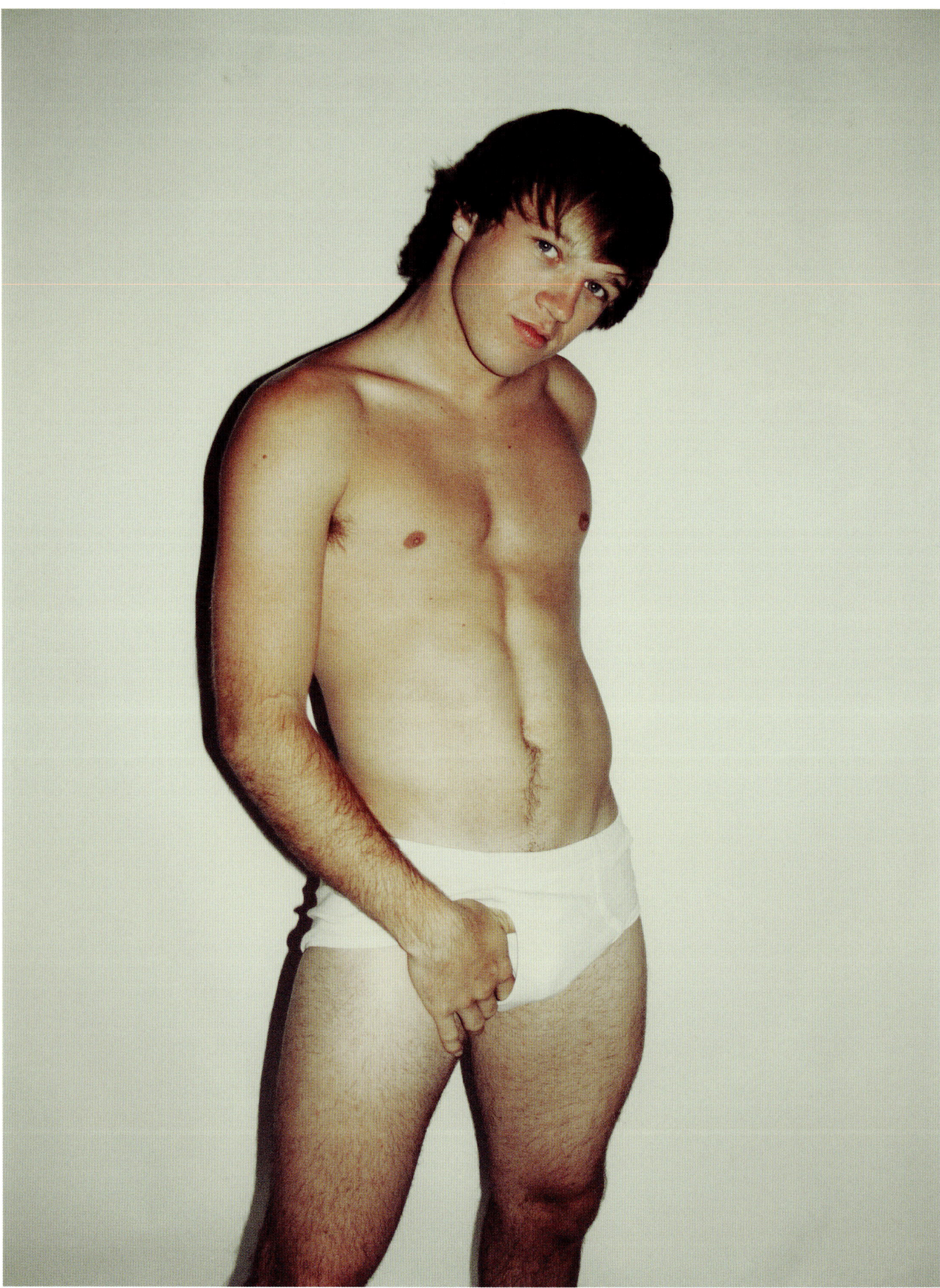

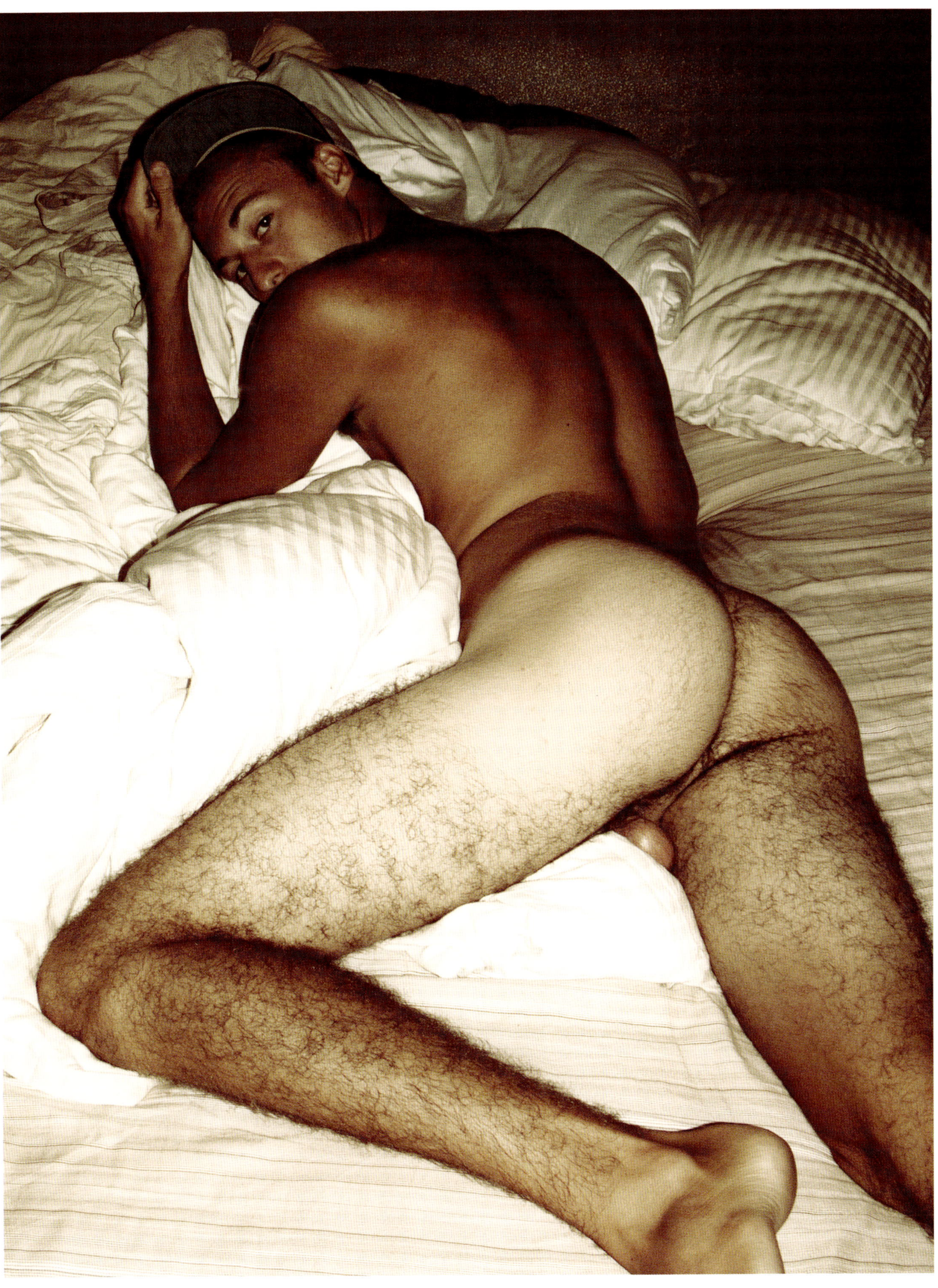

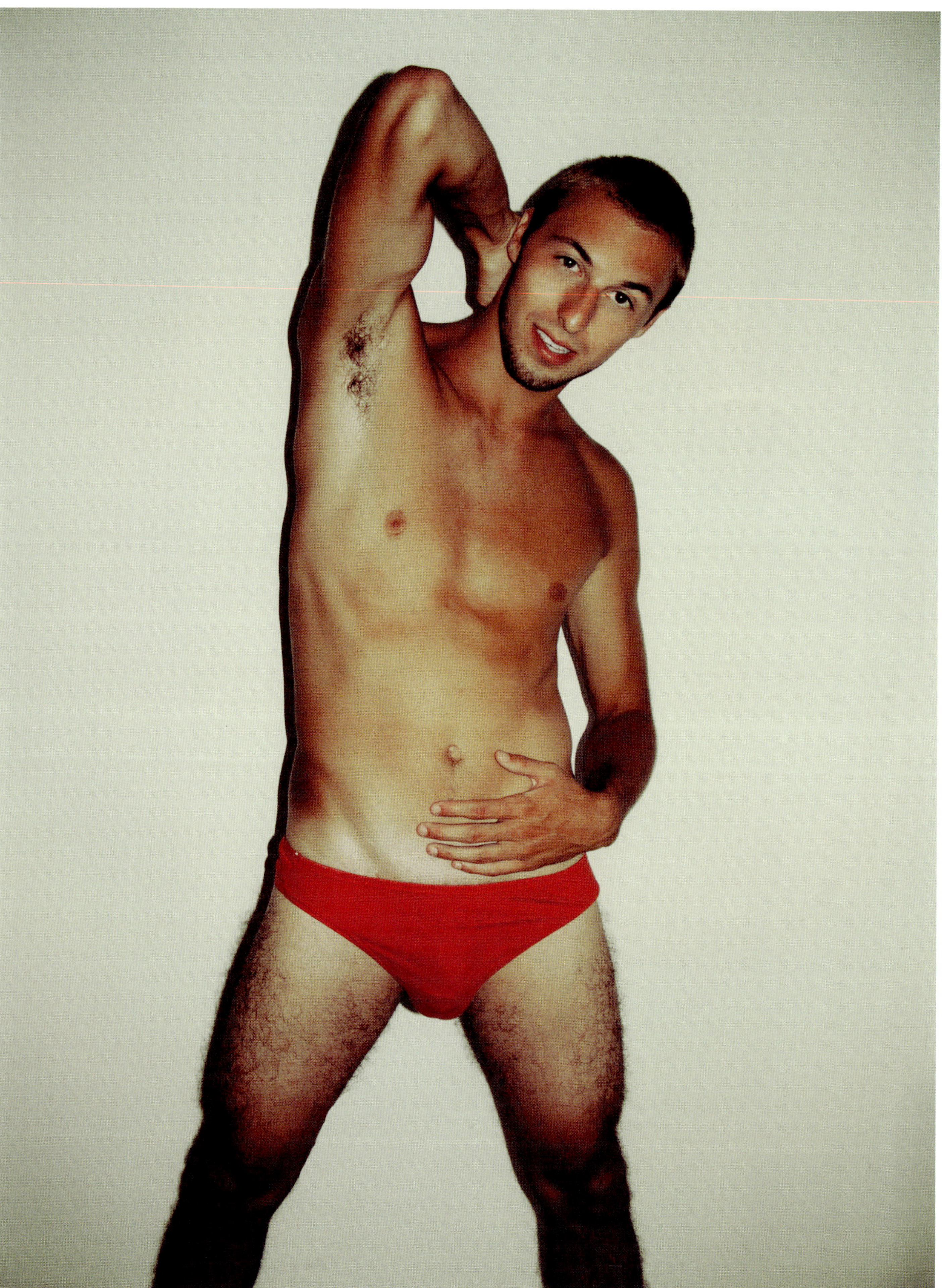

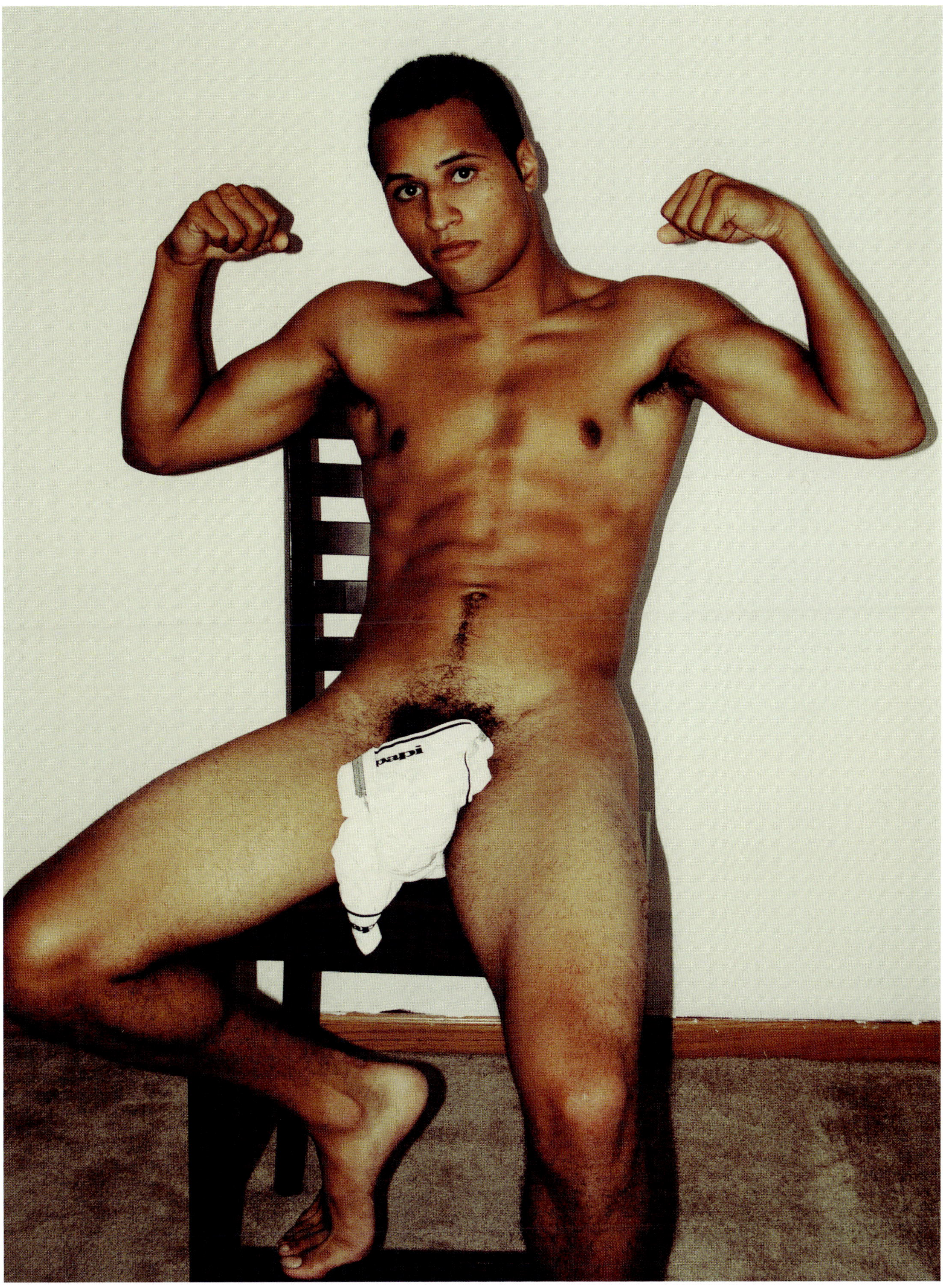

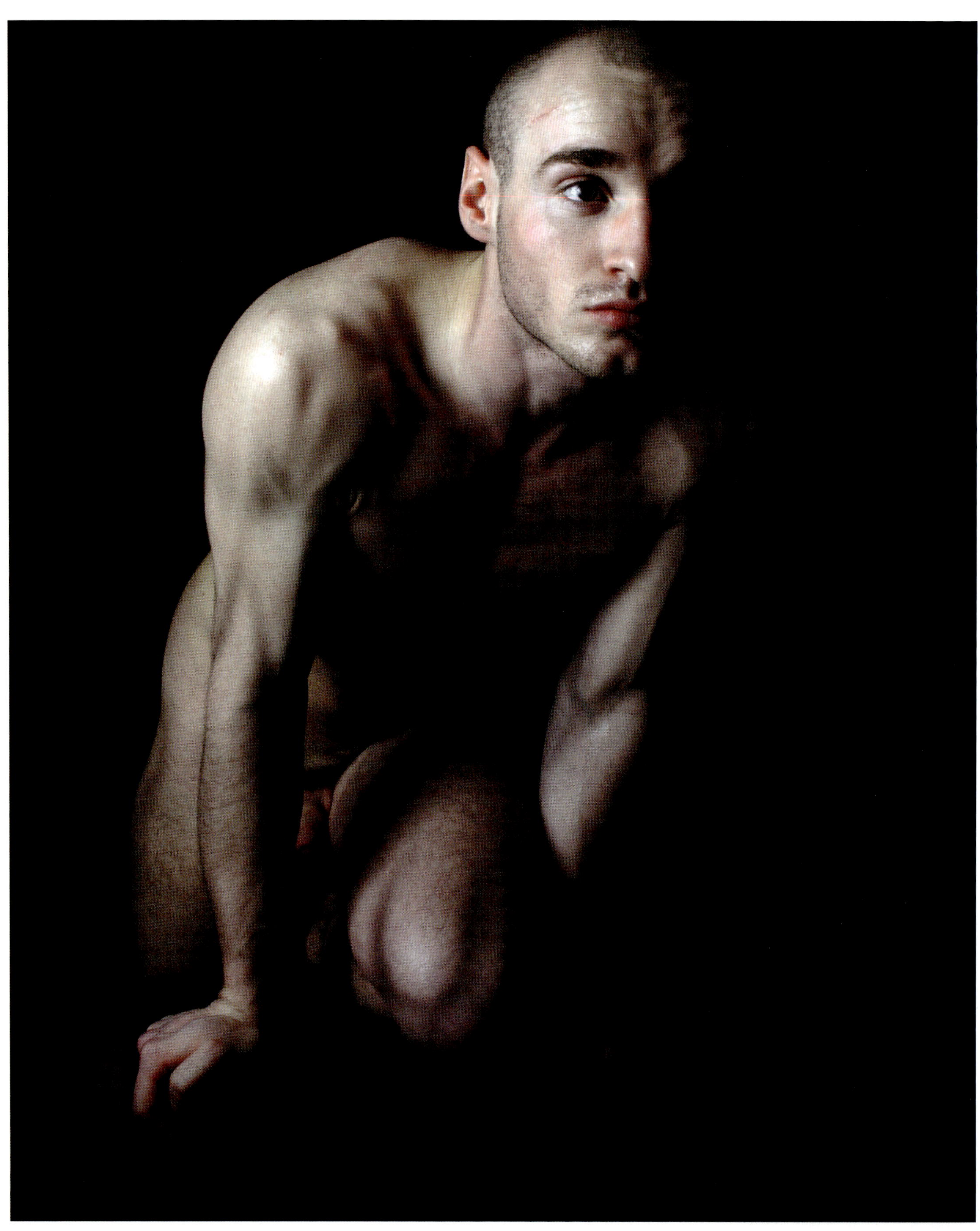

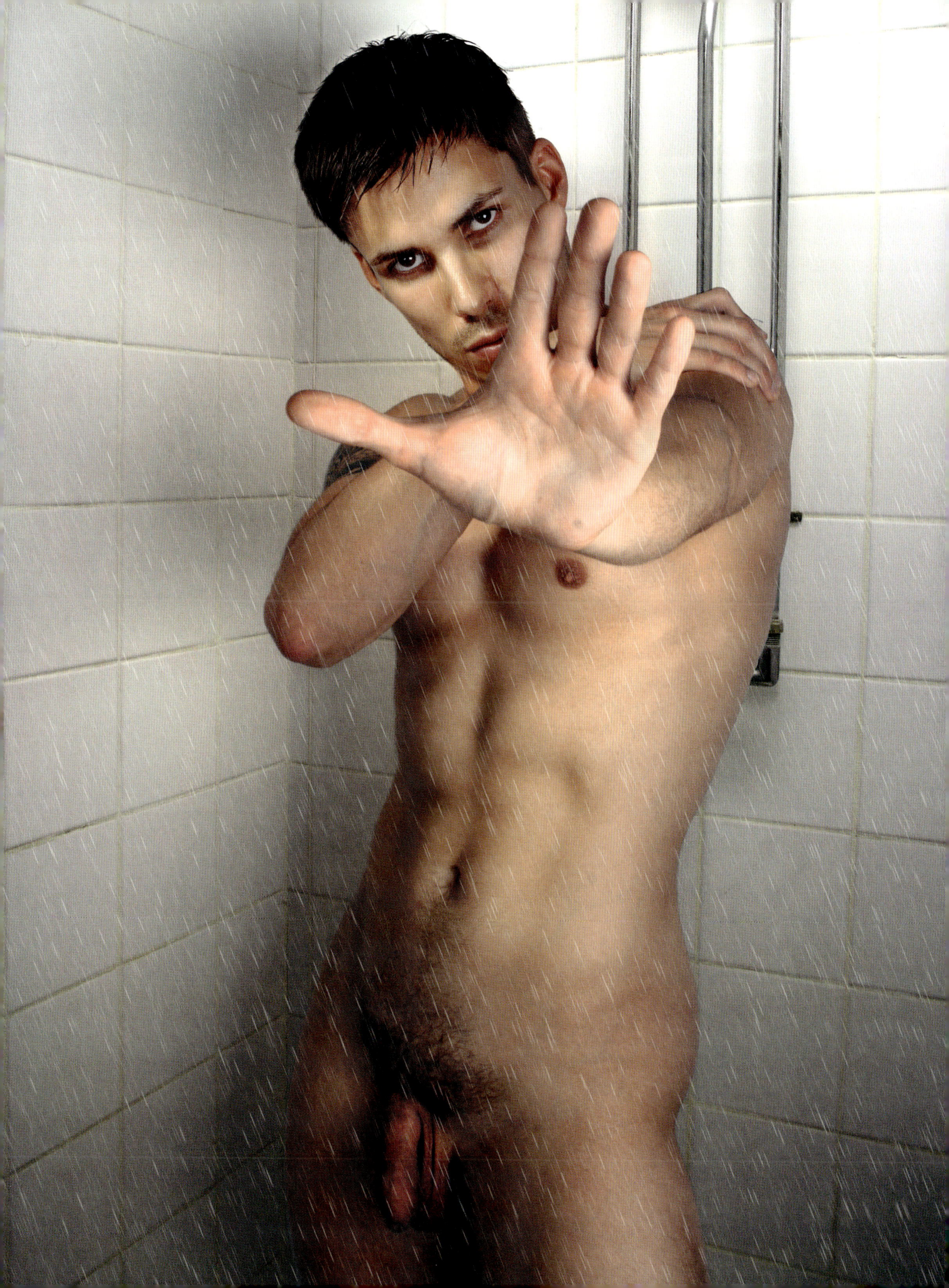

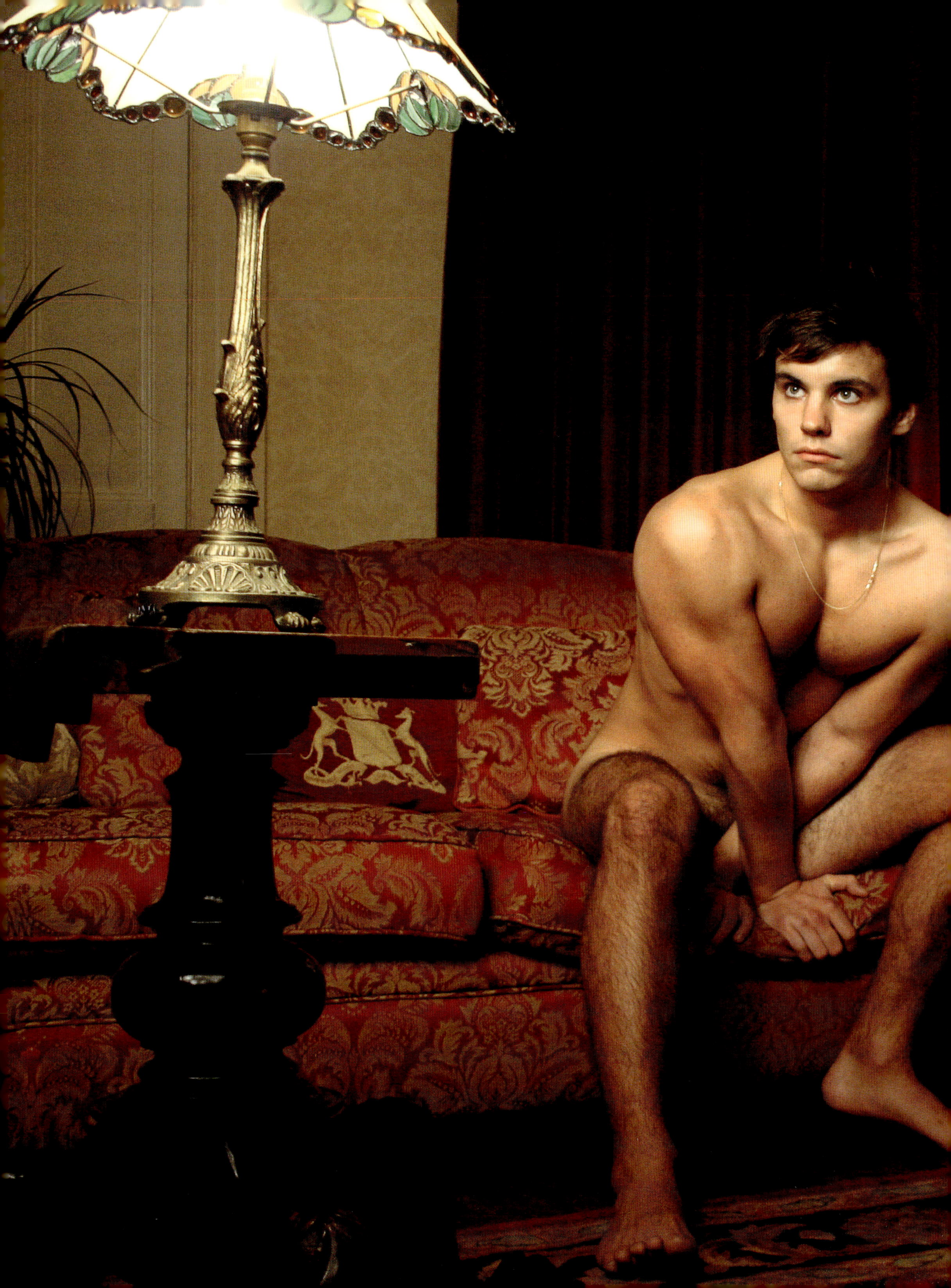

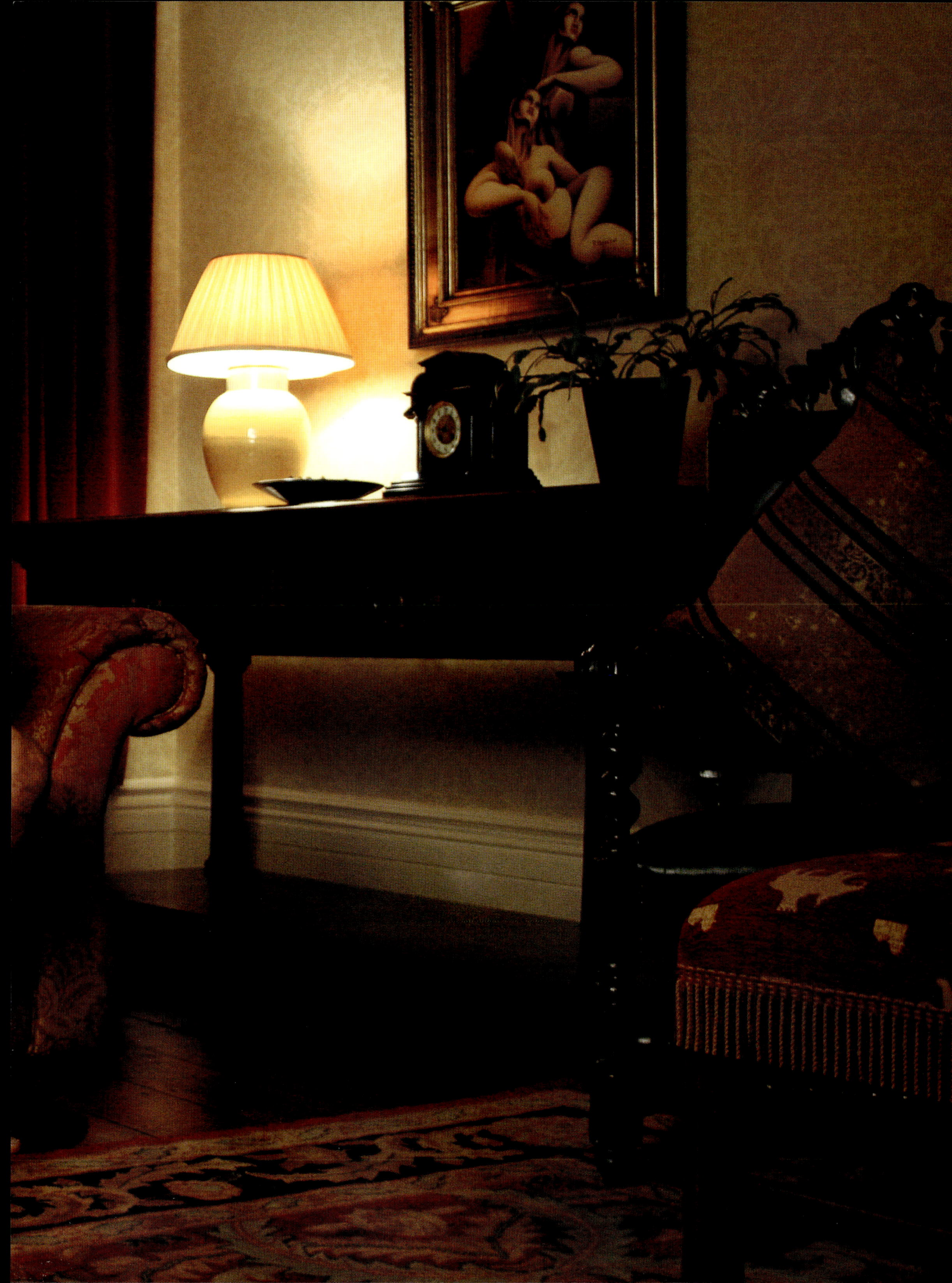

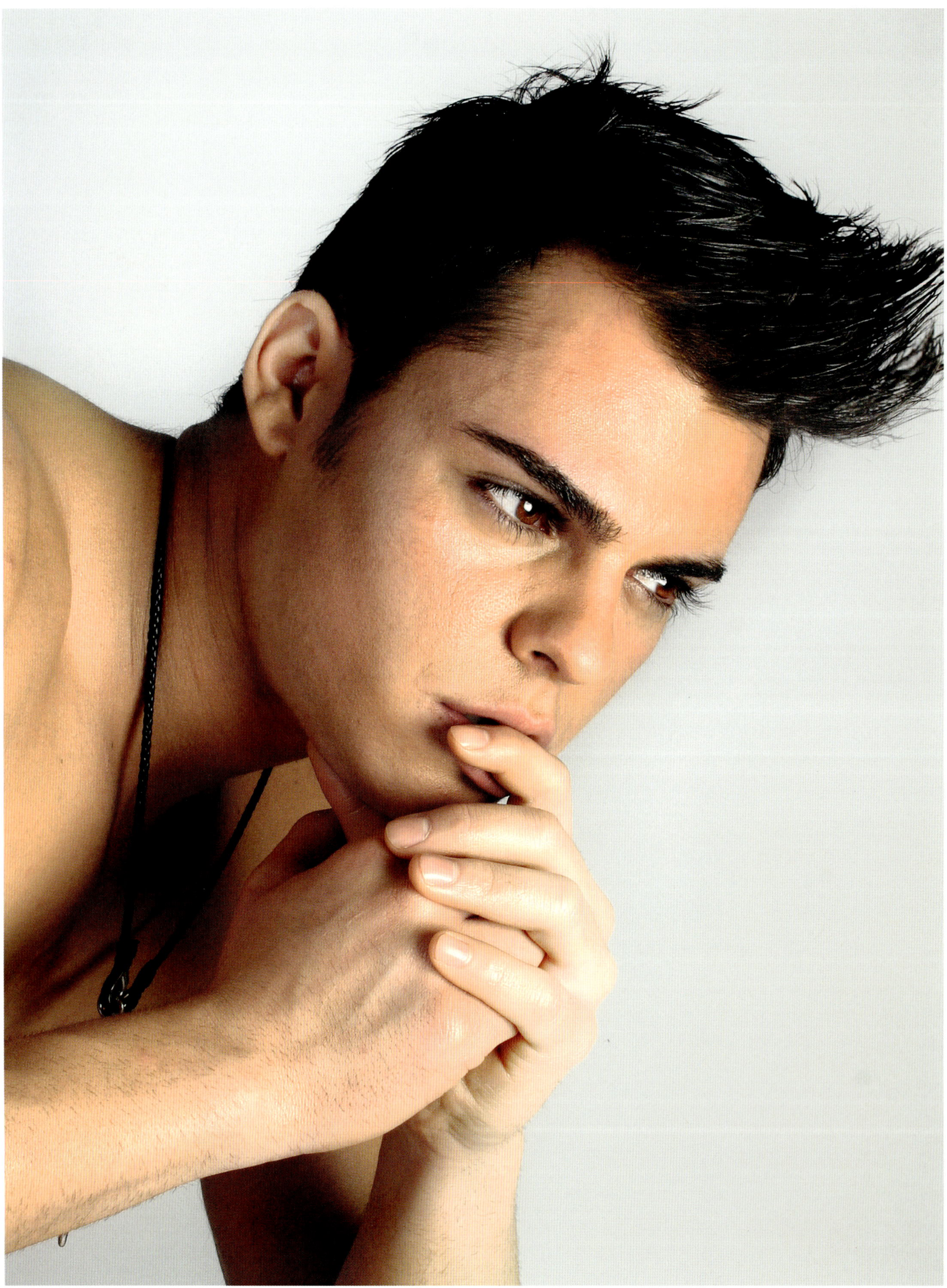

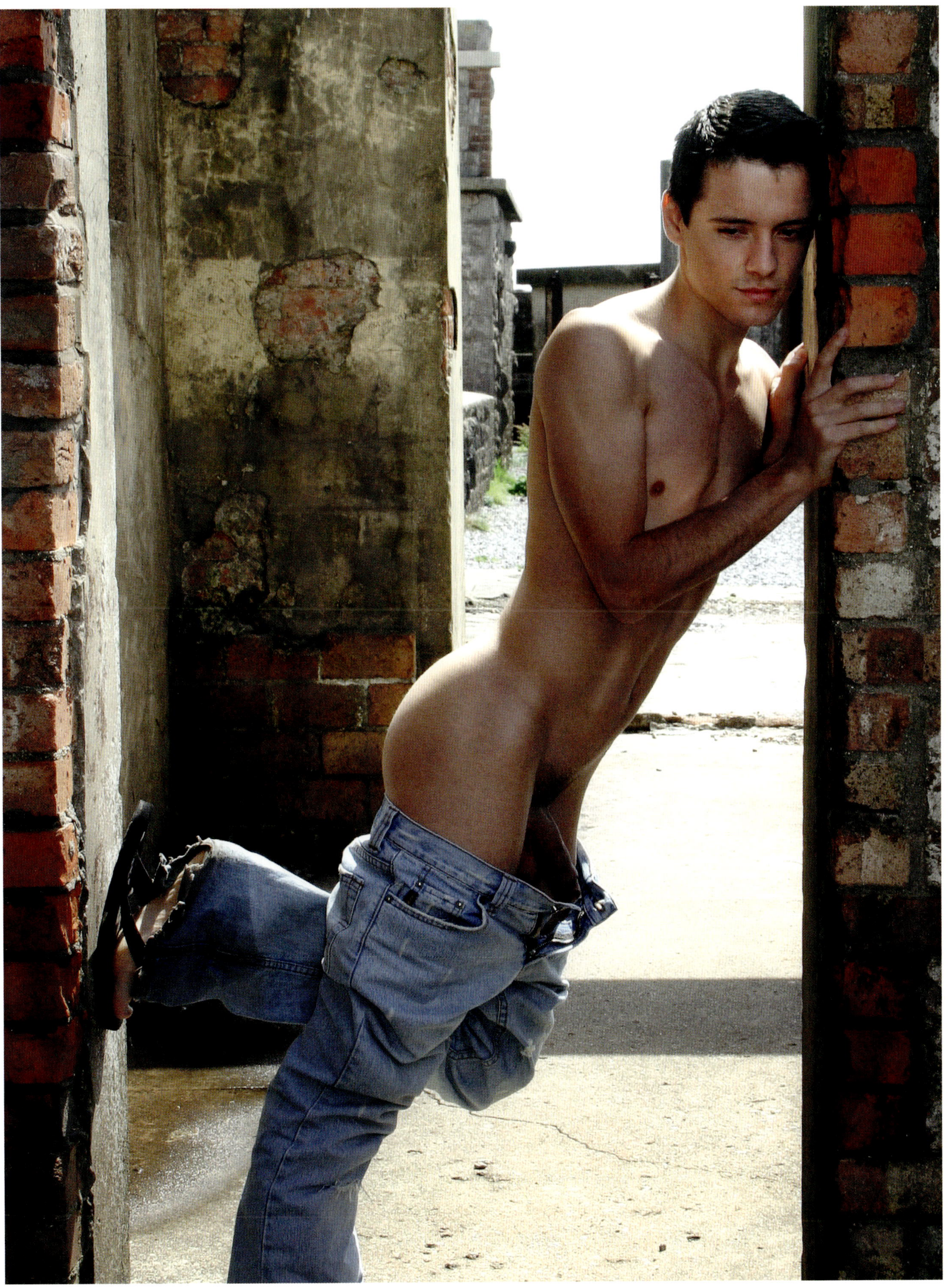

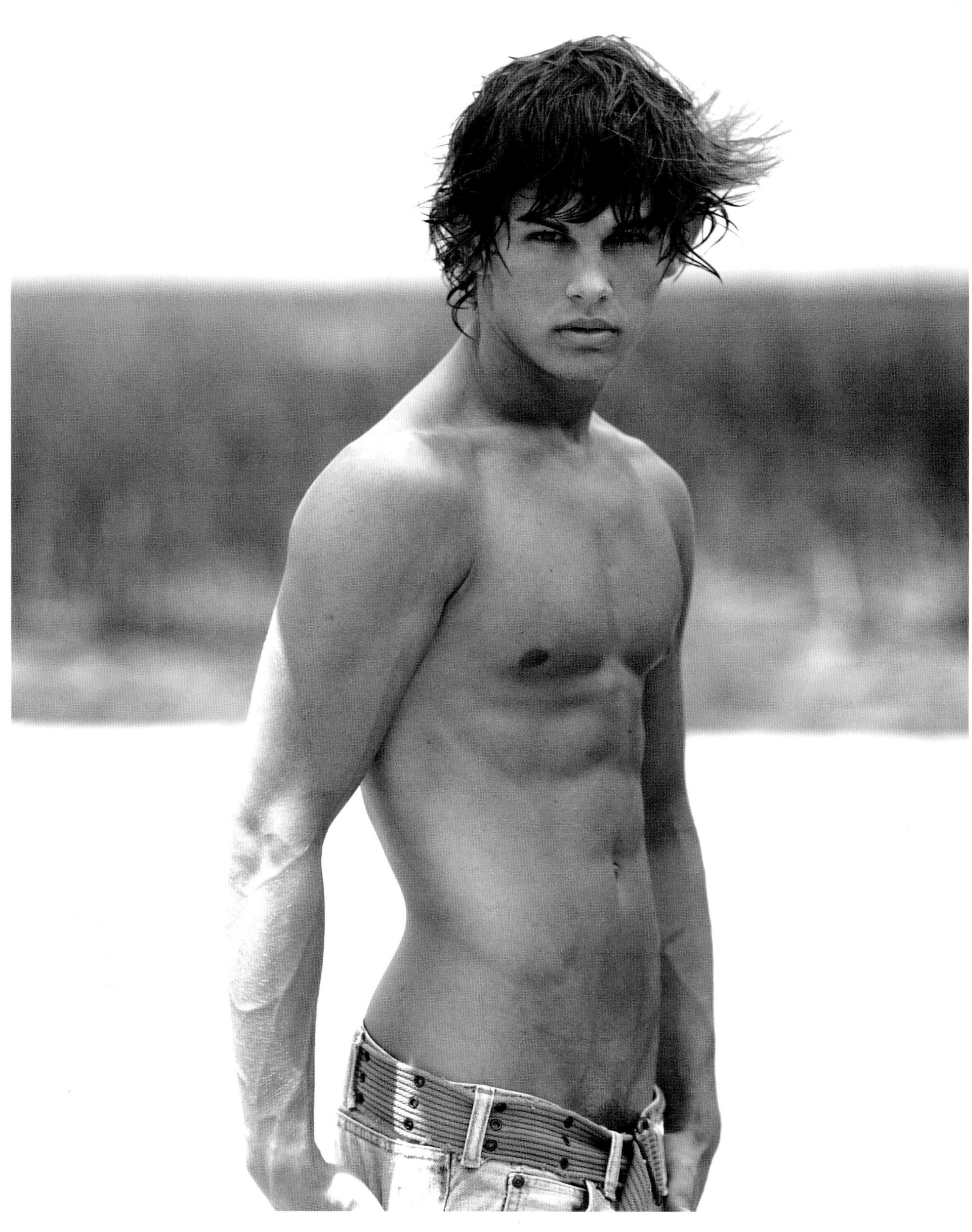

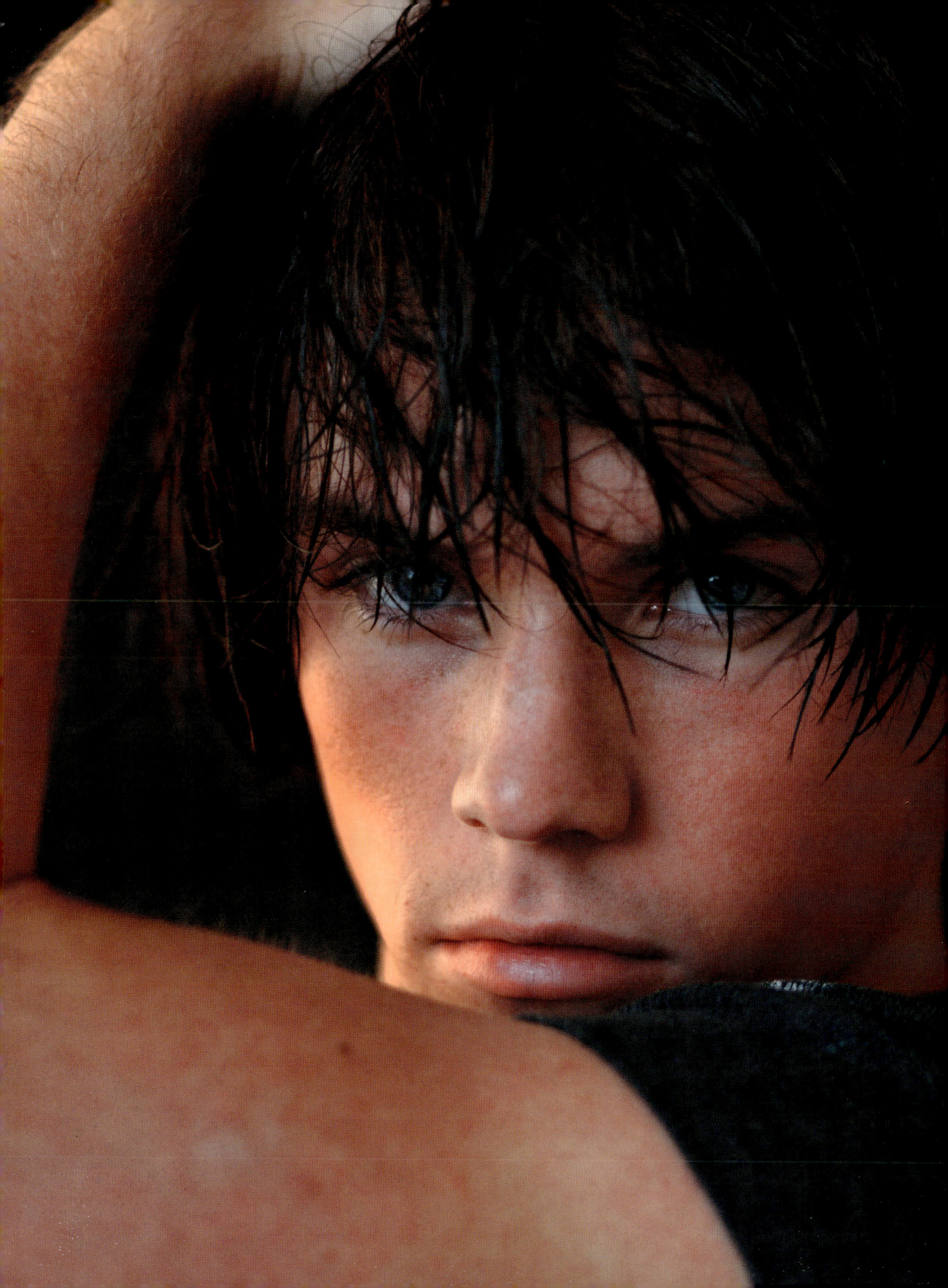

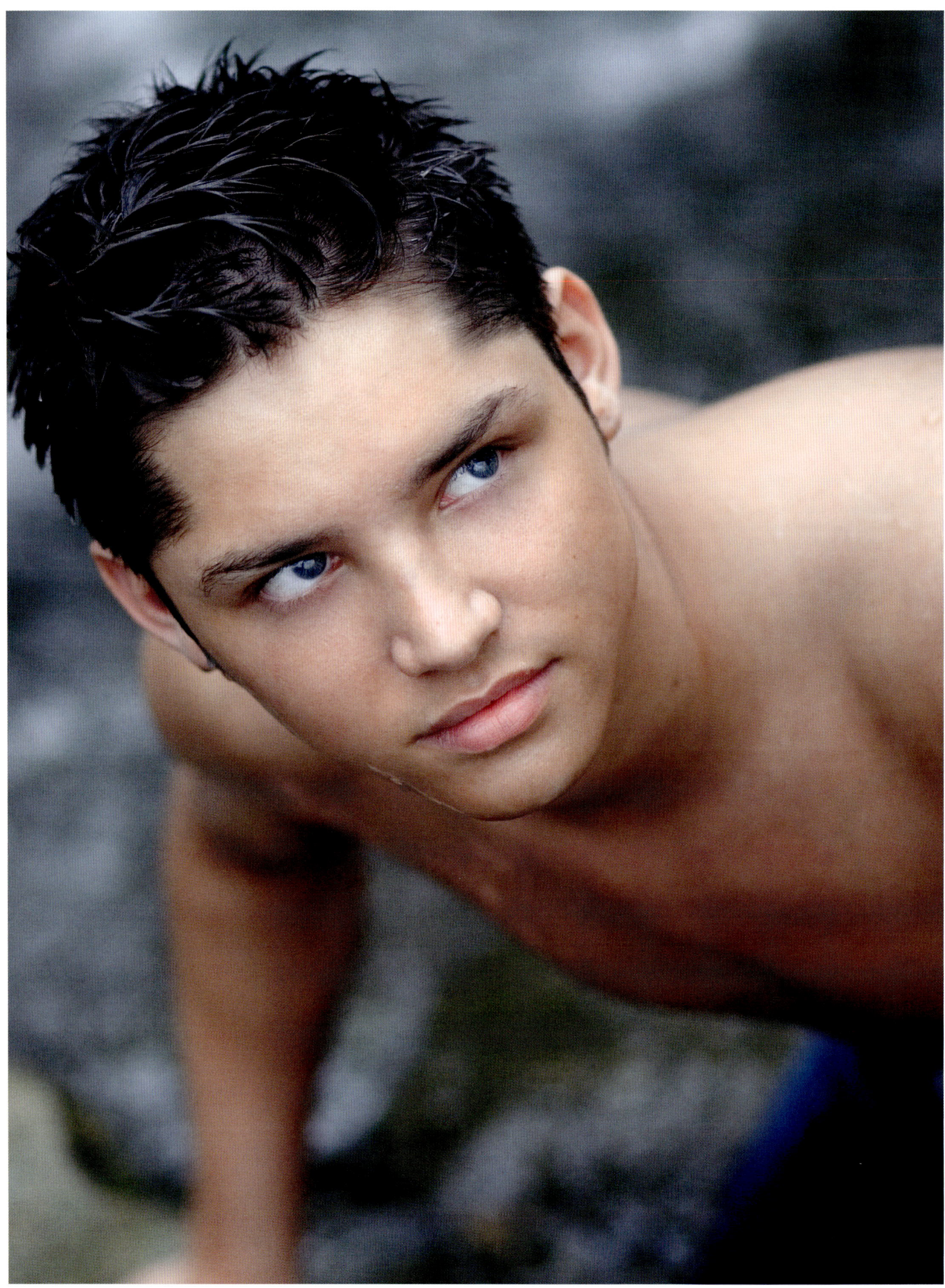

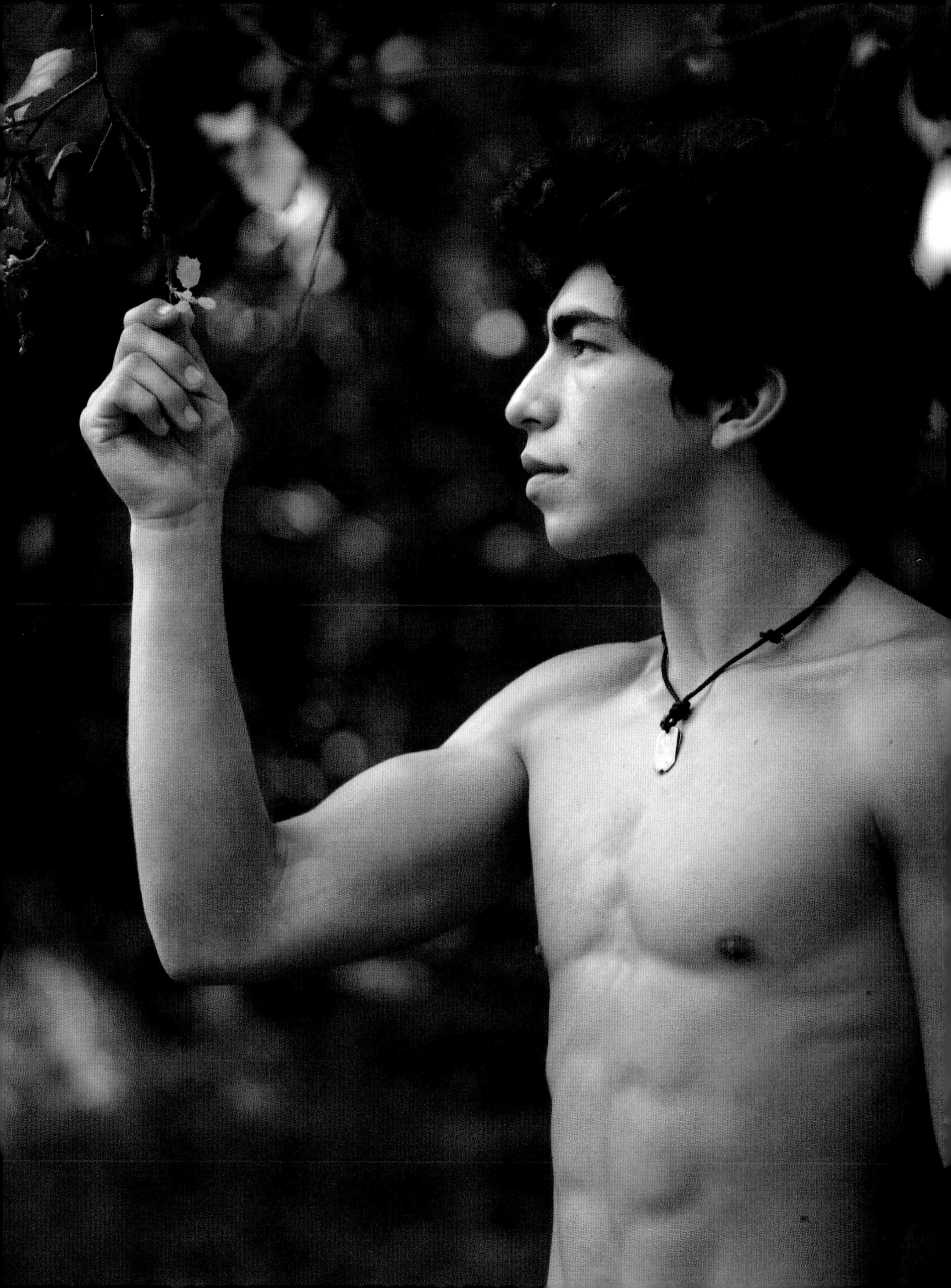

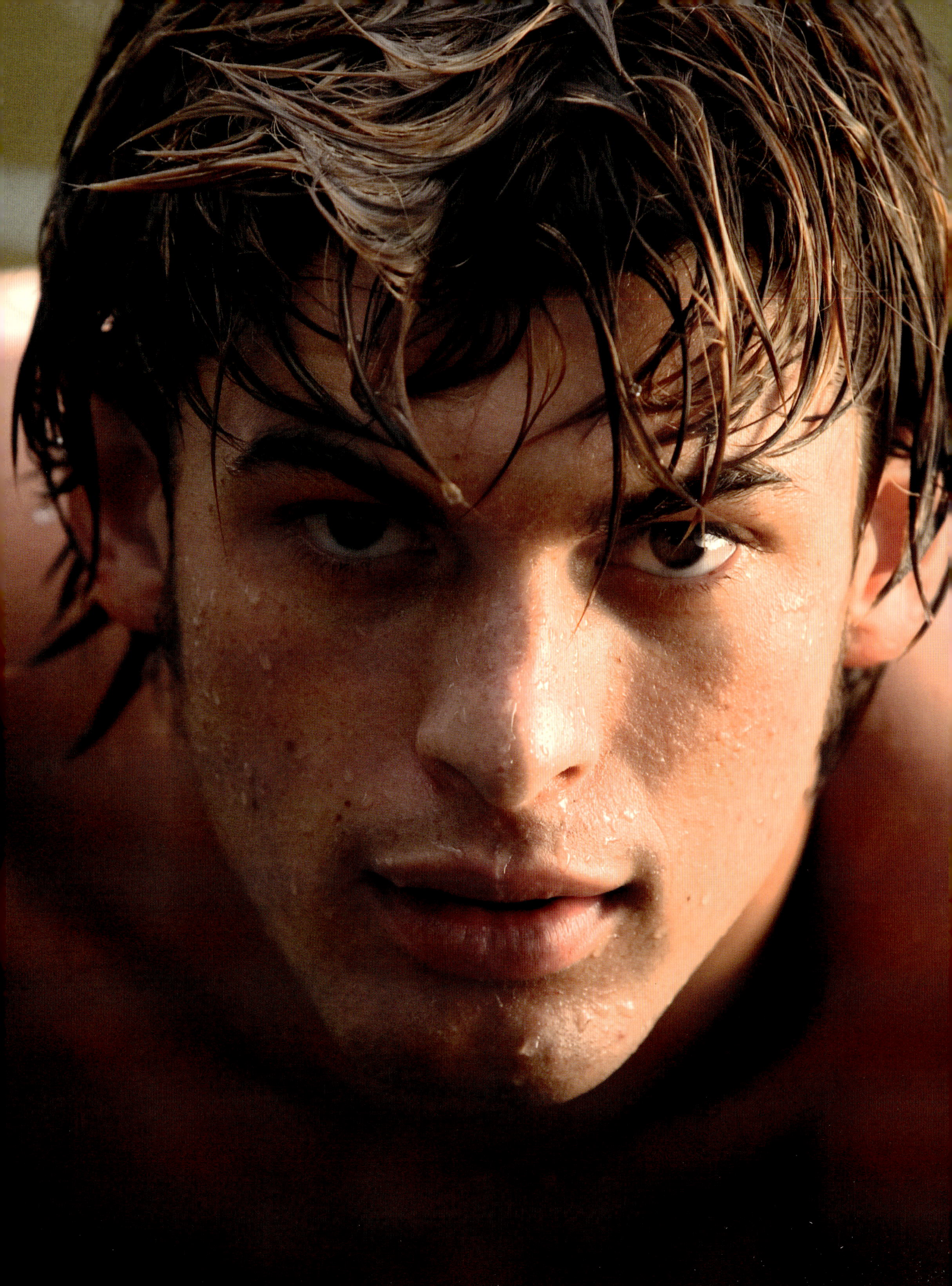

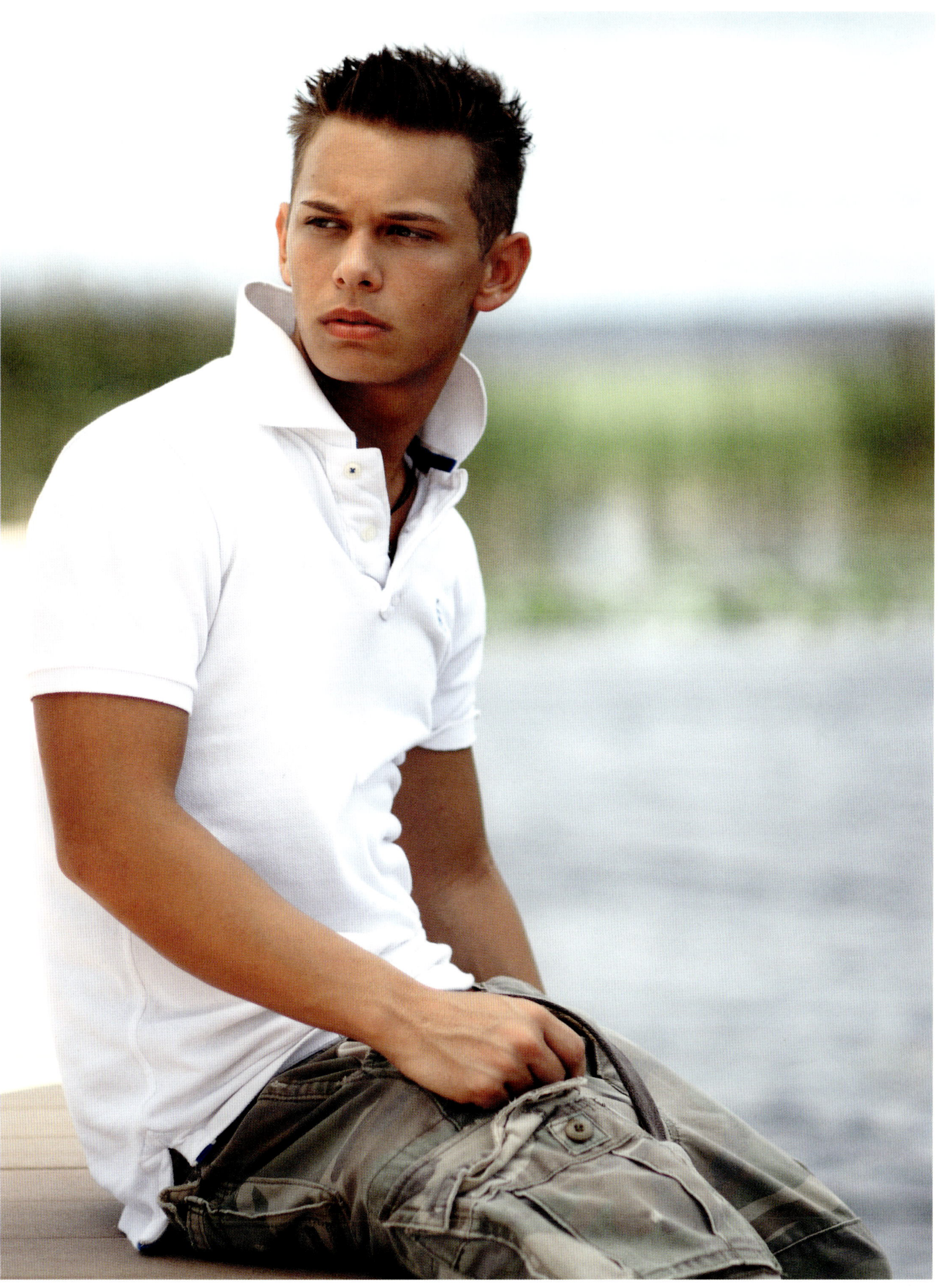

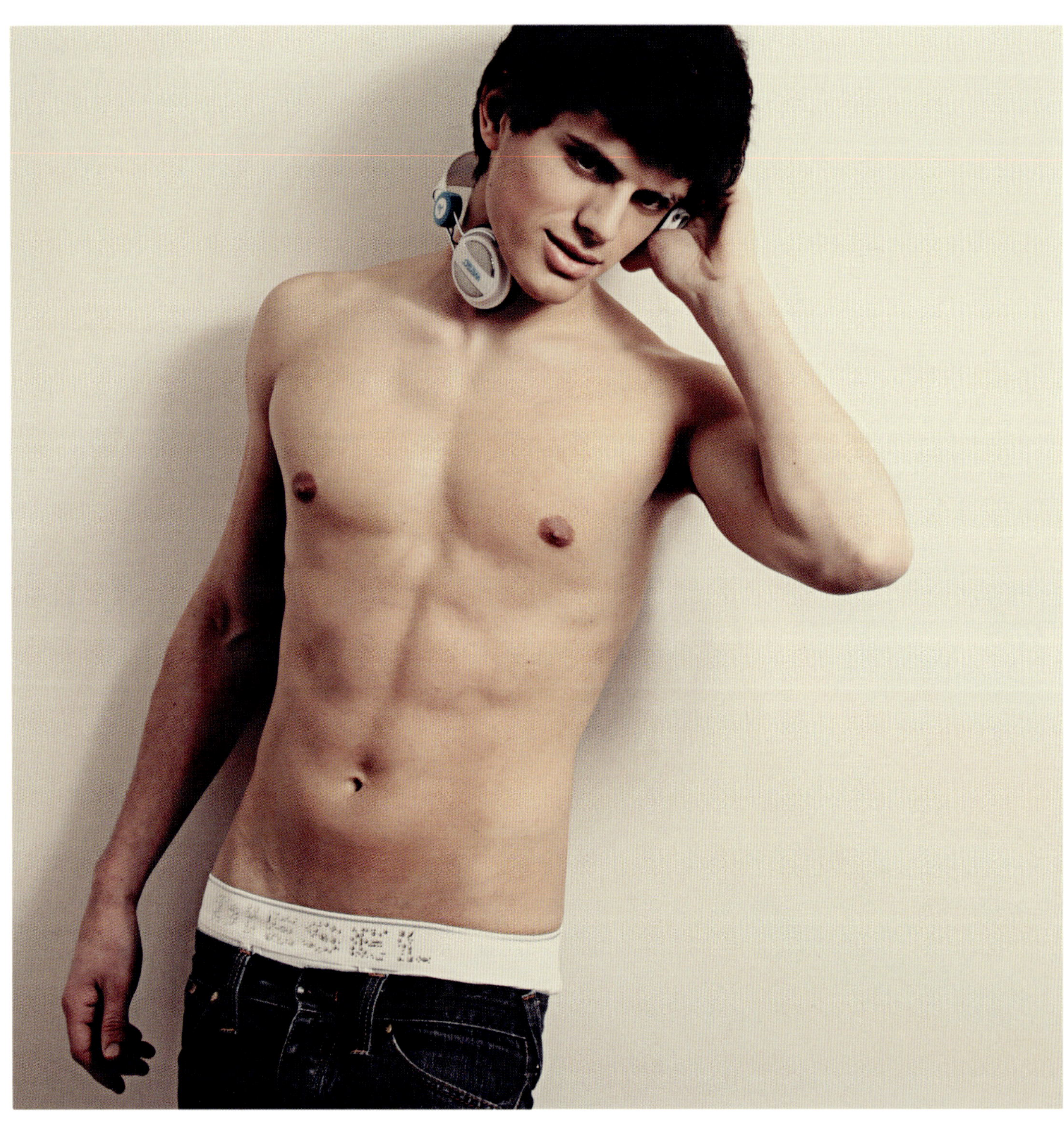

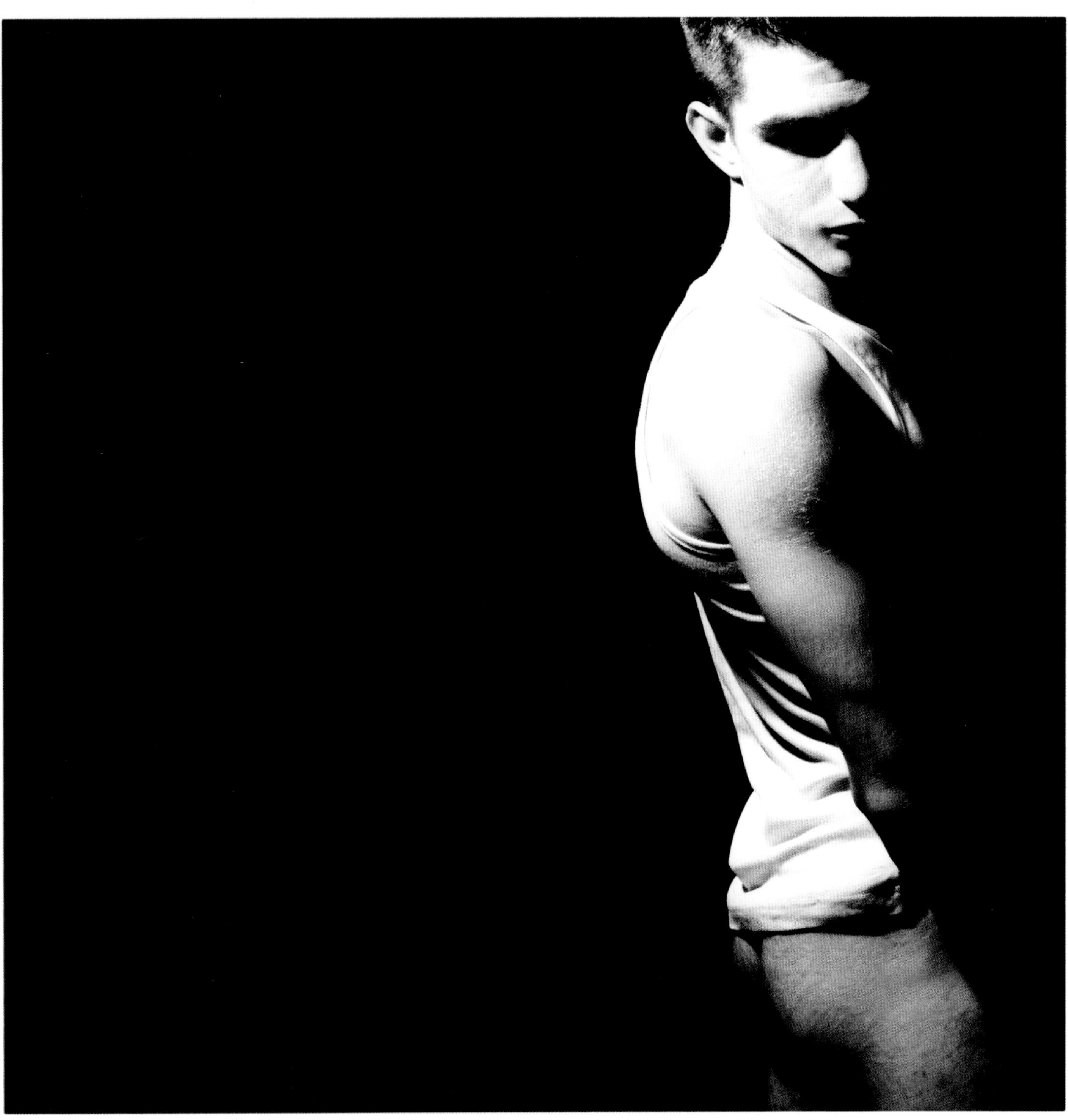

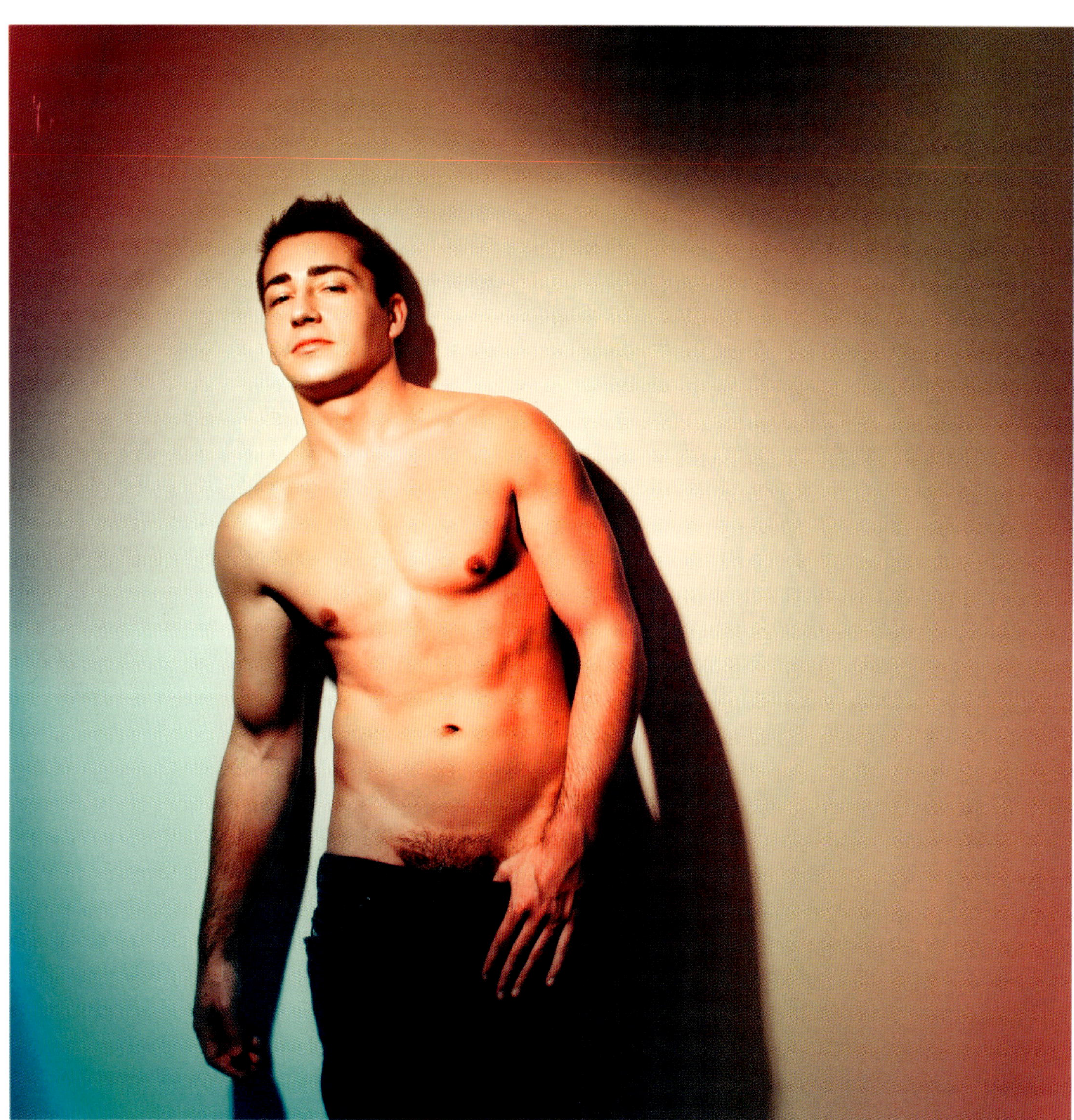

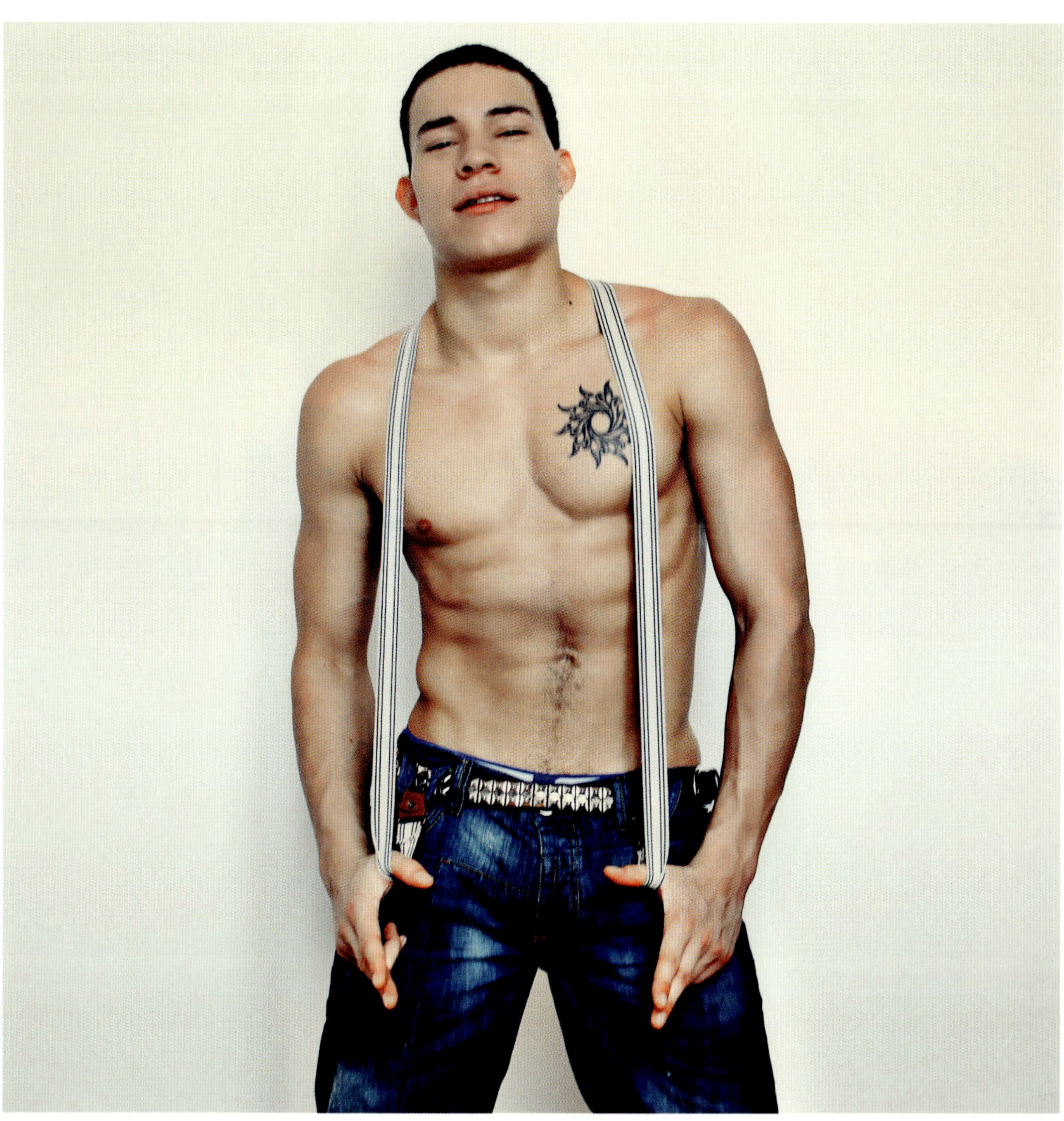

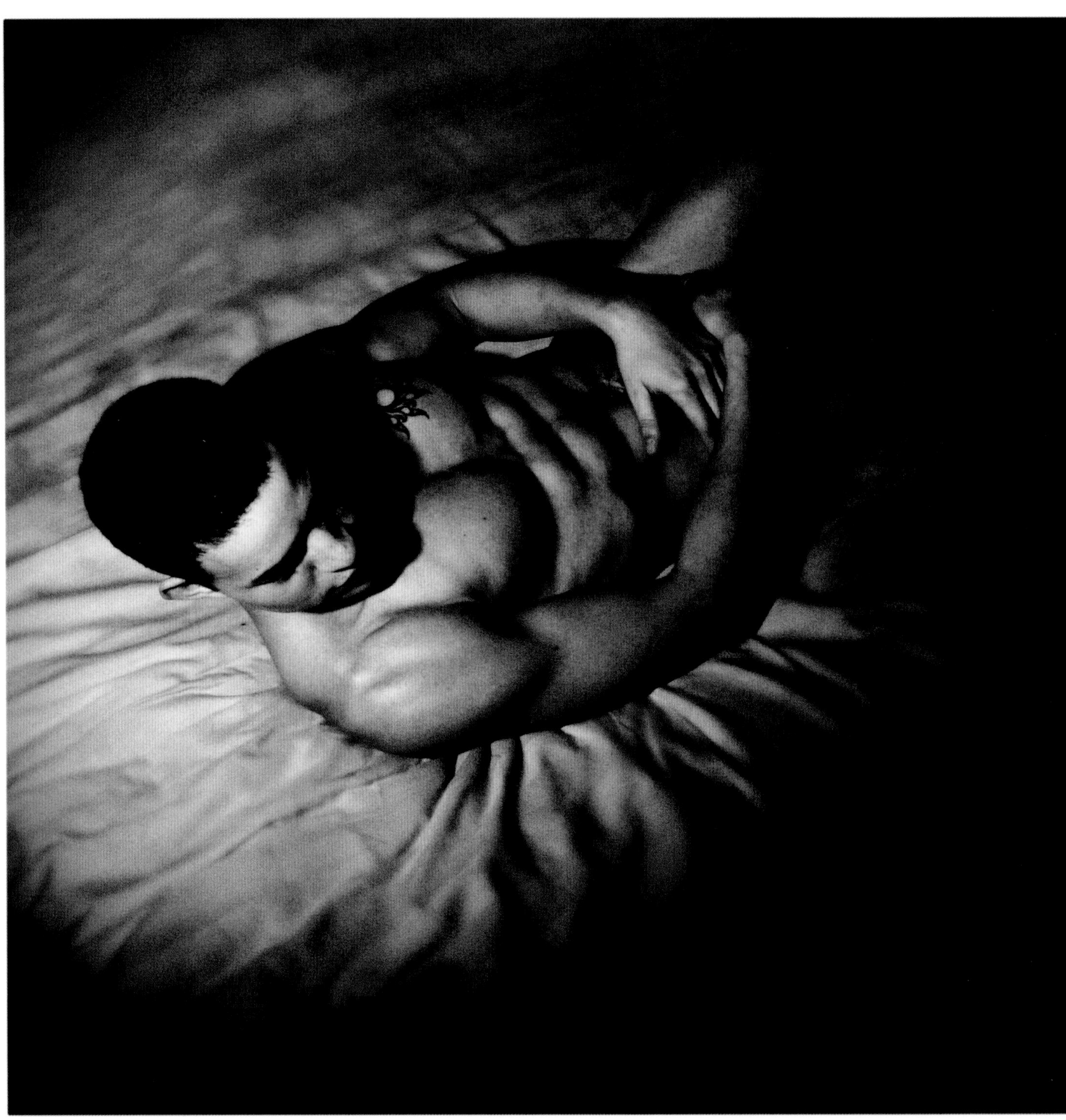

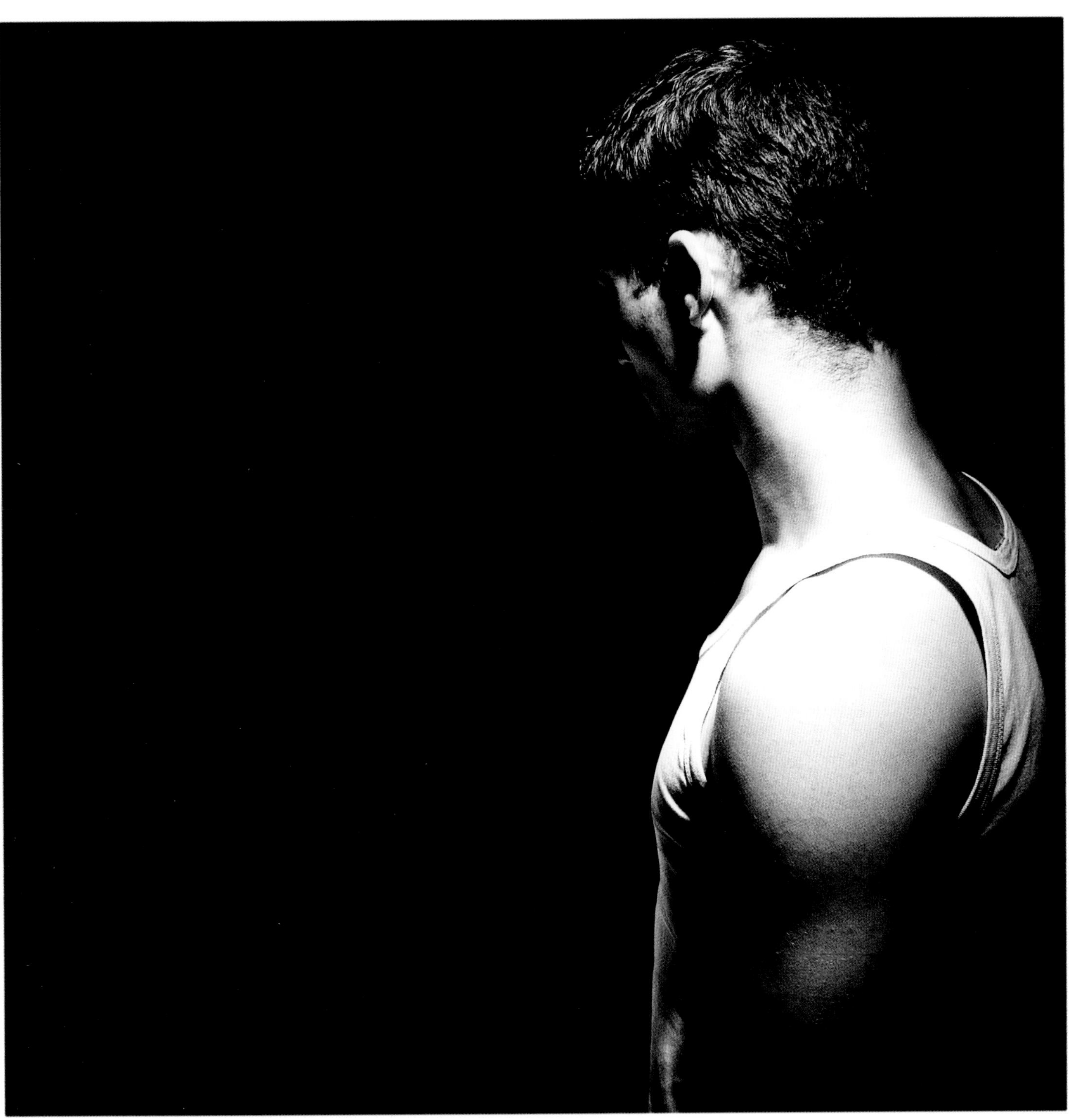

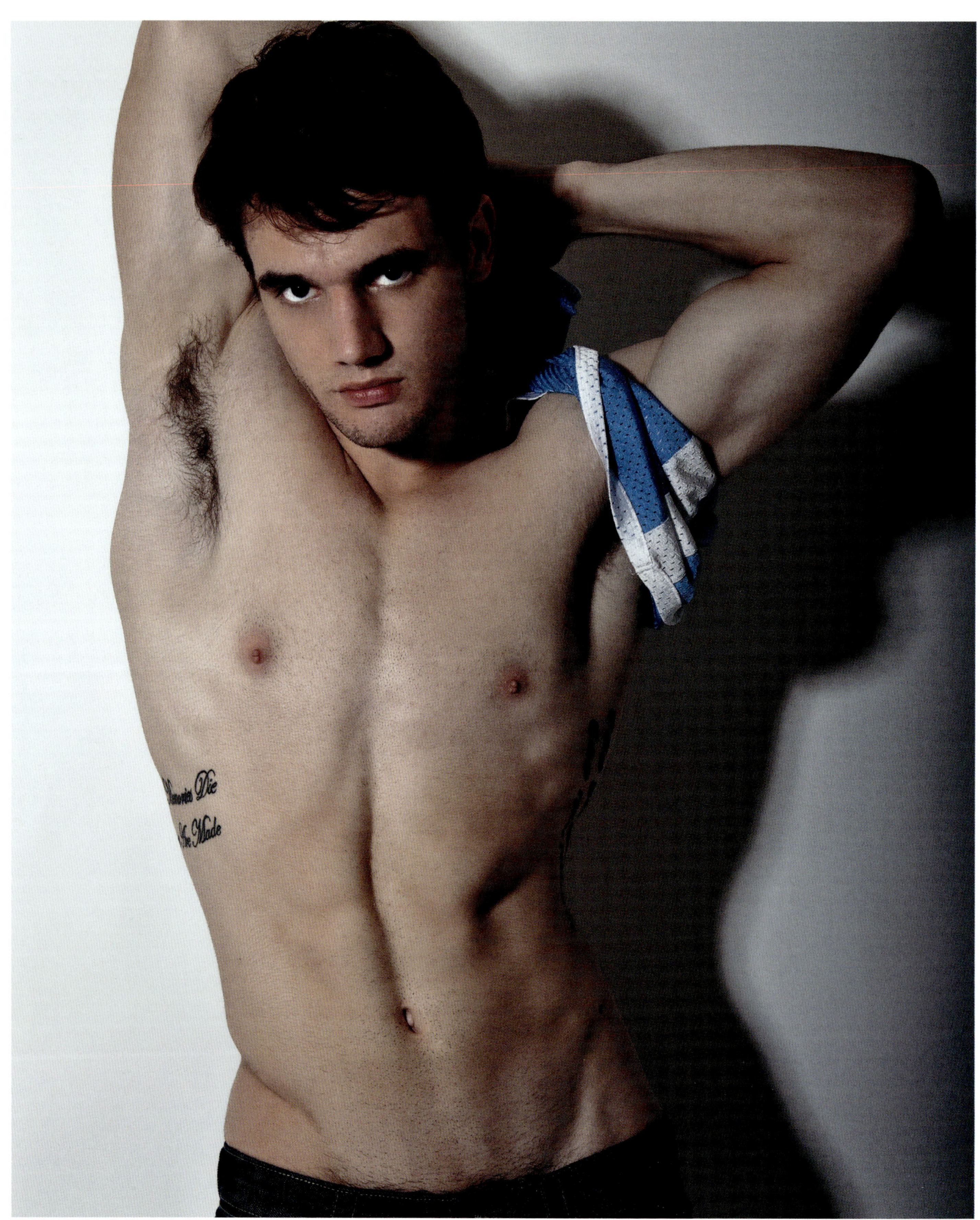

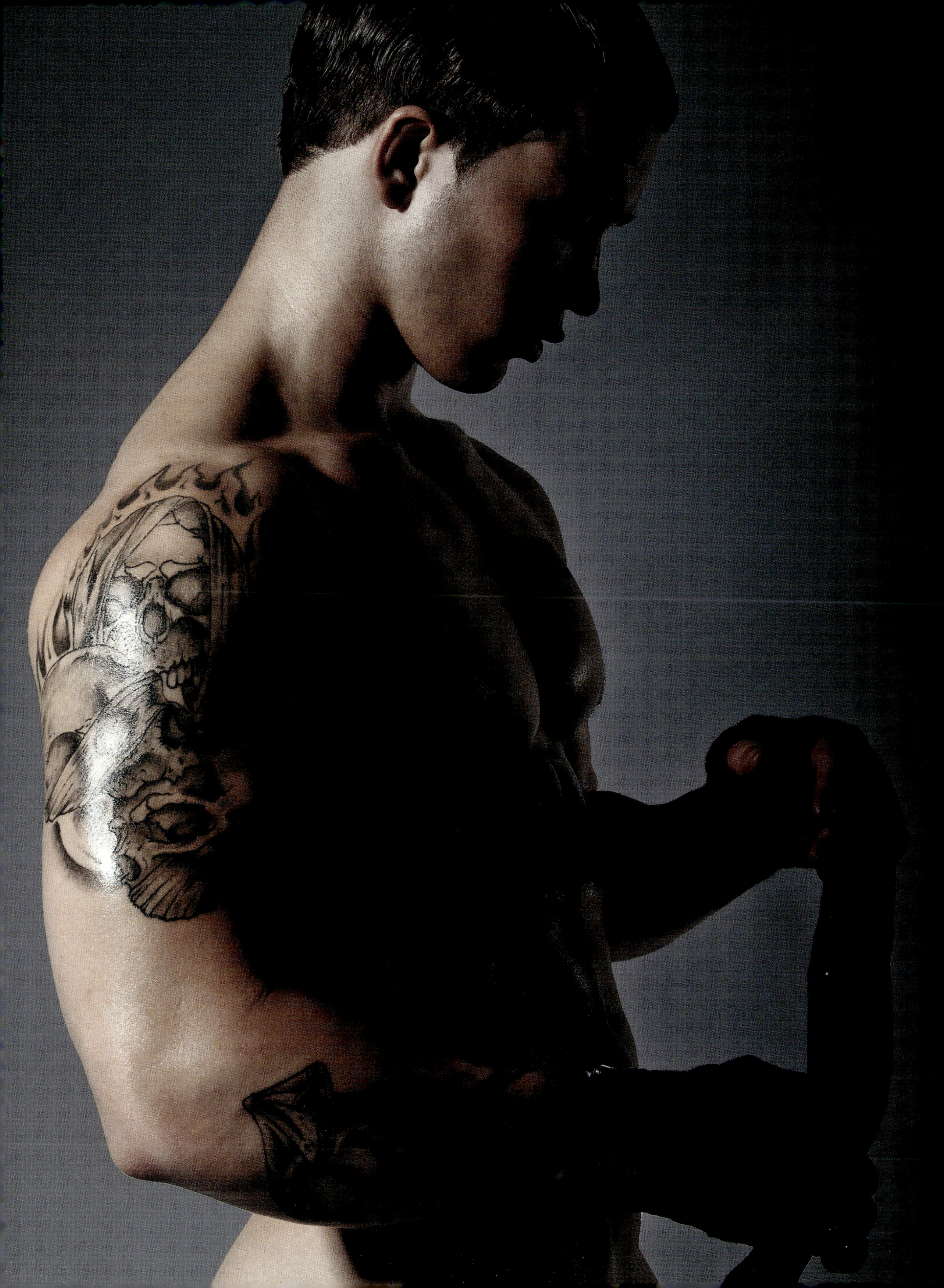

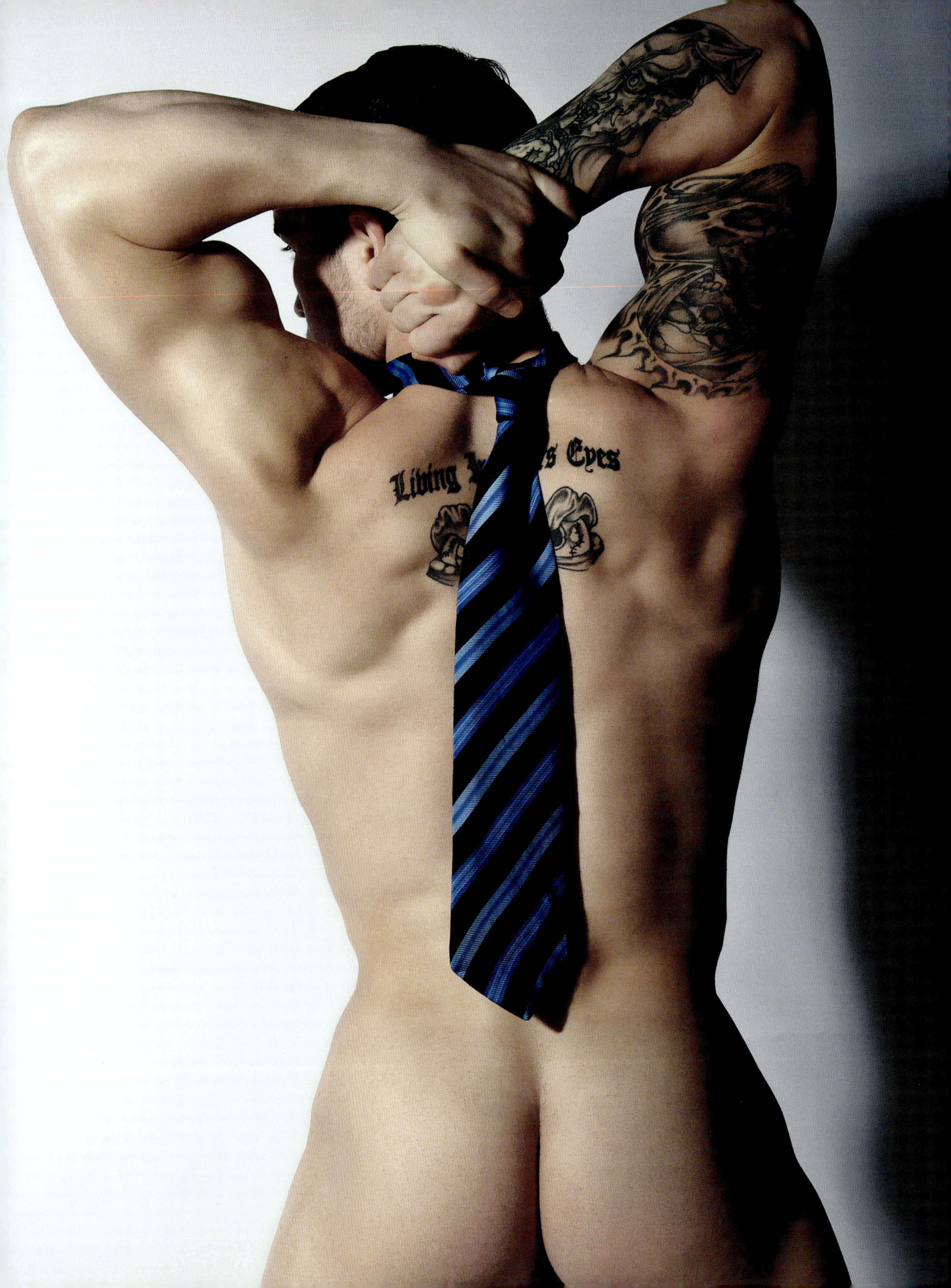
Living   Eyes

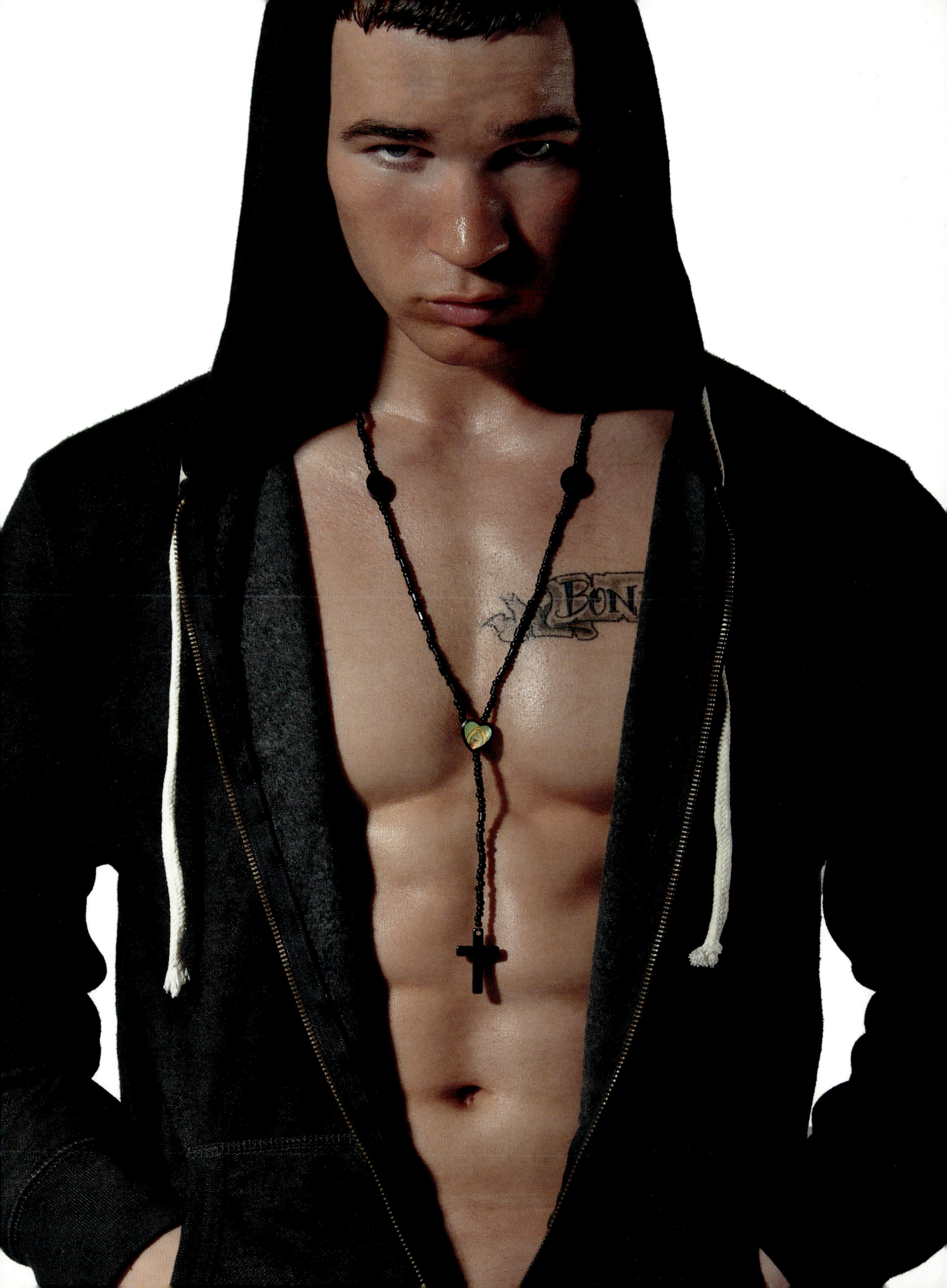

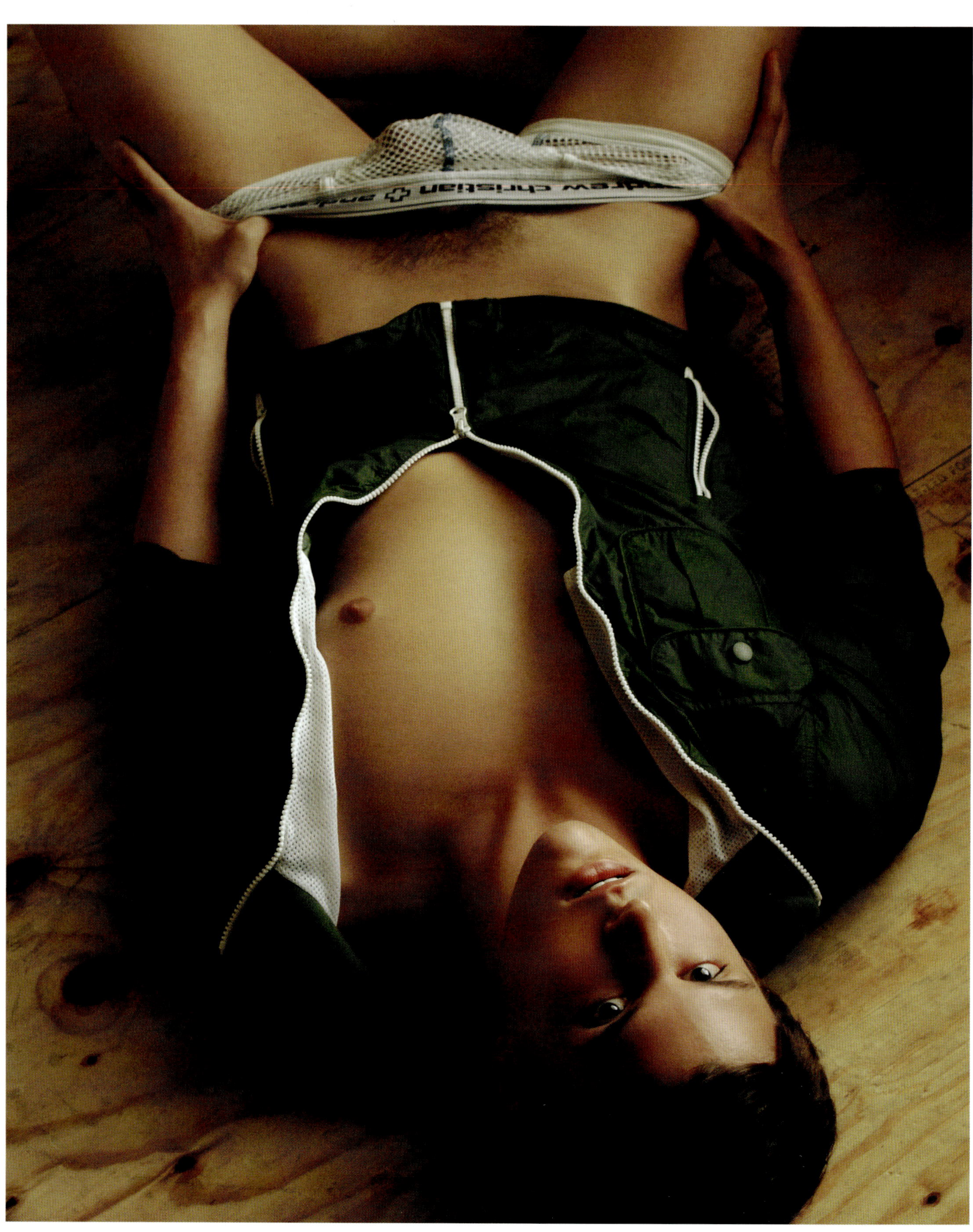

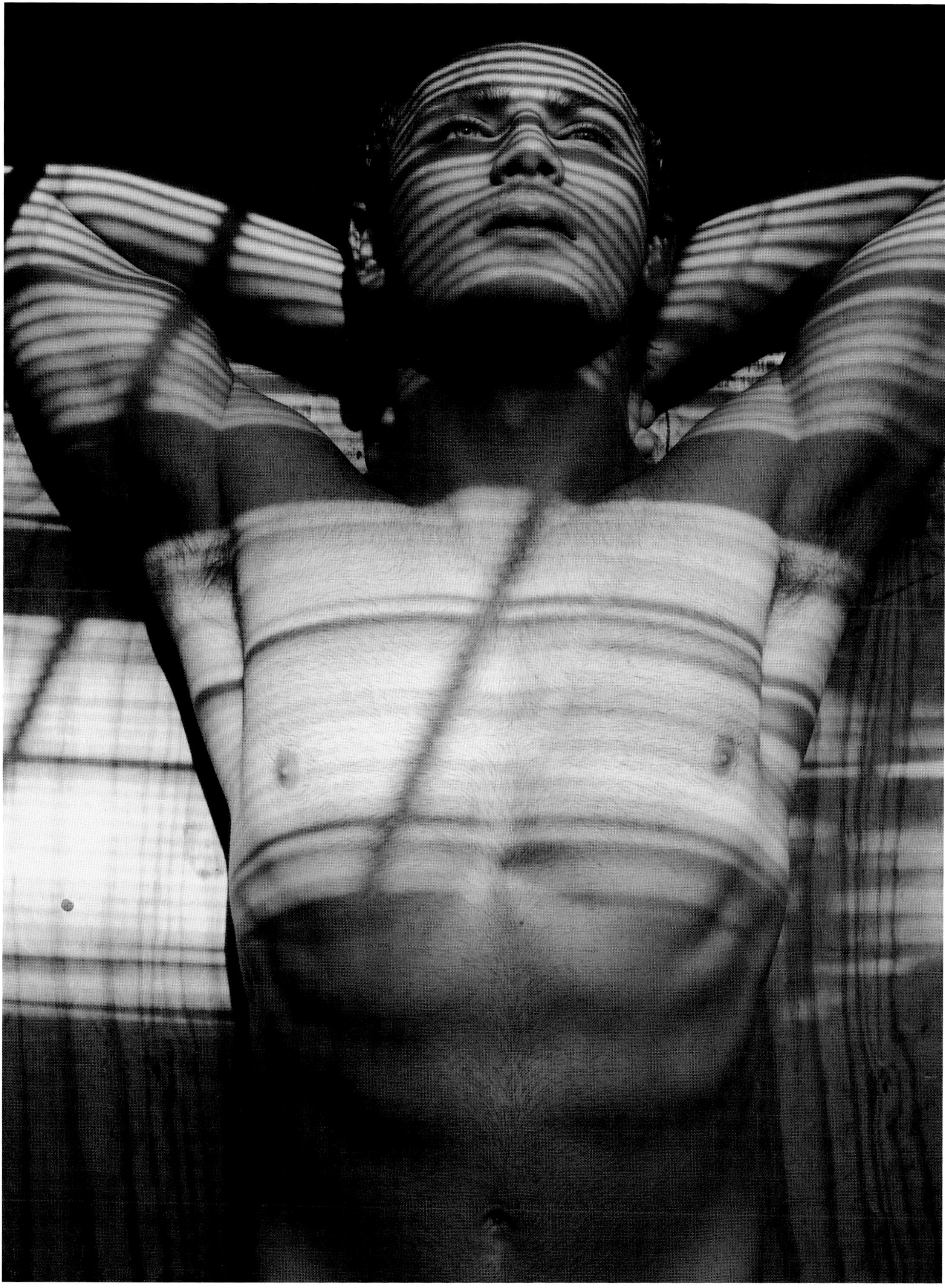

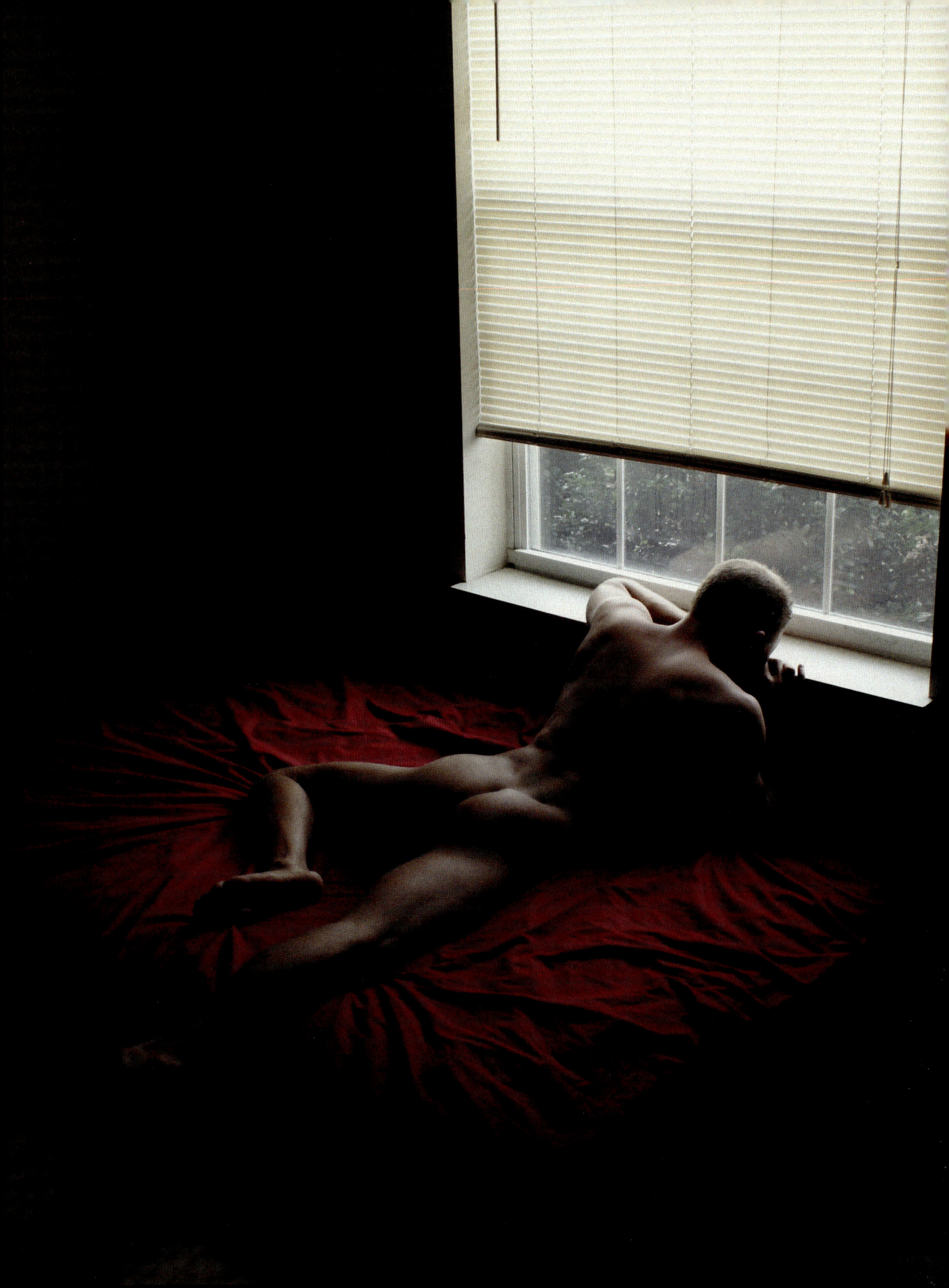

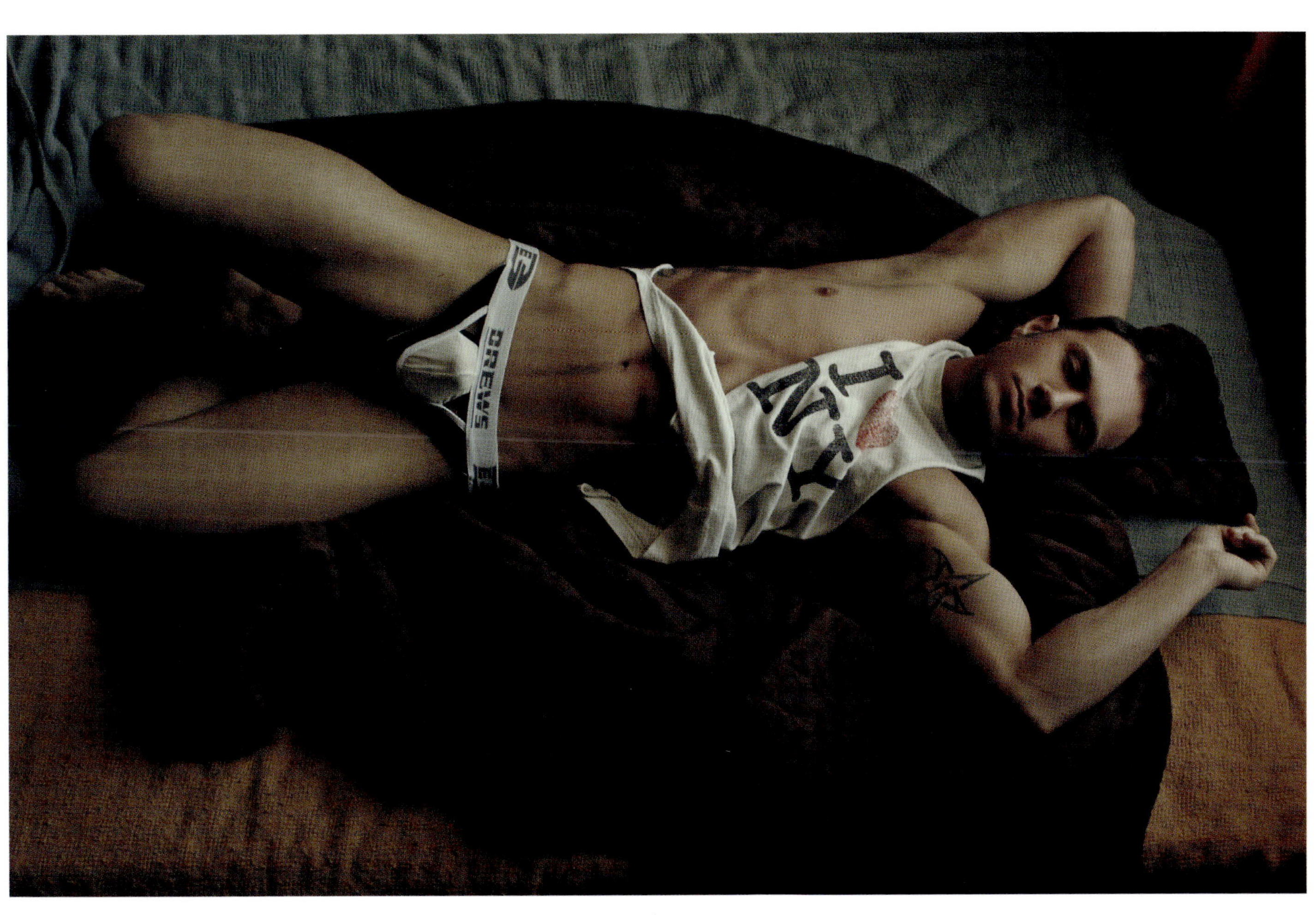

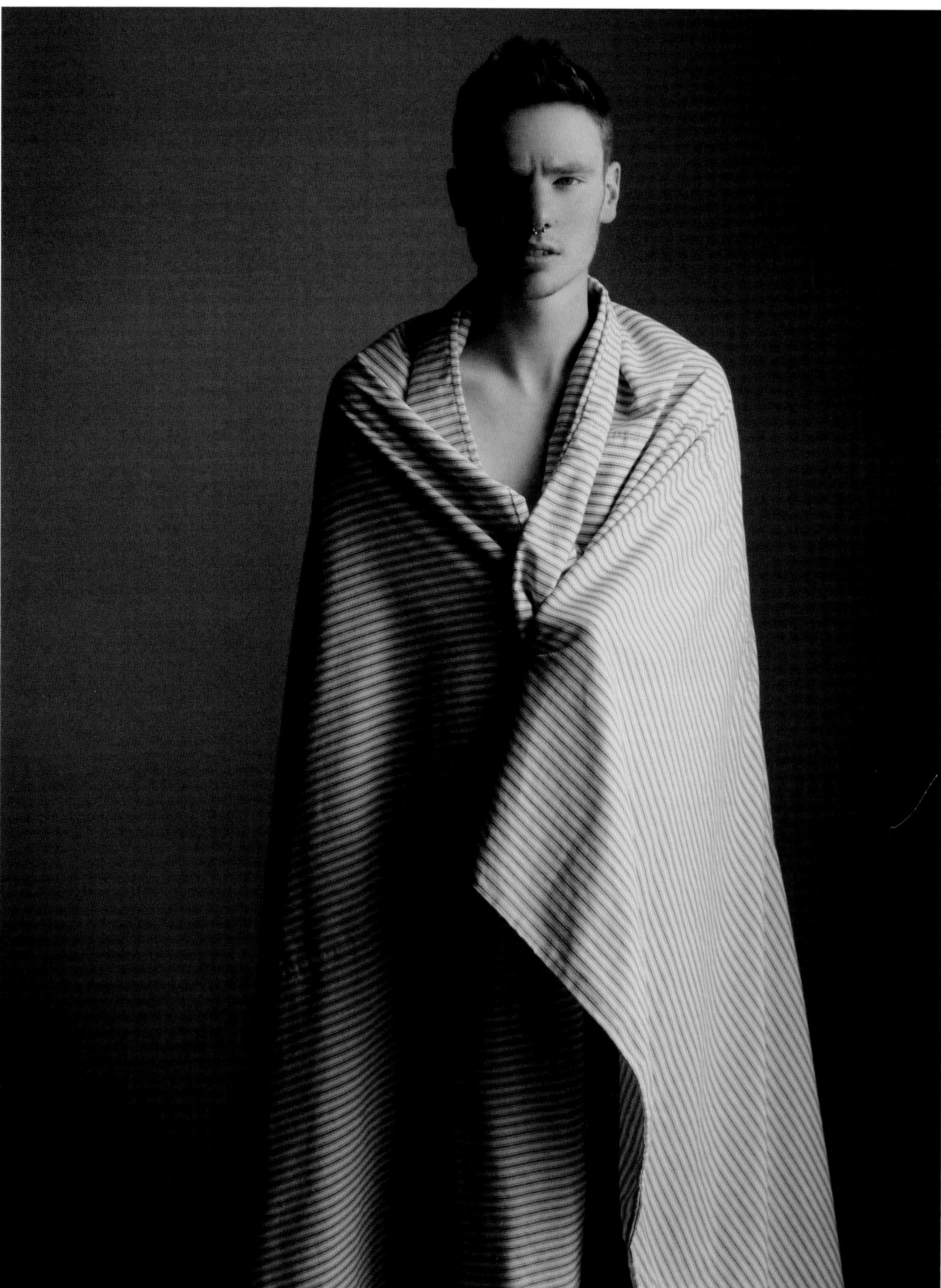

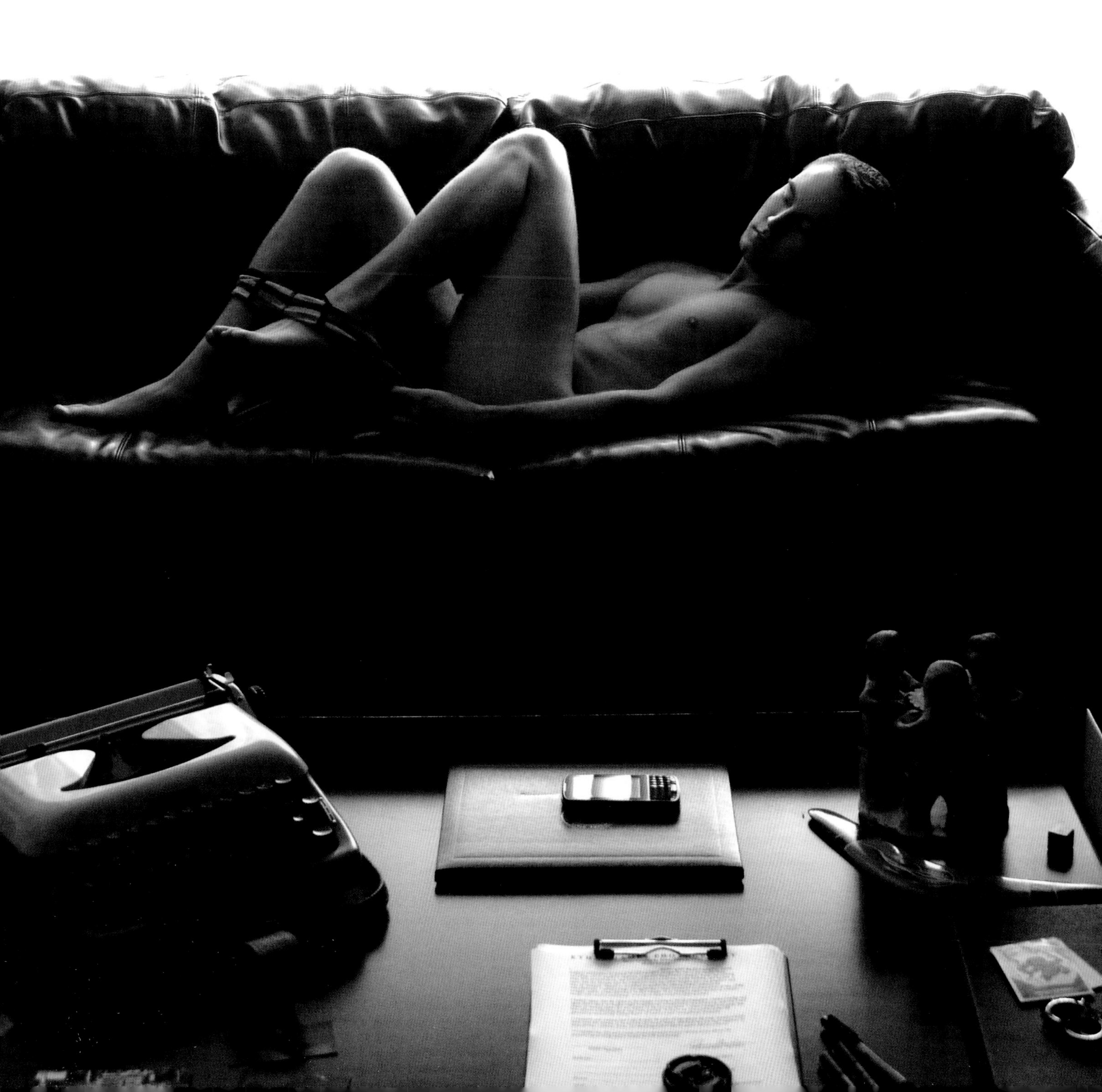

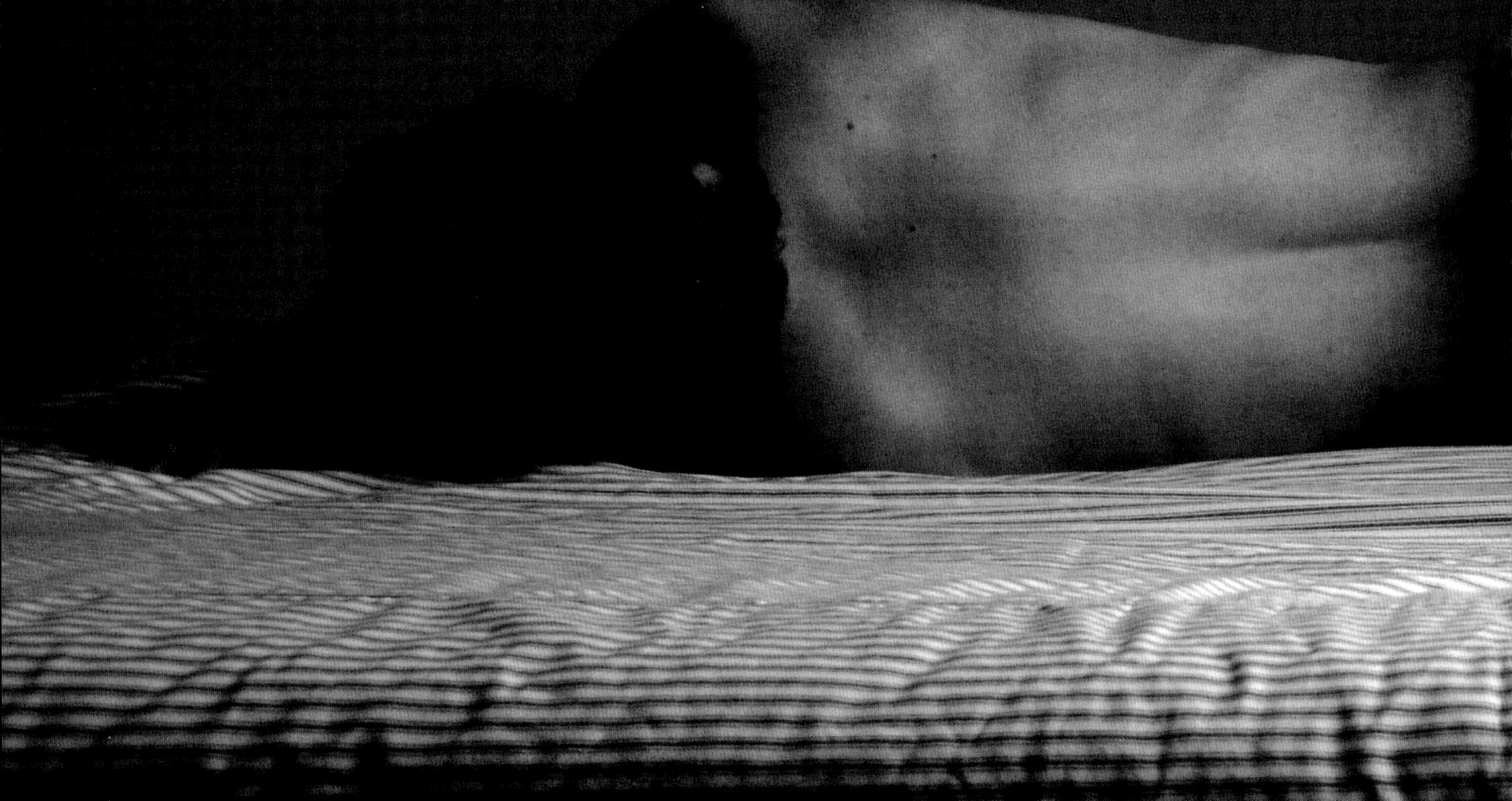

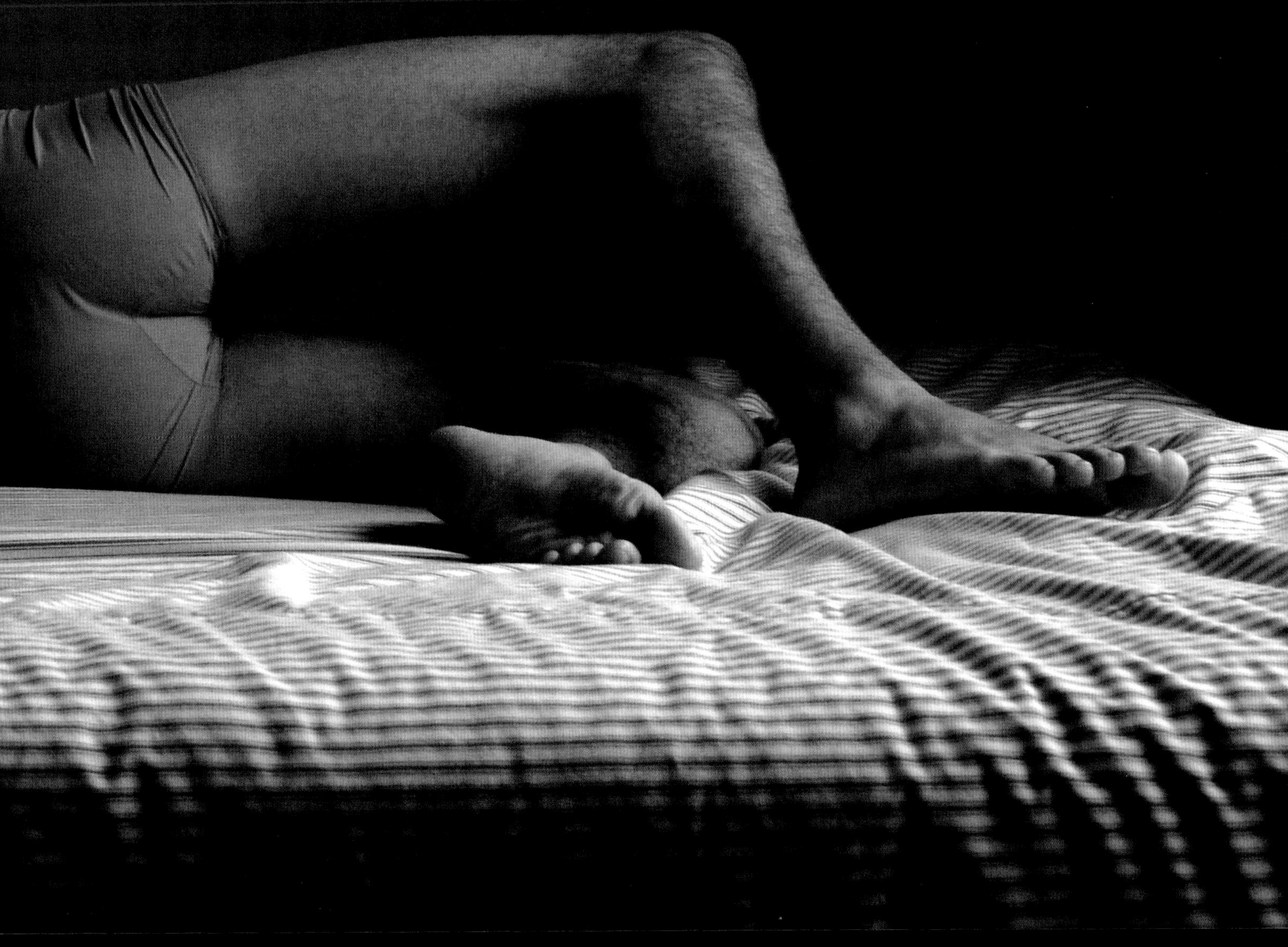

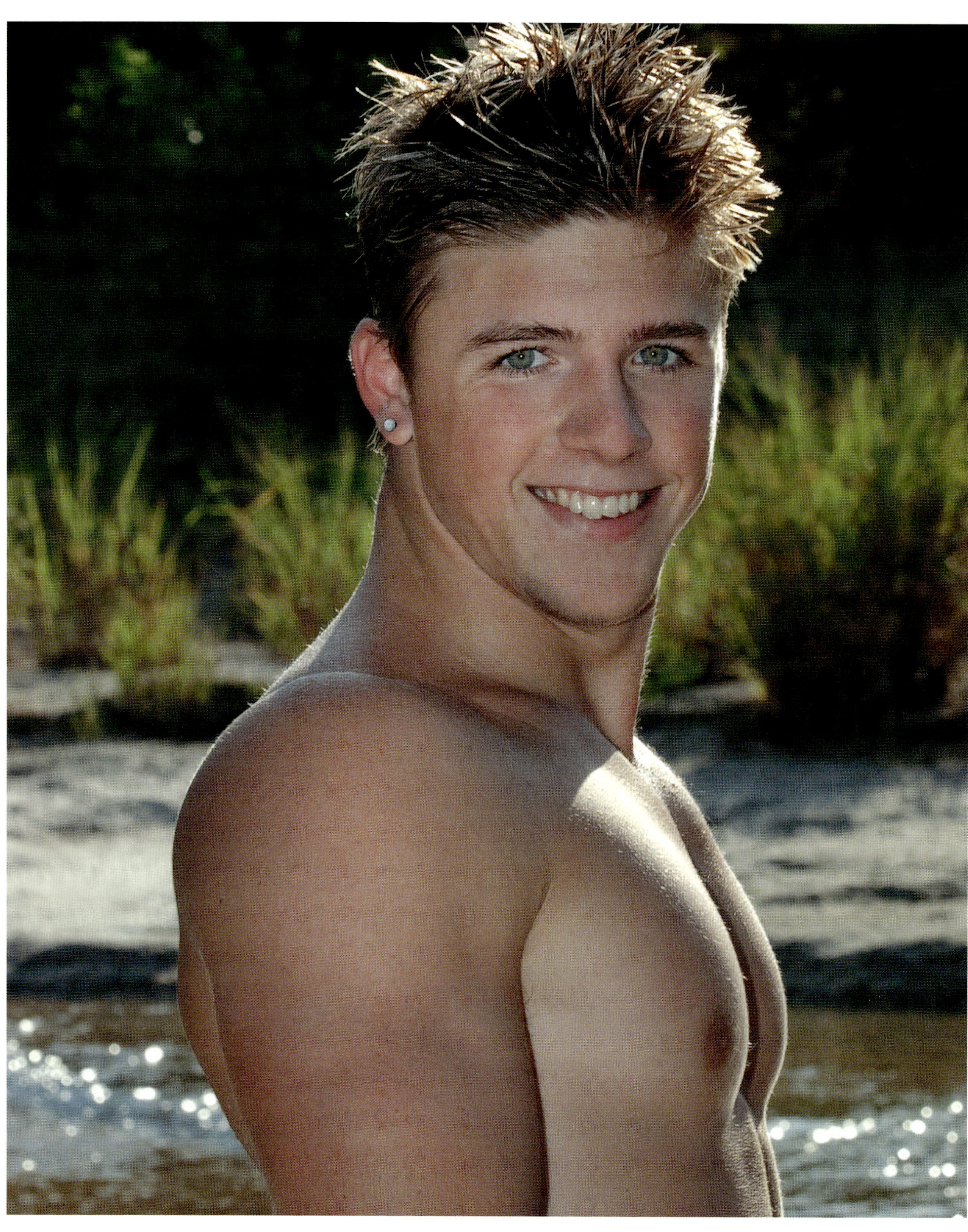

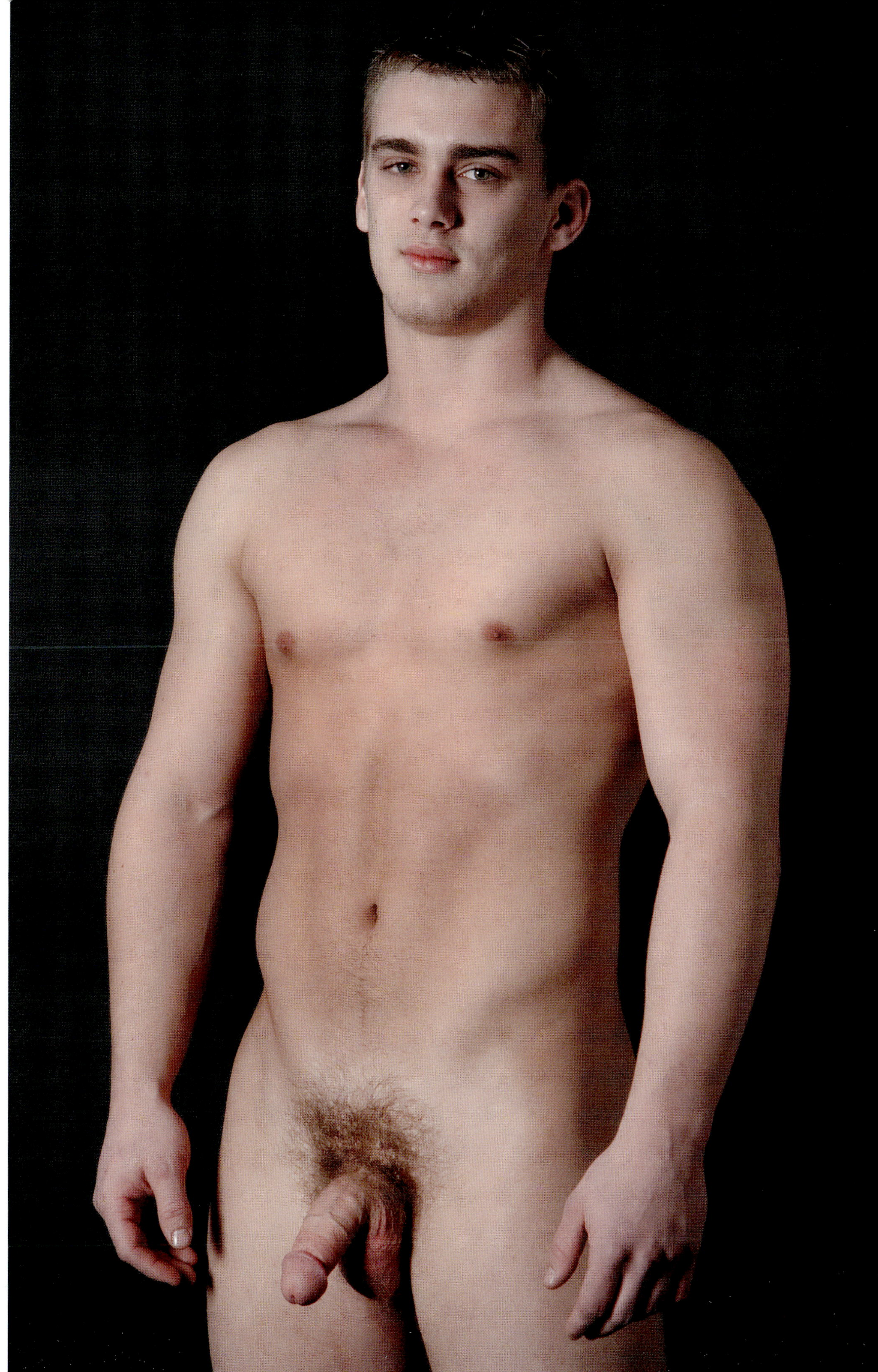

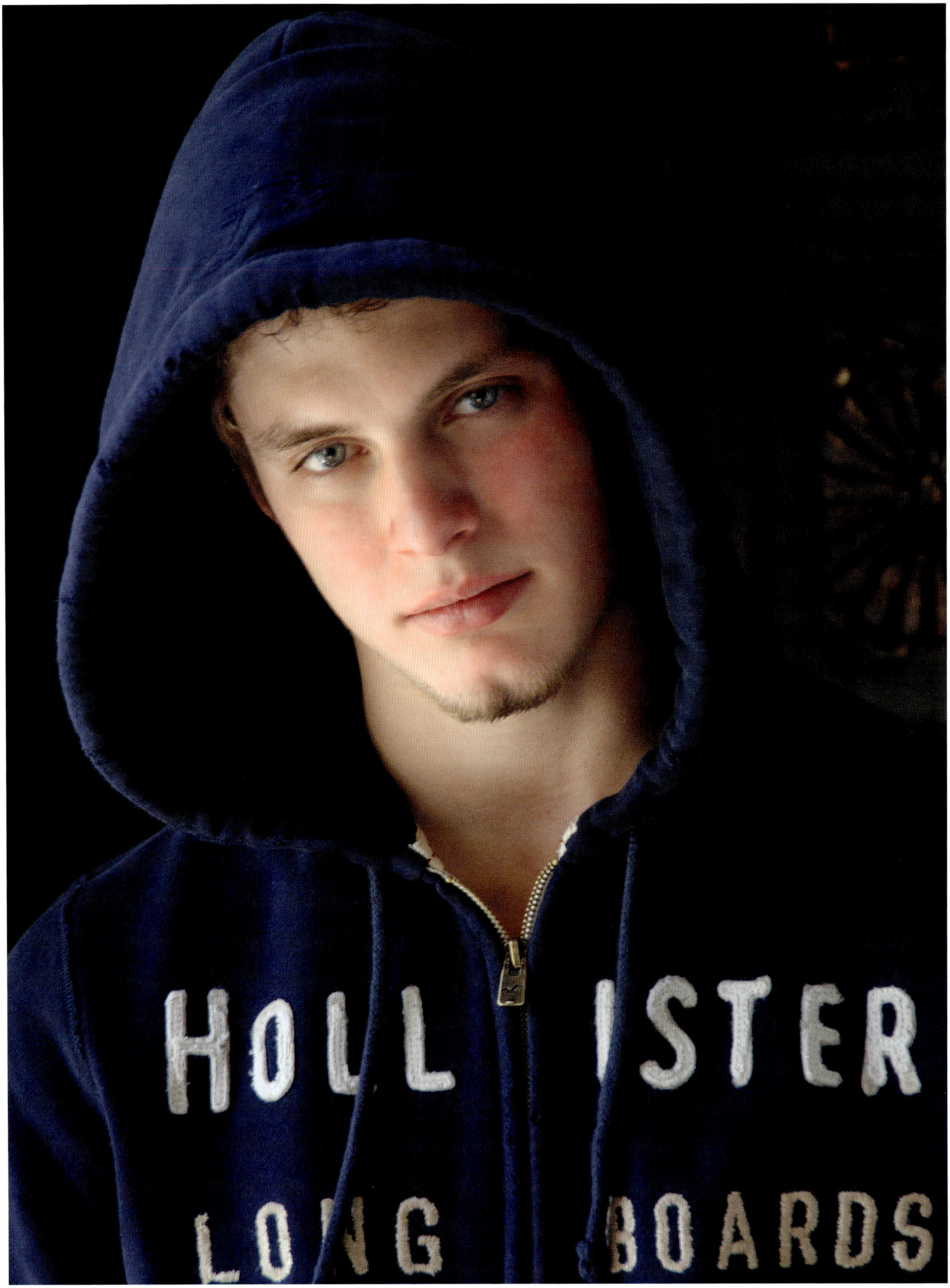

HOLLISTER
LONG BOARDS

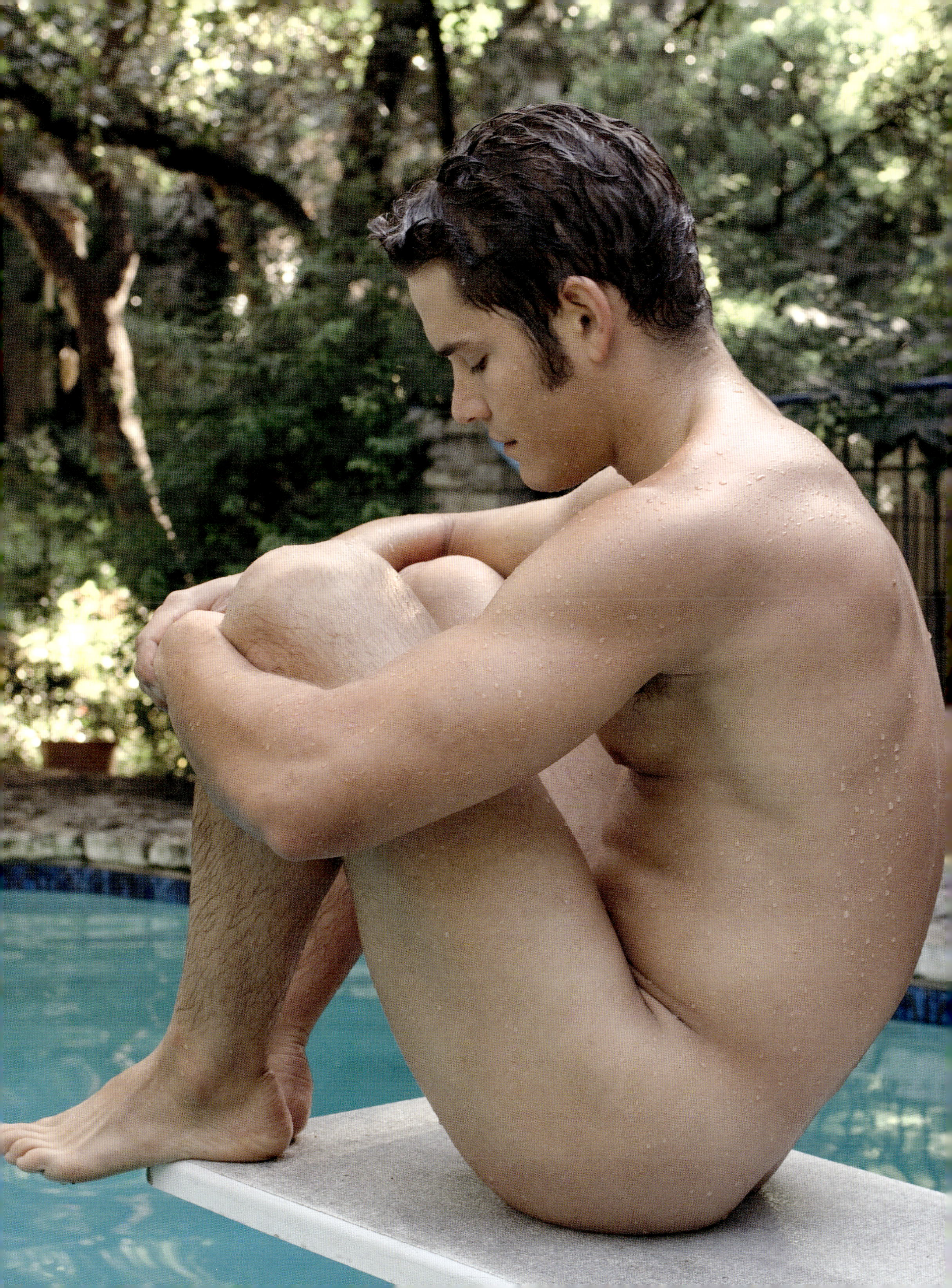

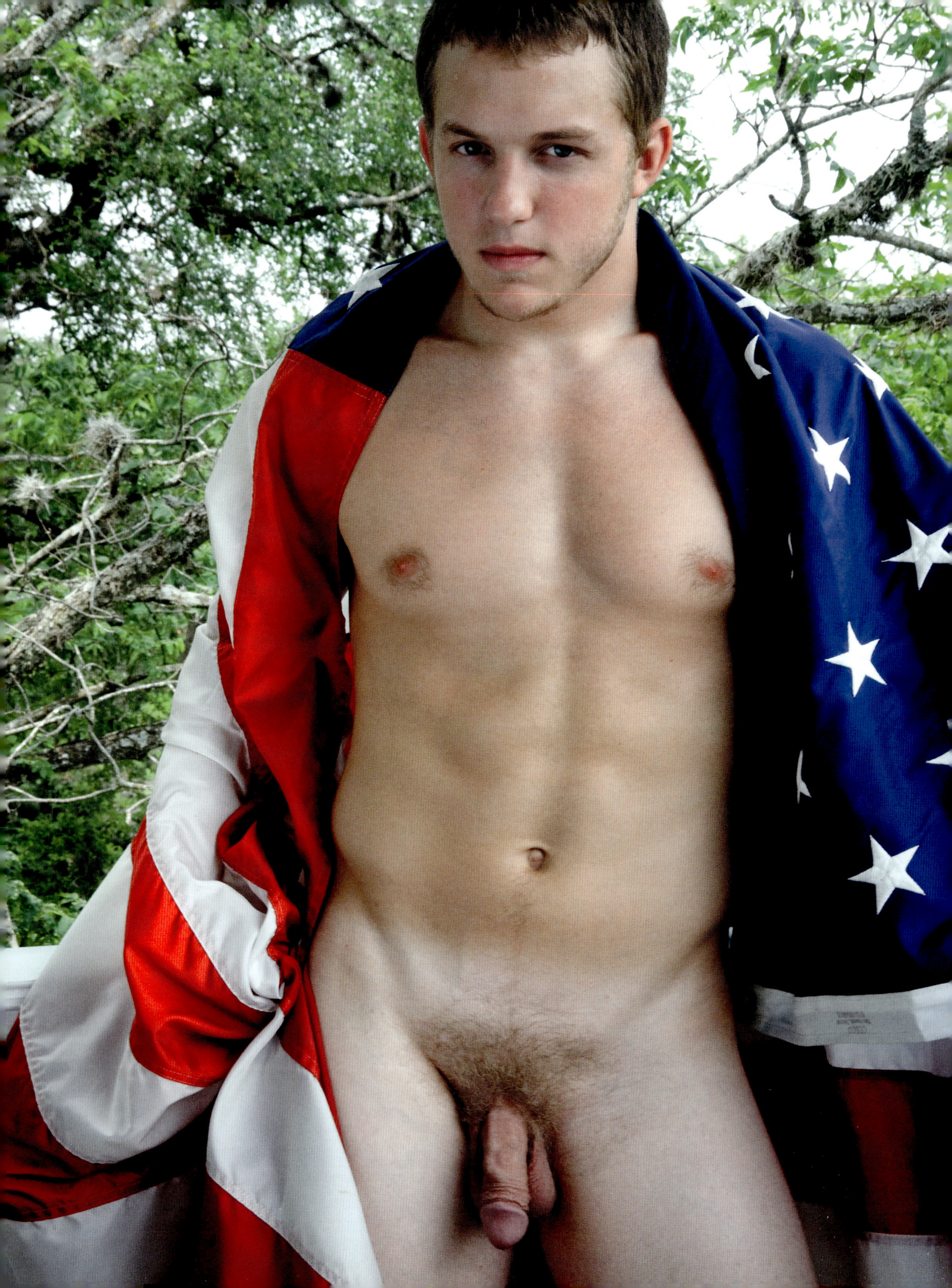

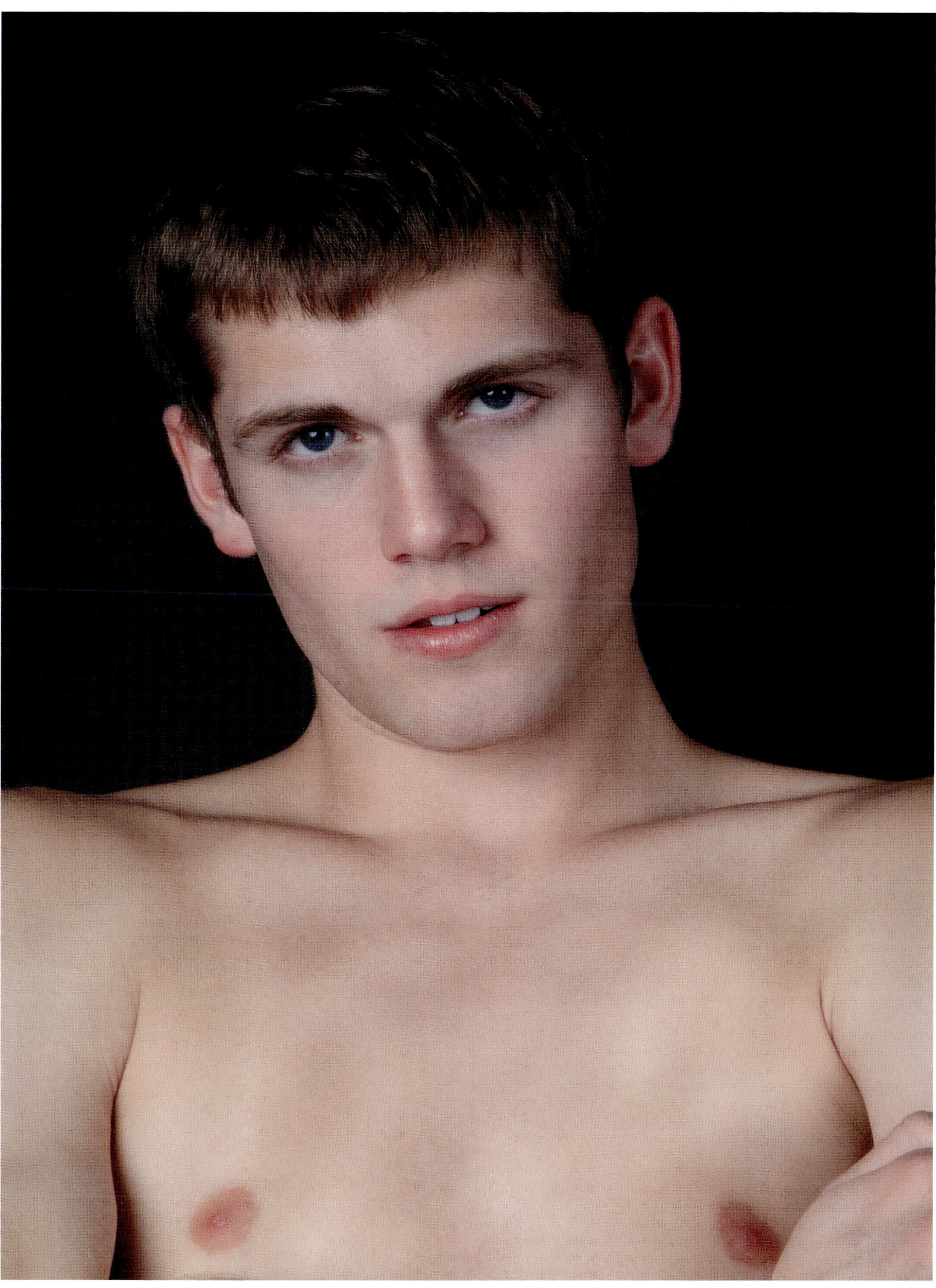

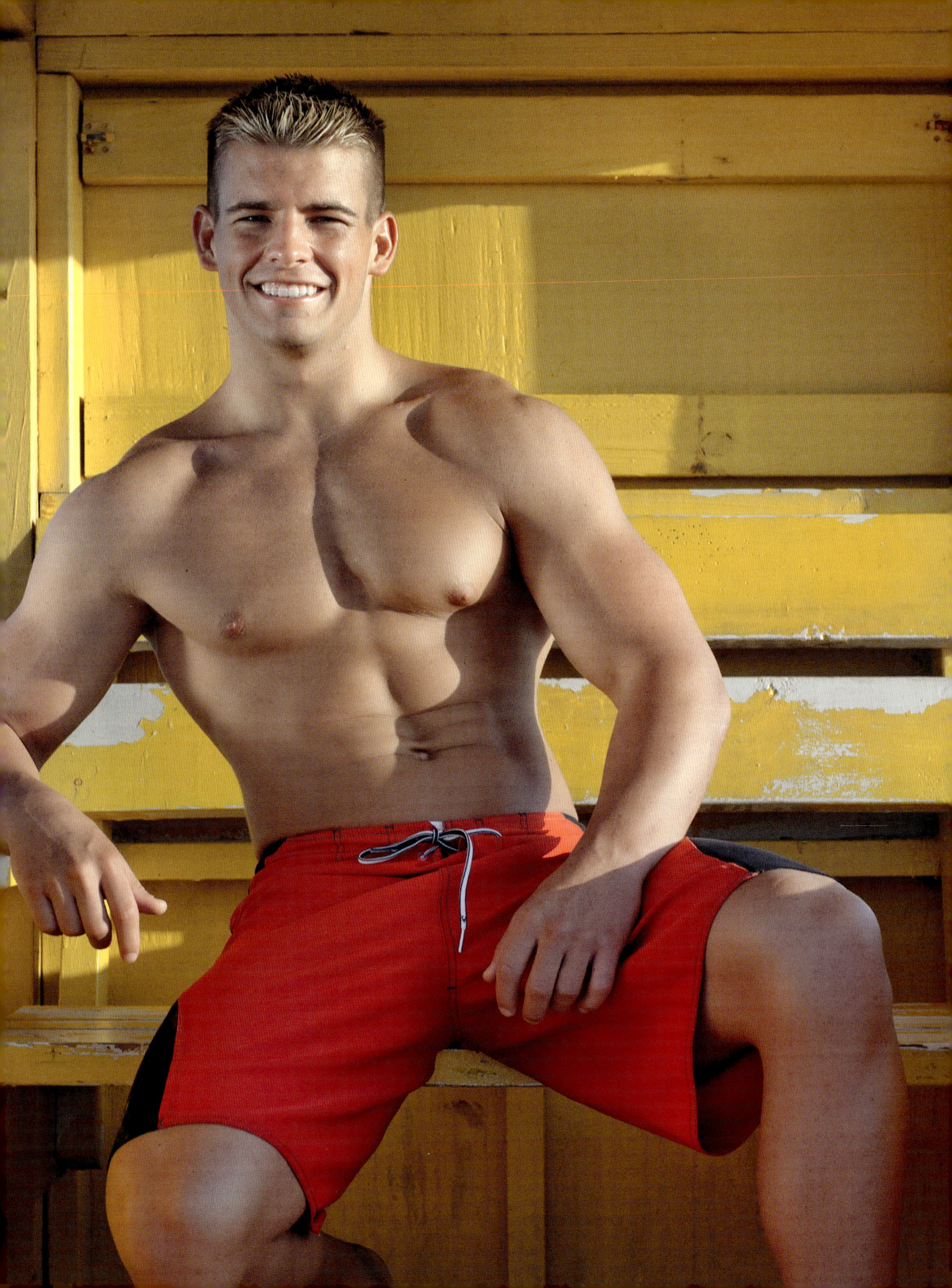

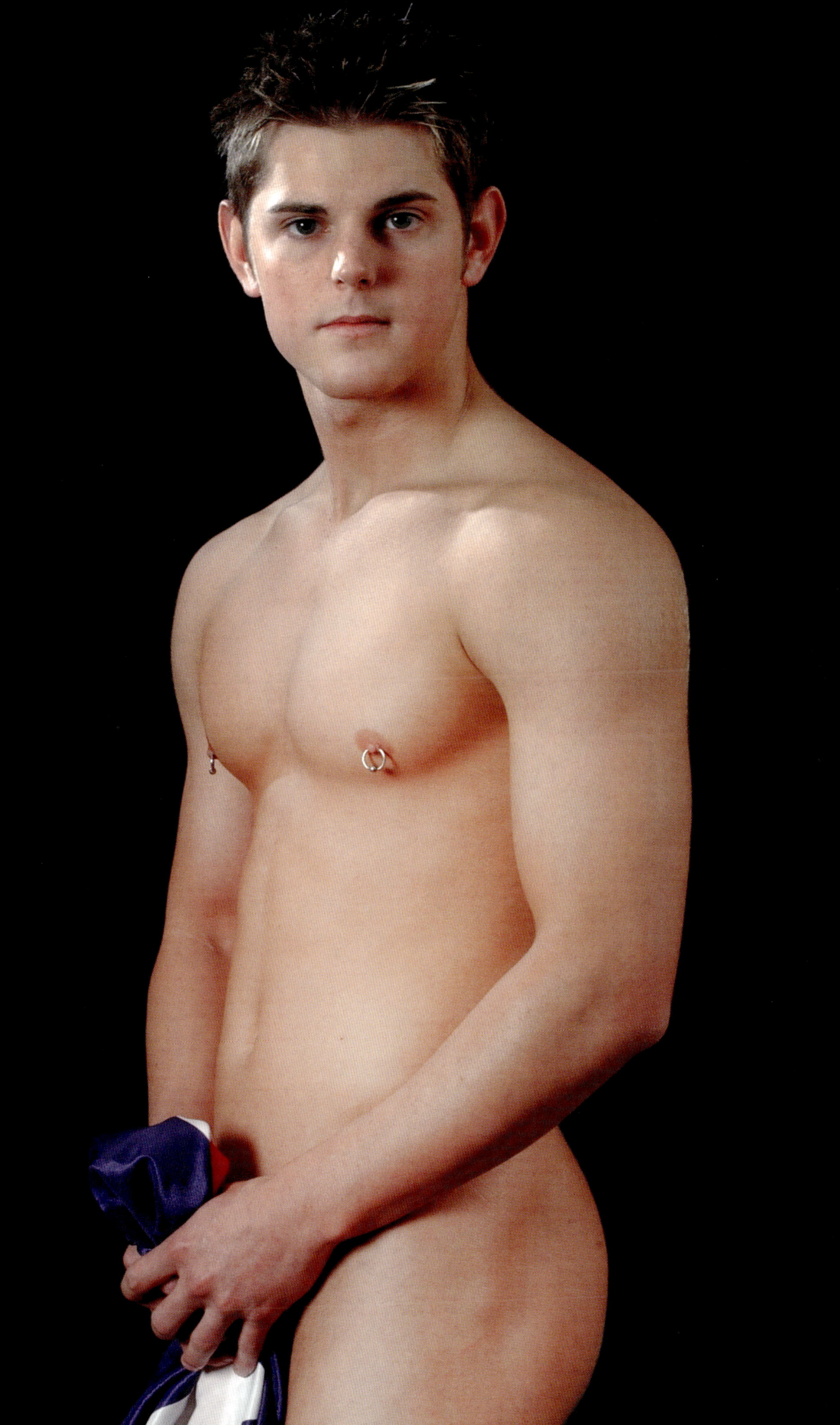

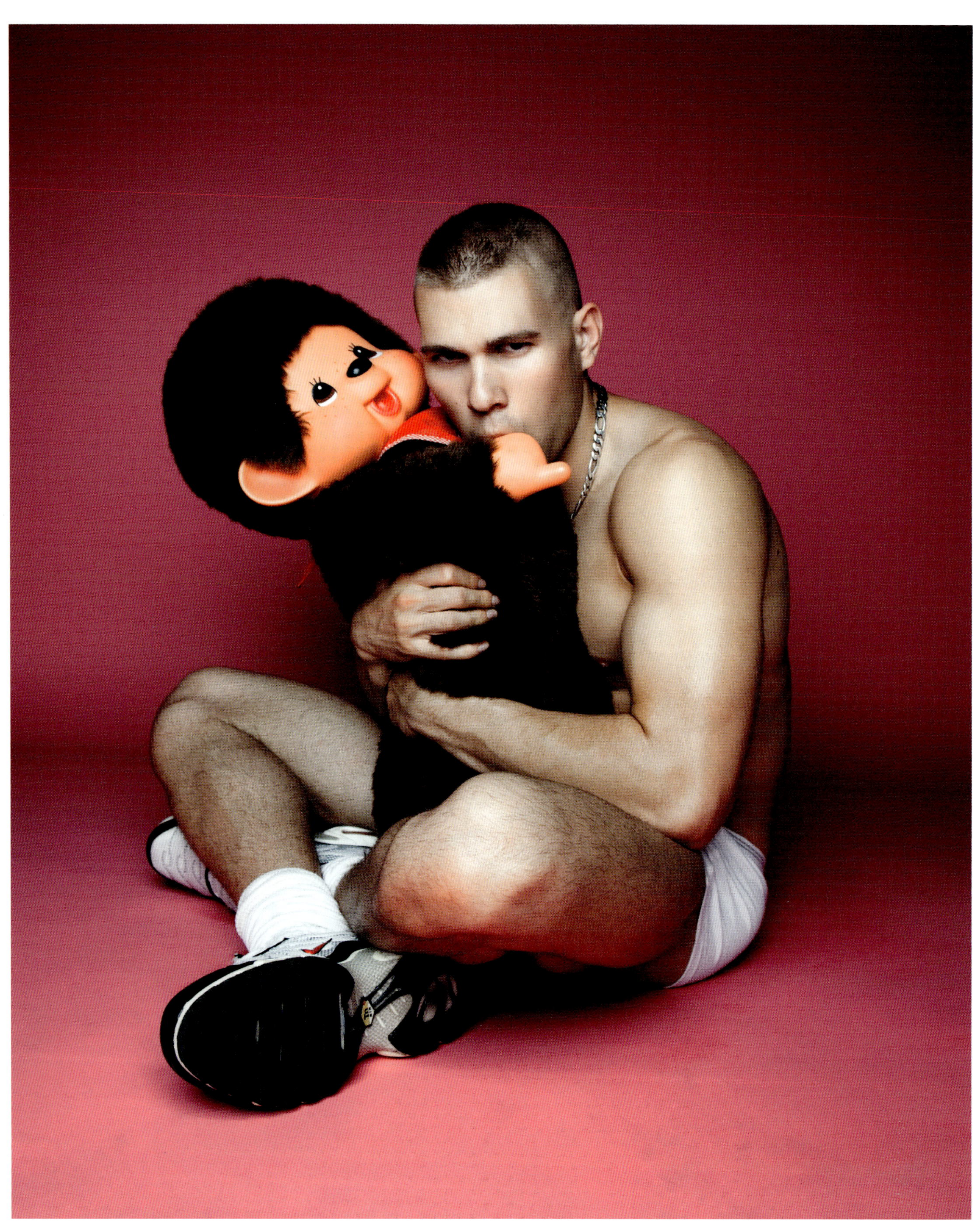

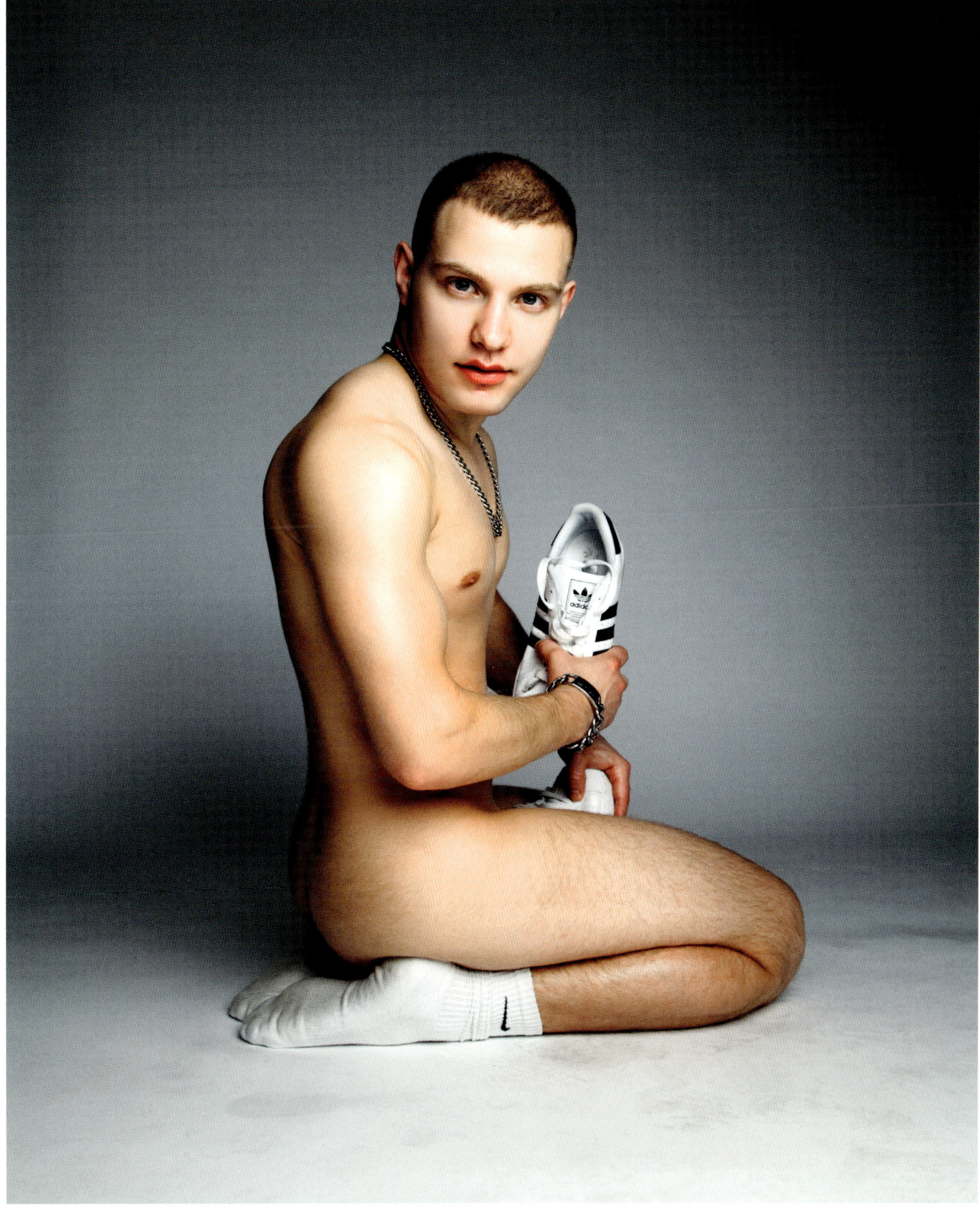

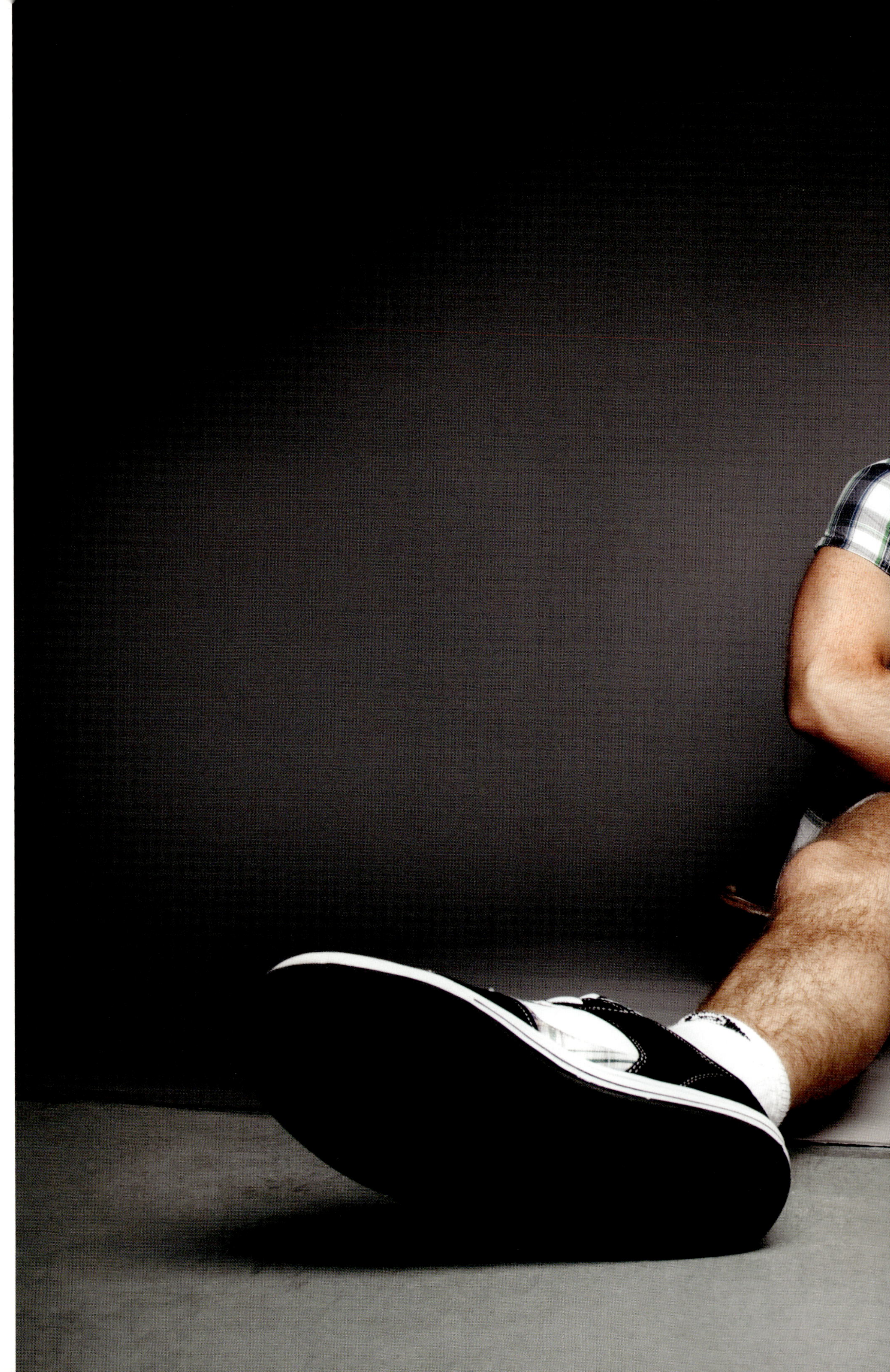

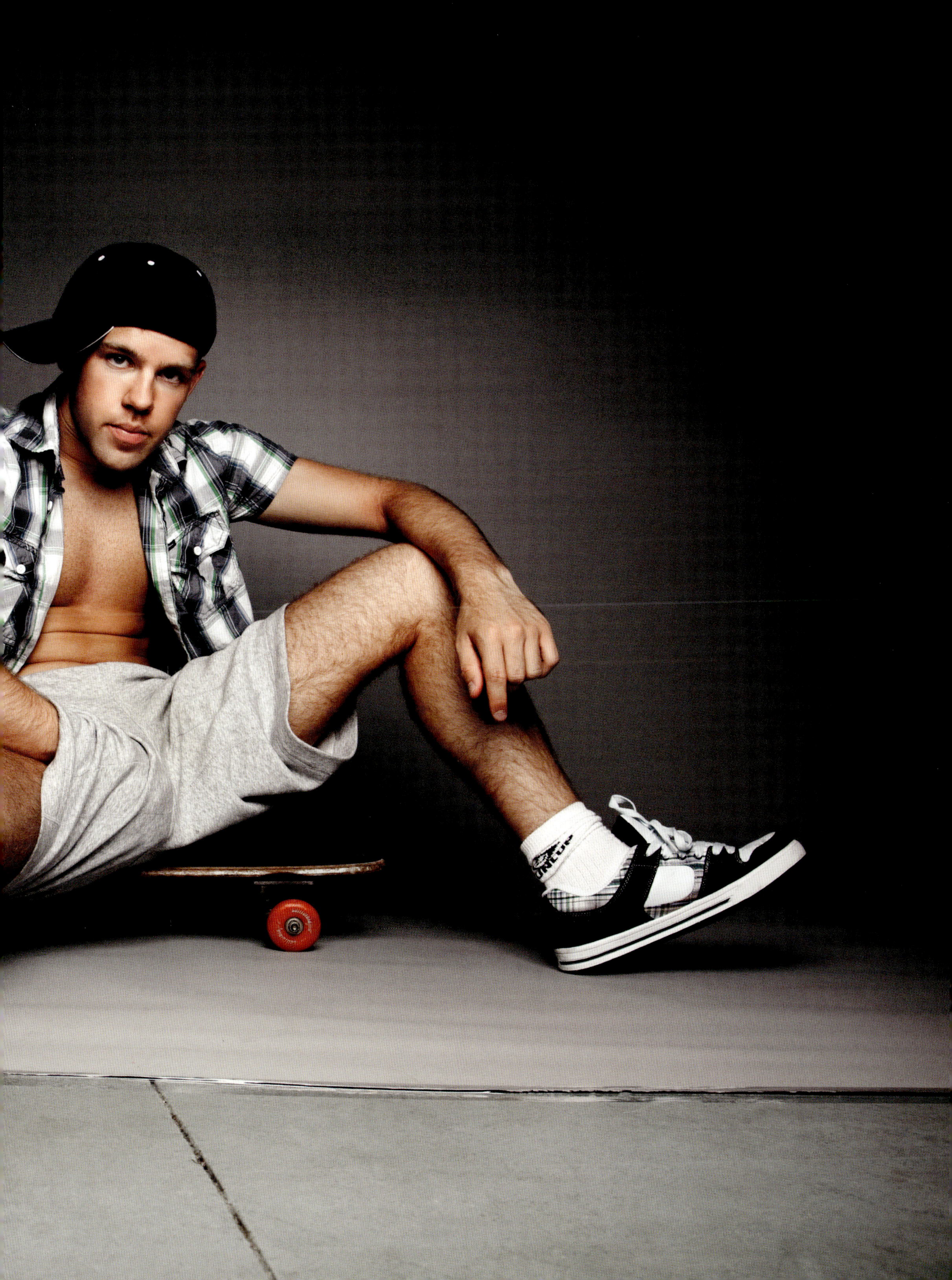

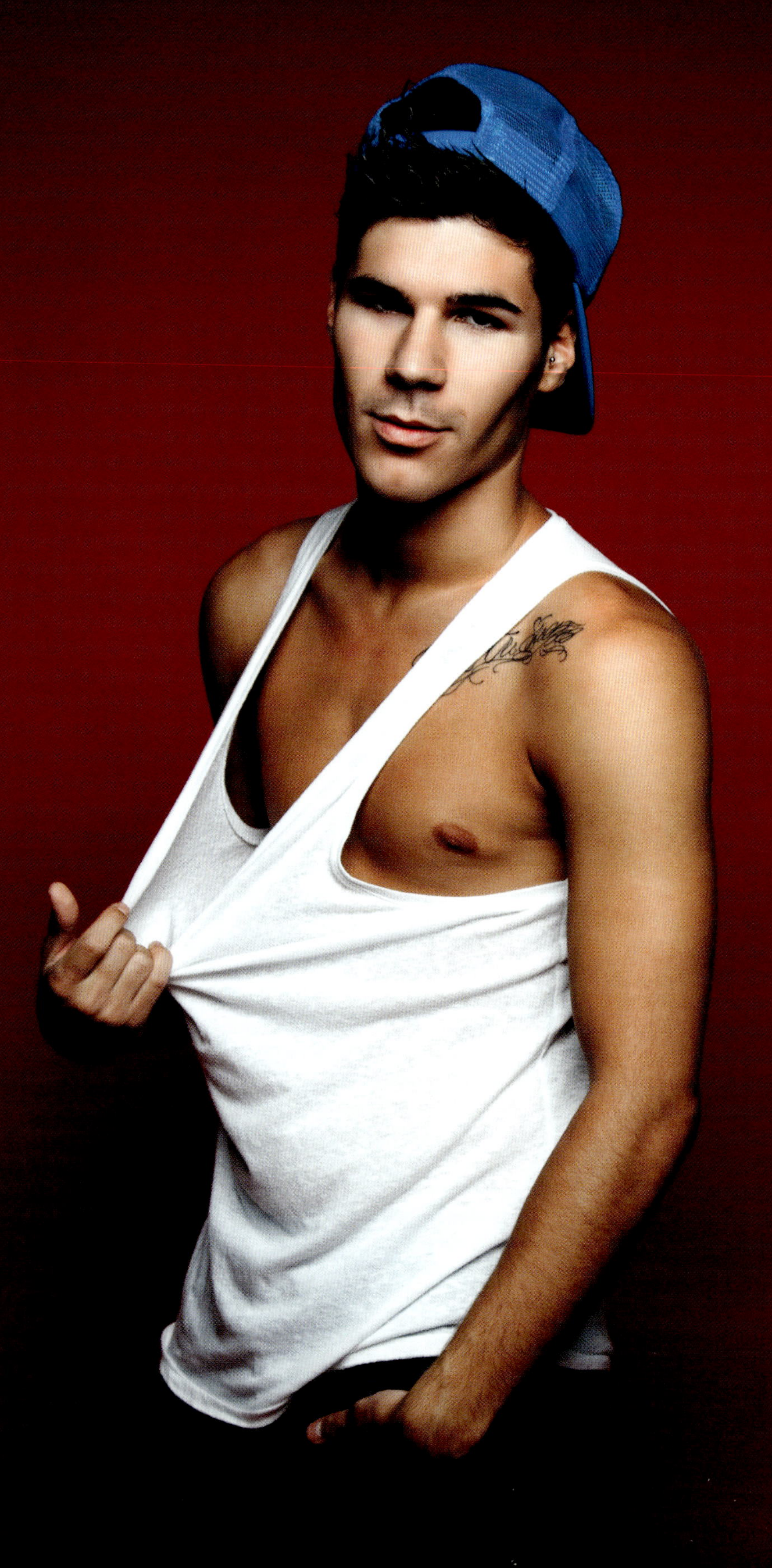

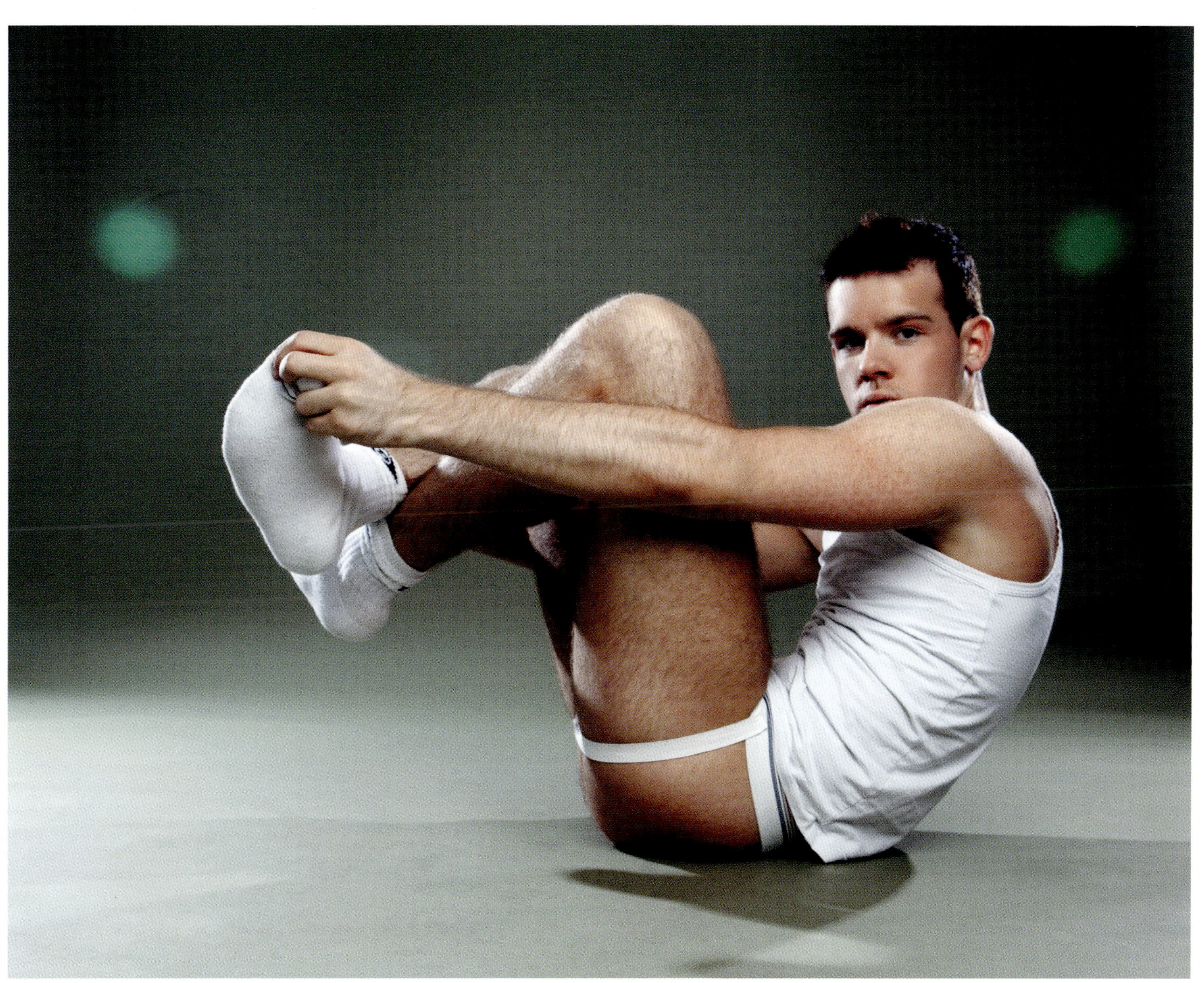

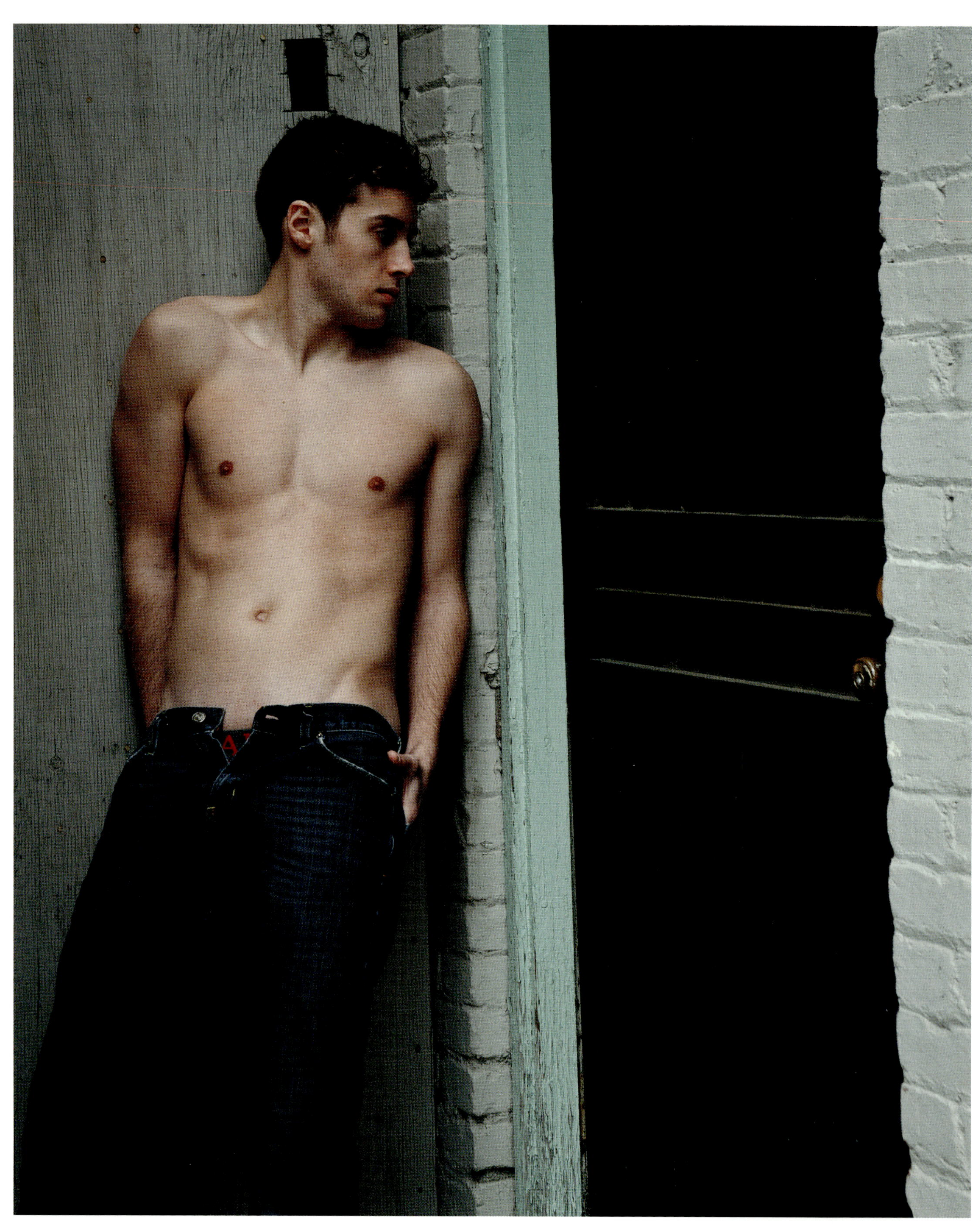

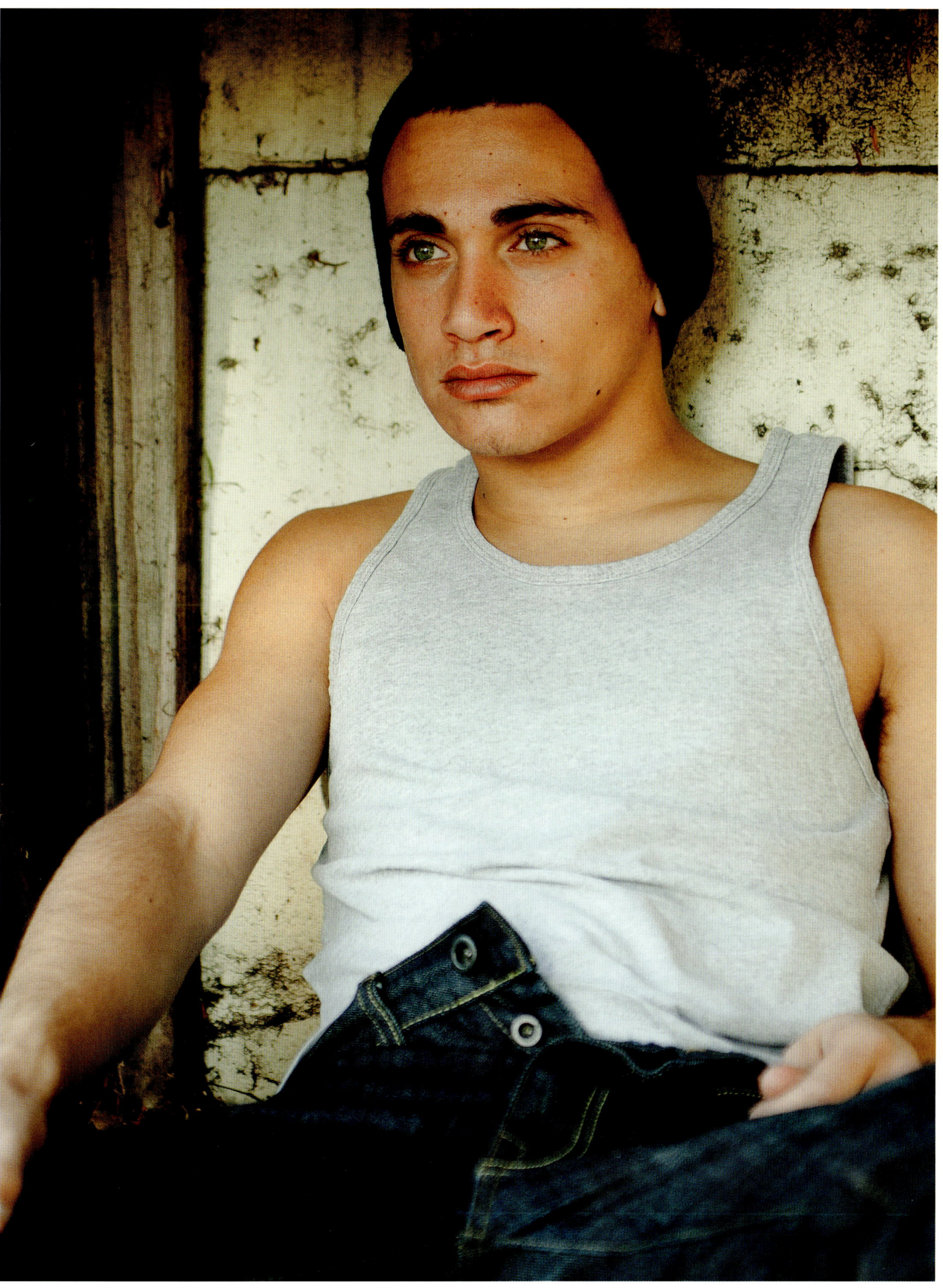

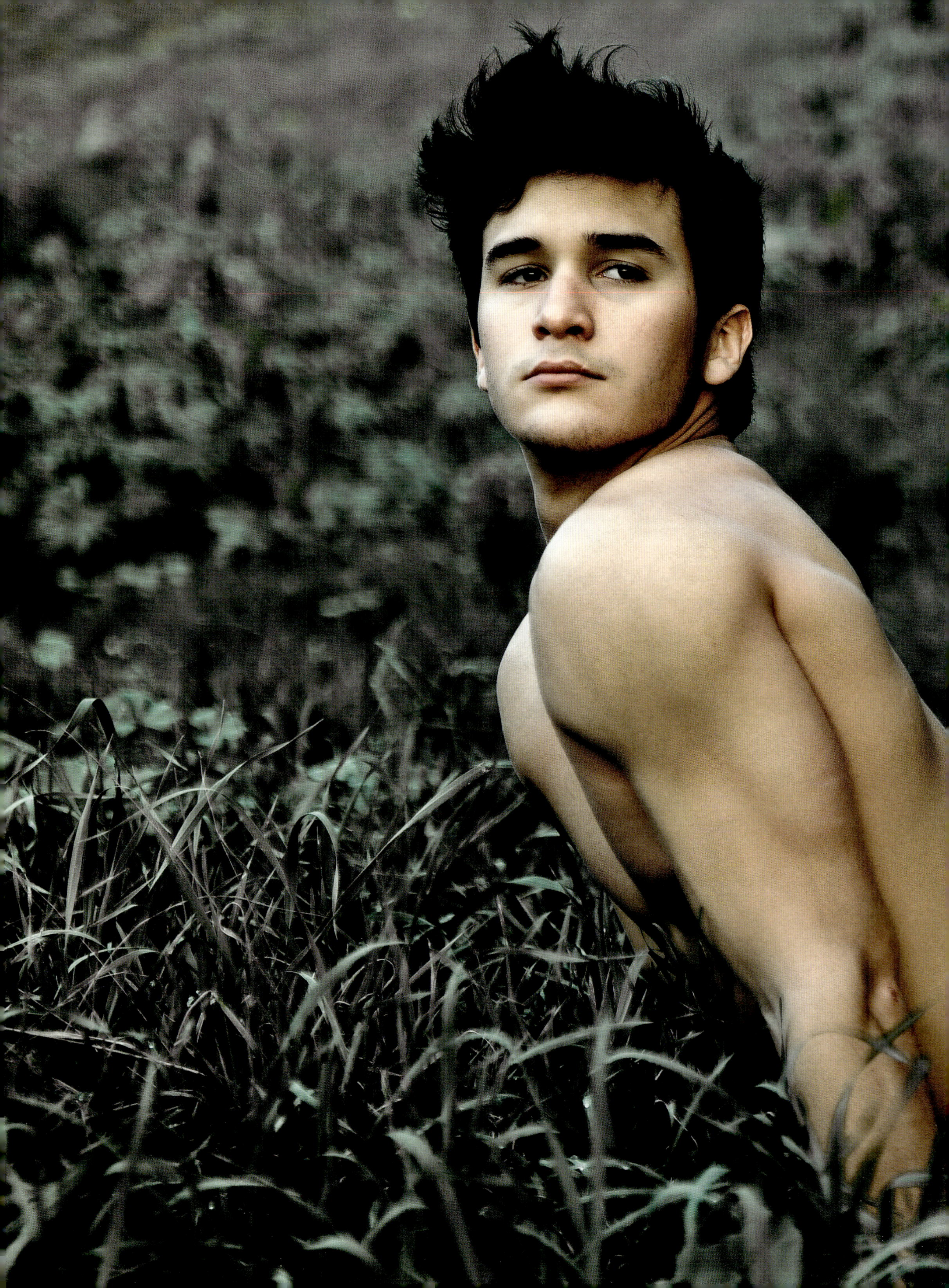

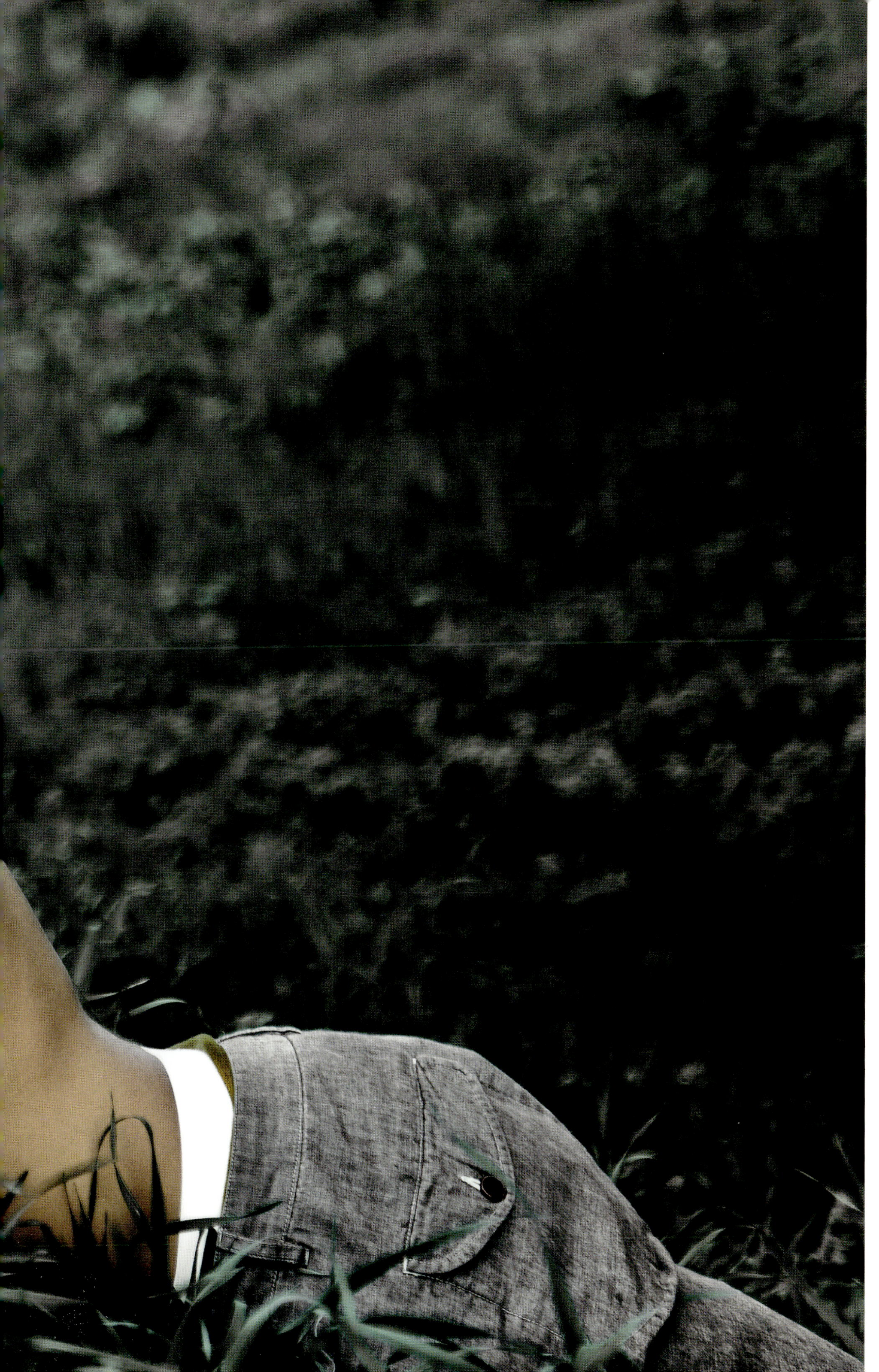

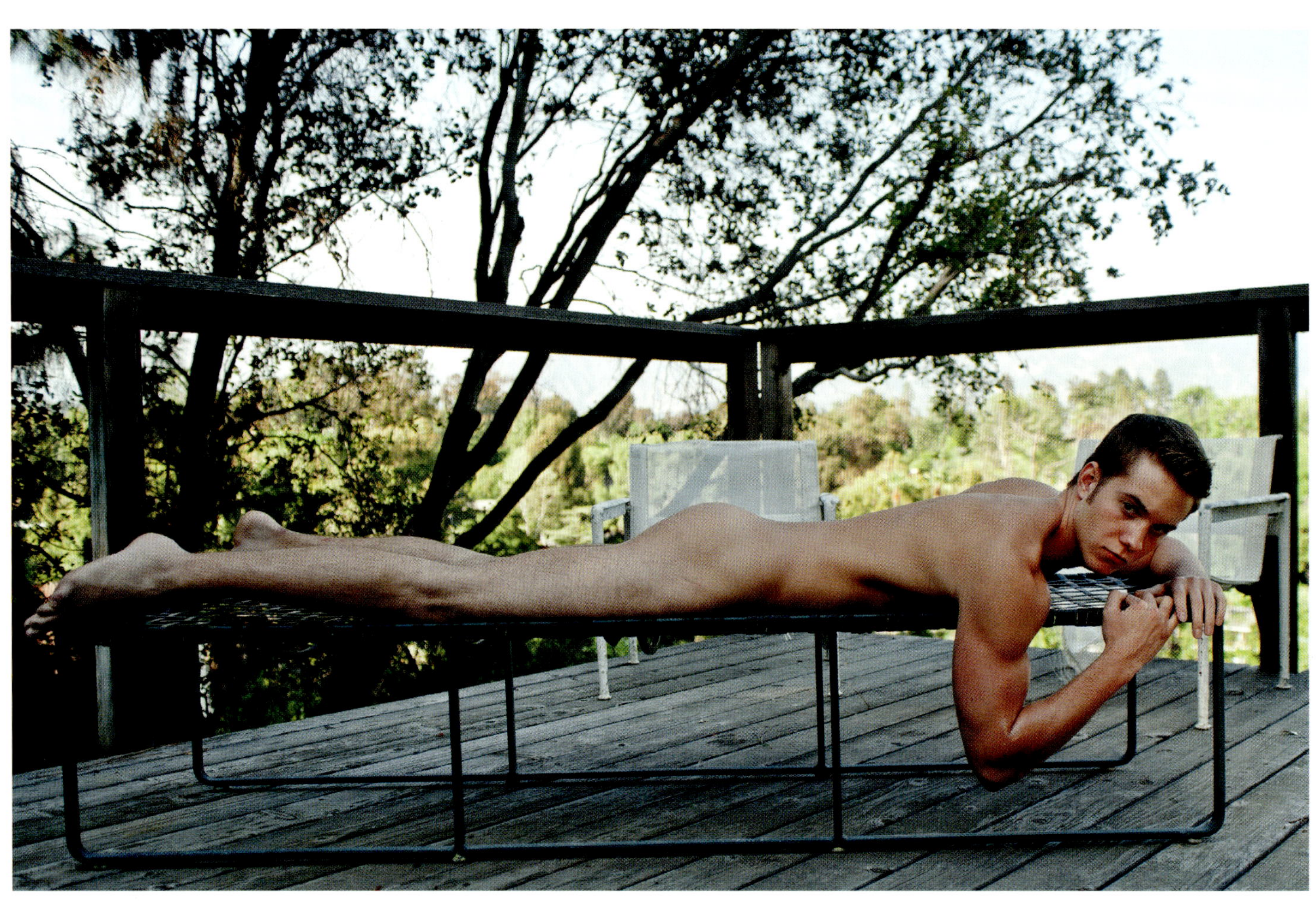

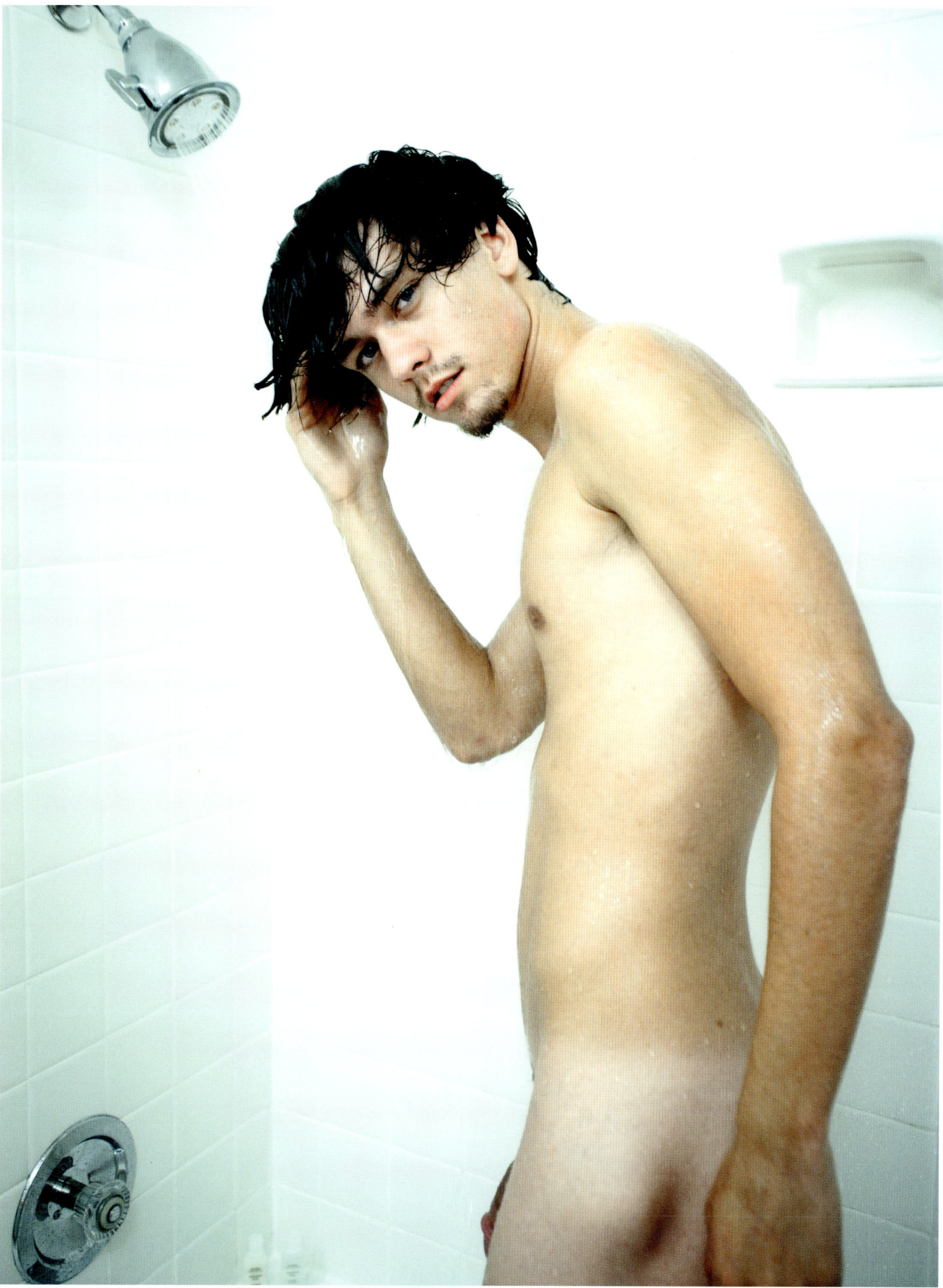

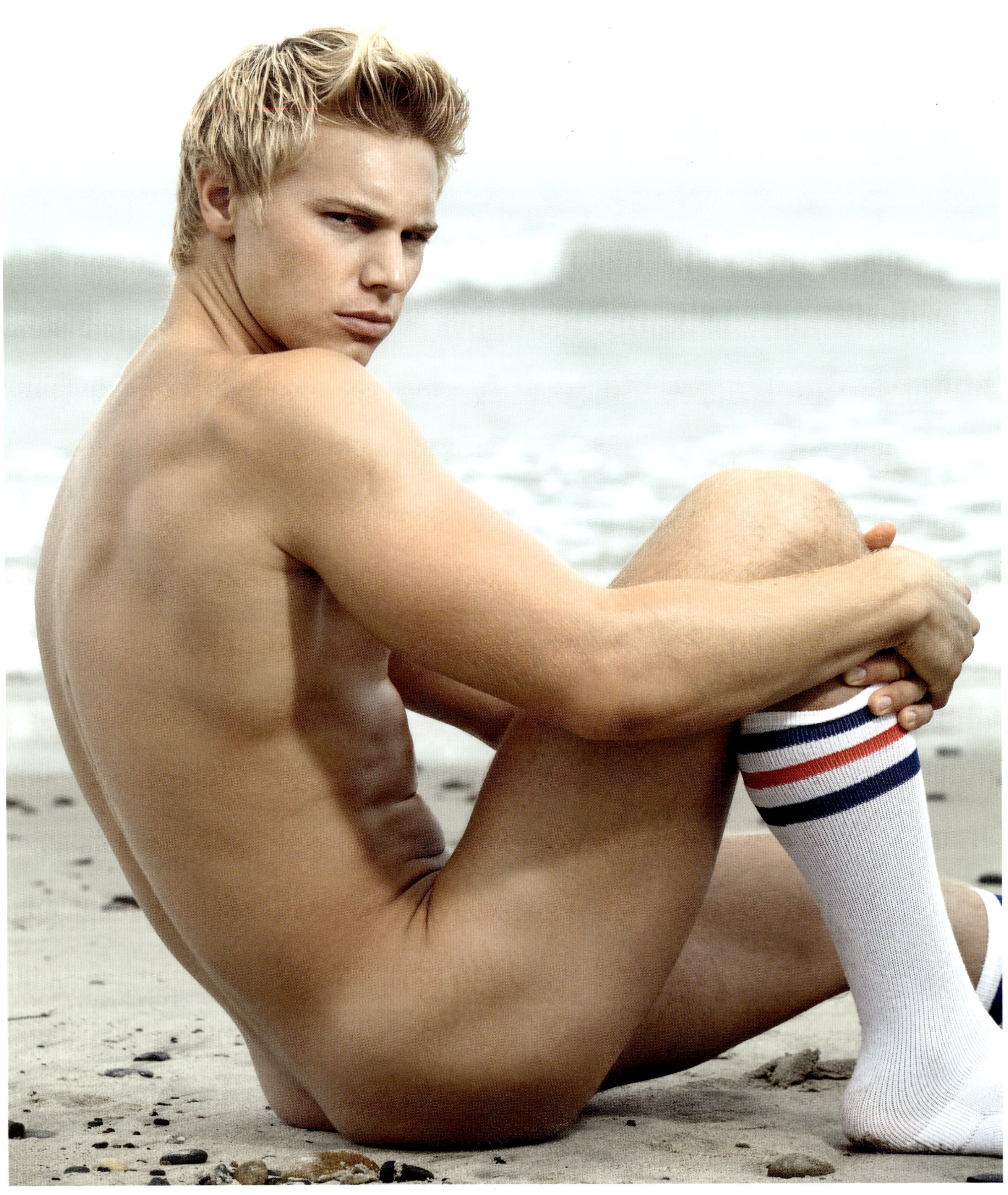

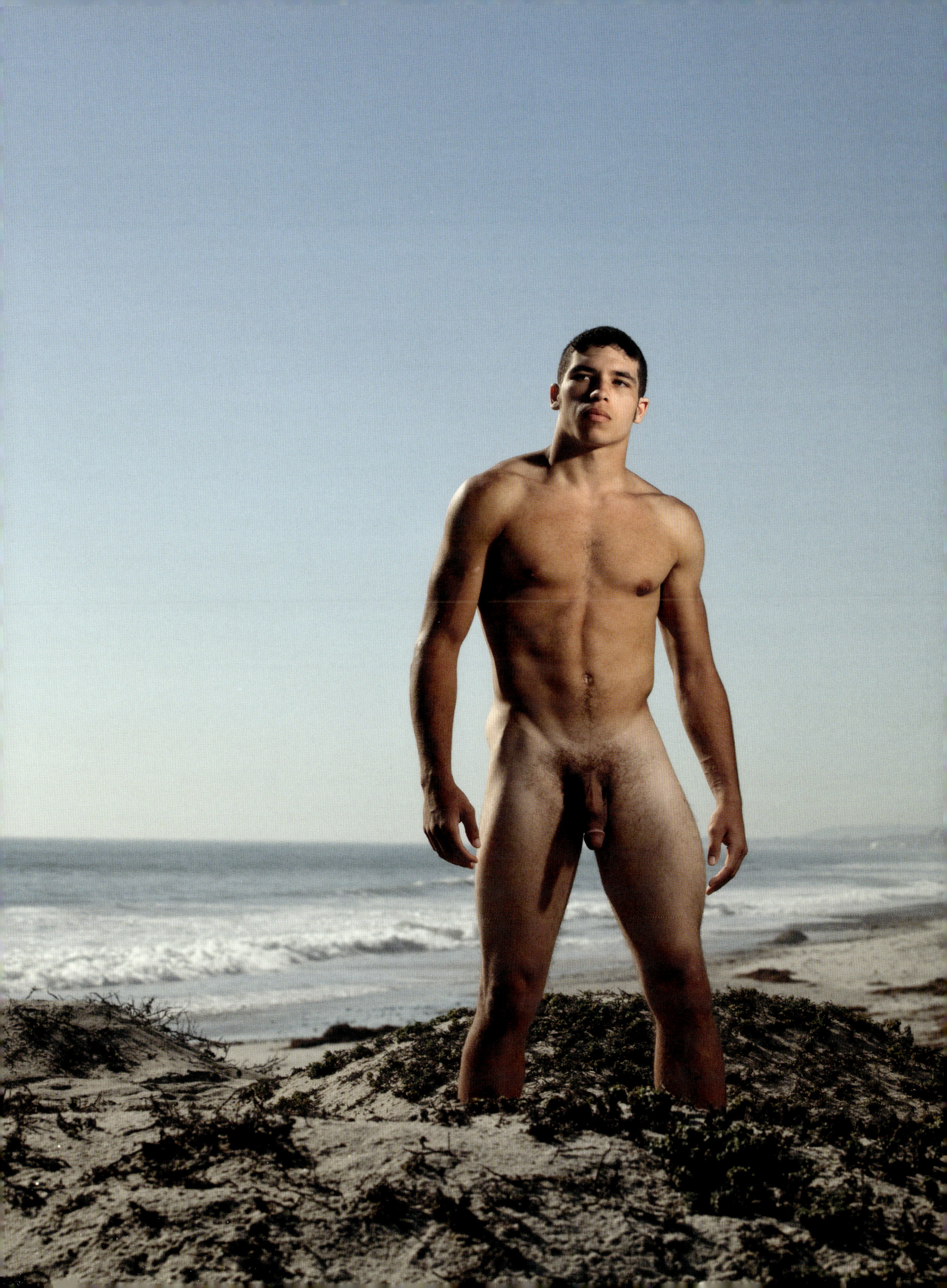

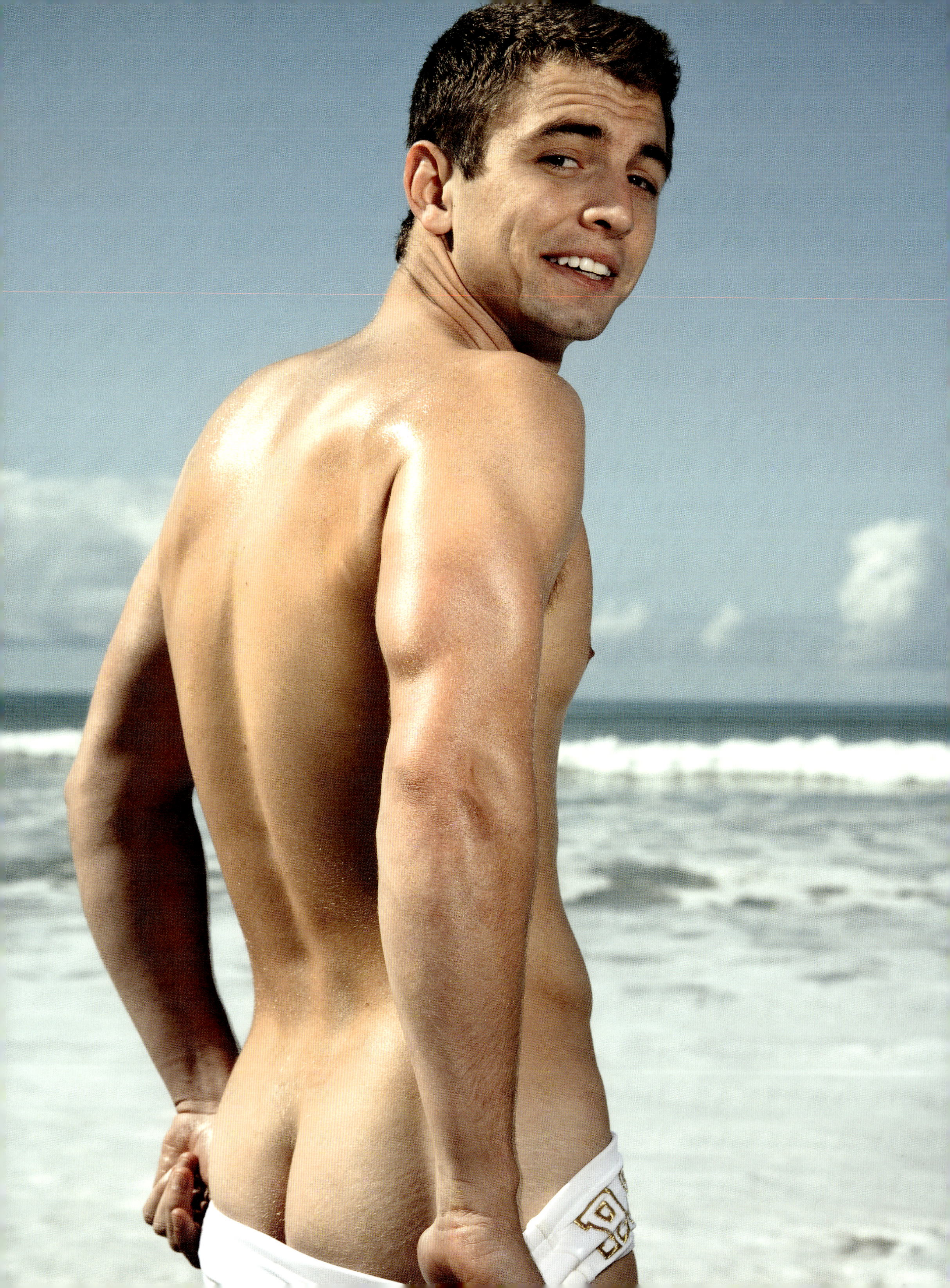

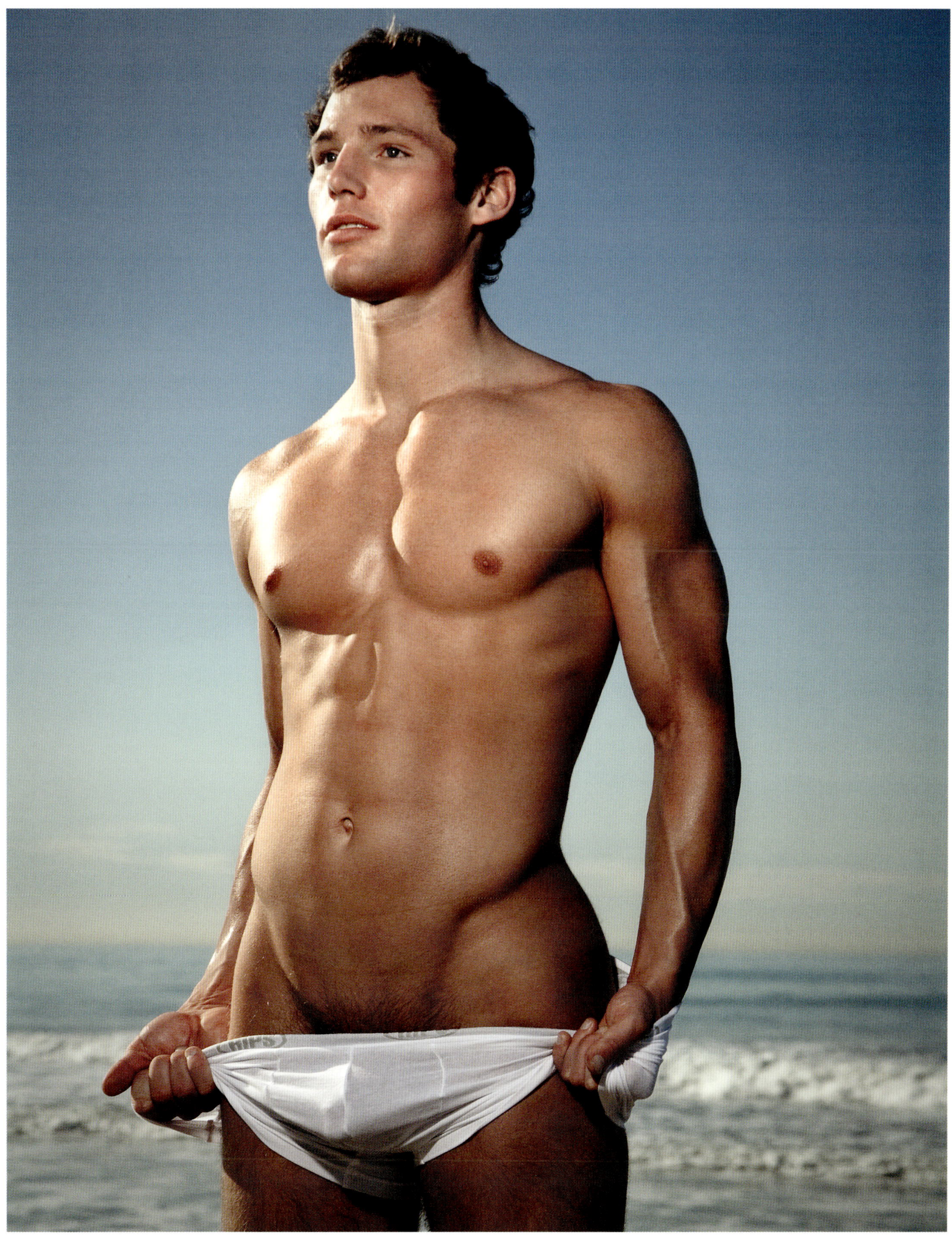

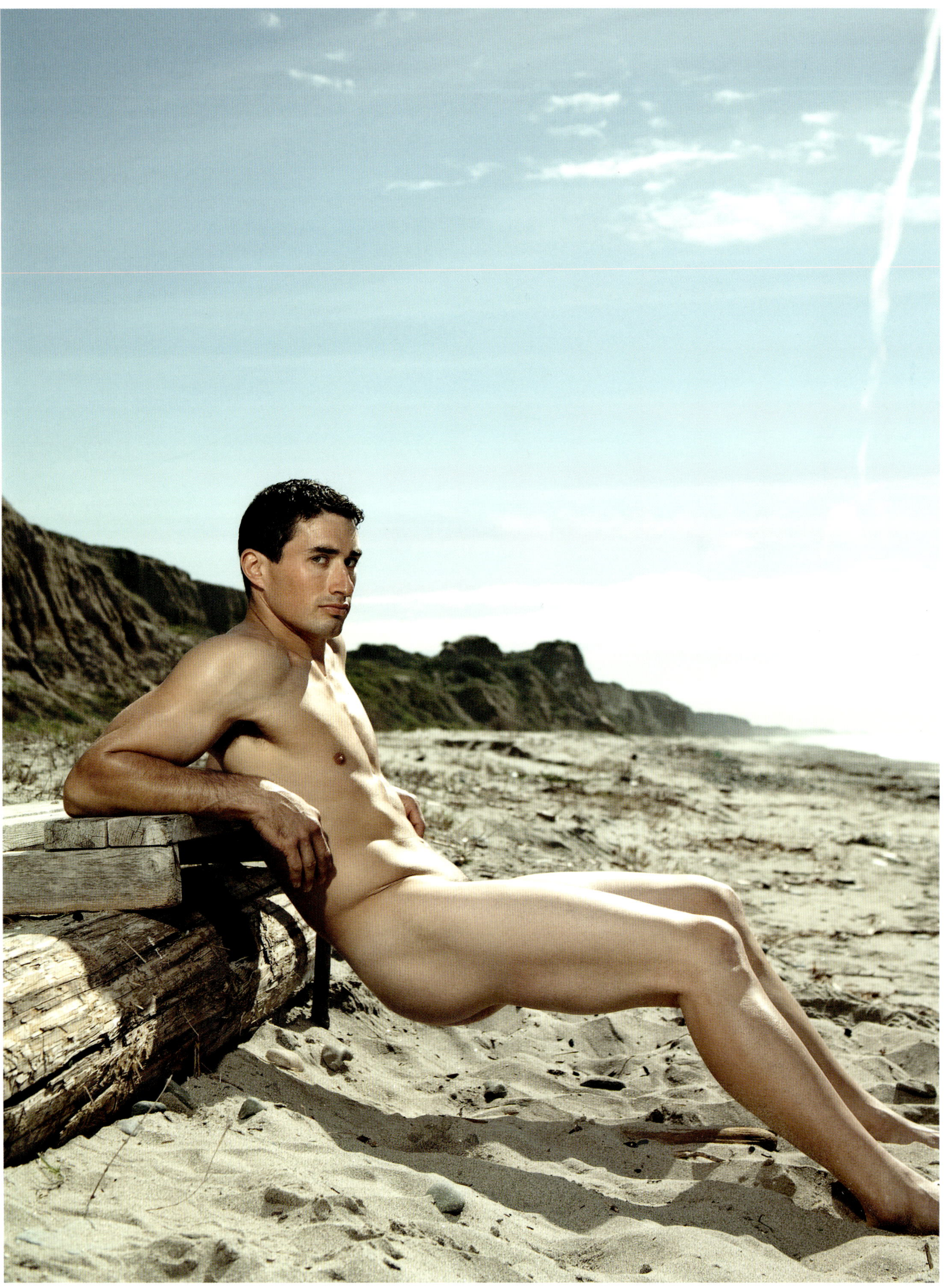

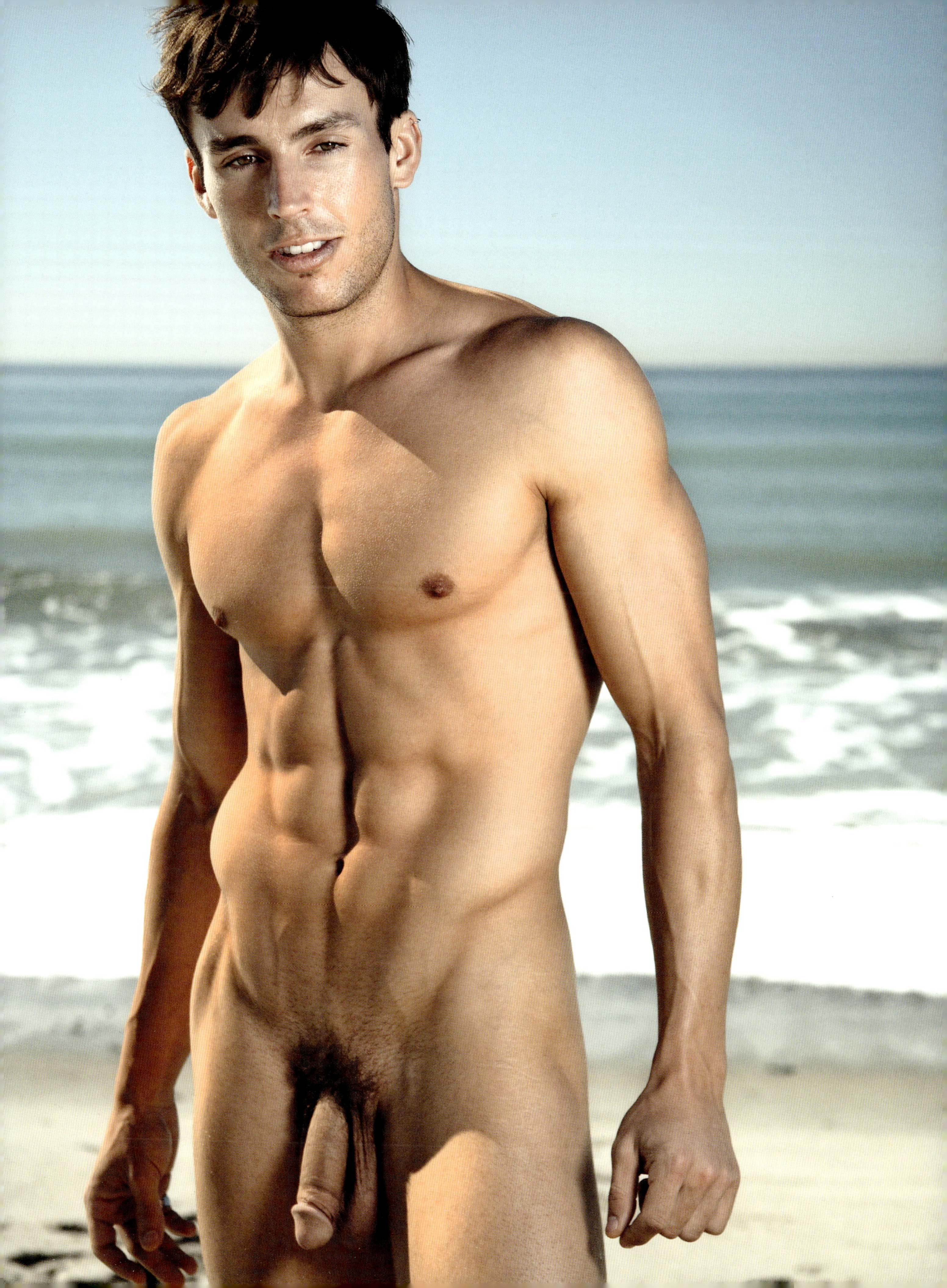

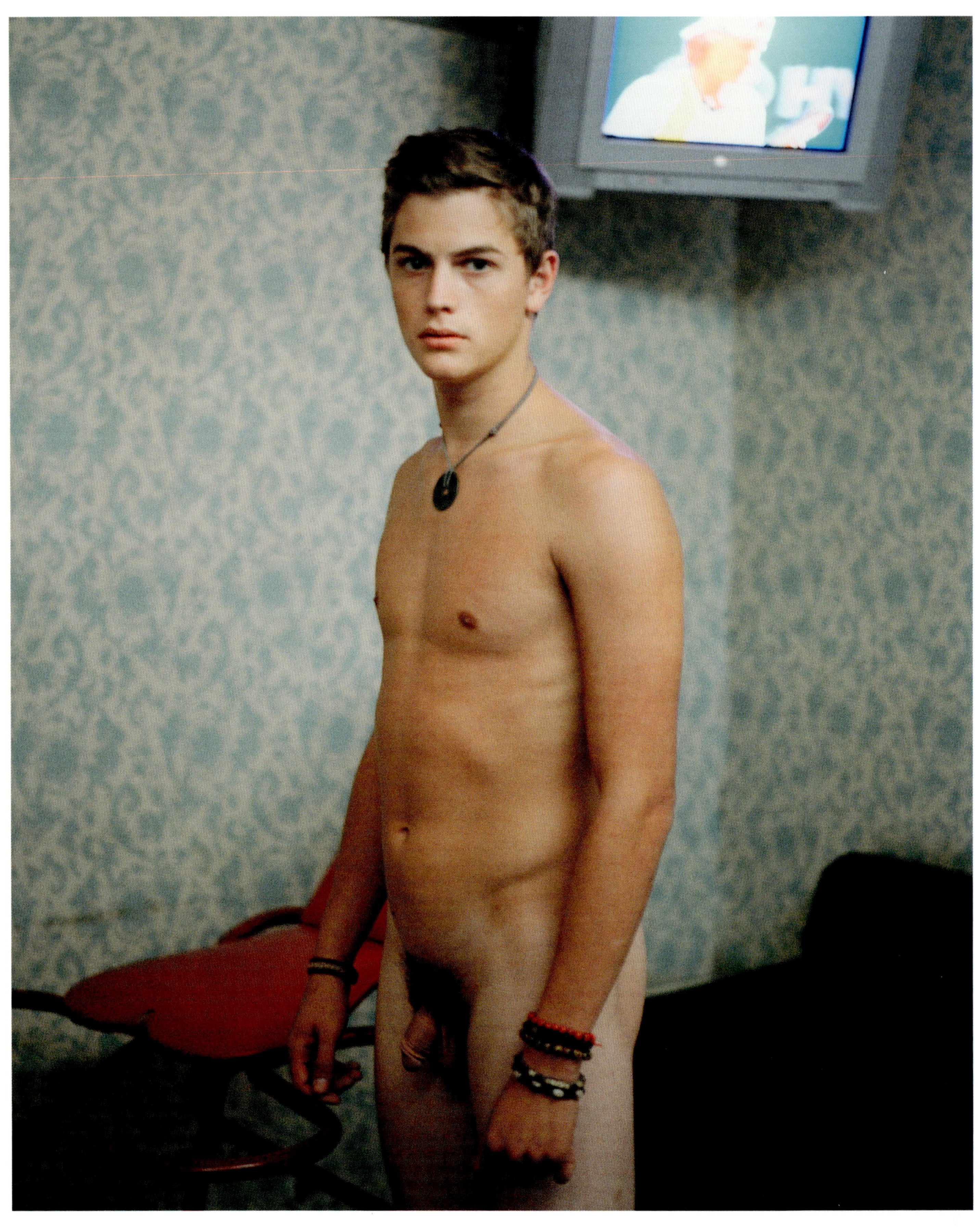

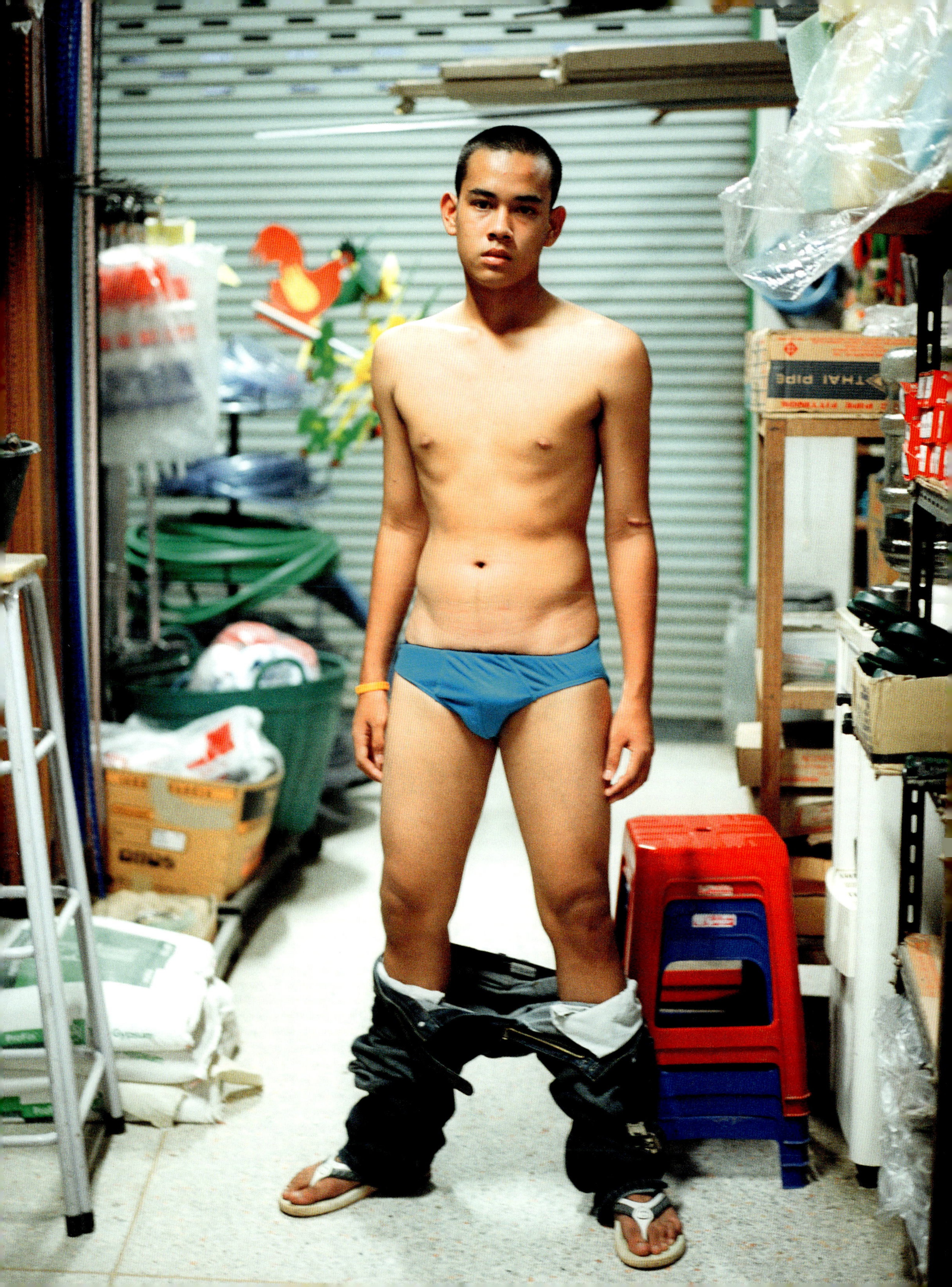

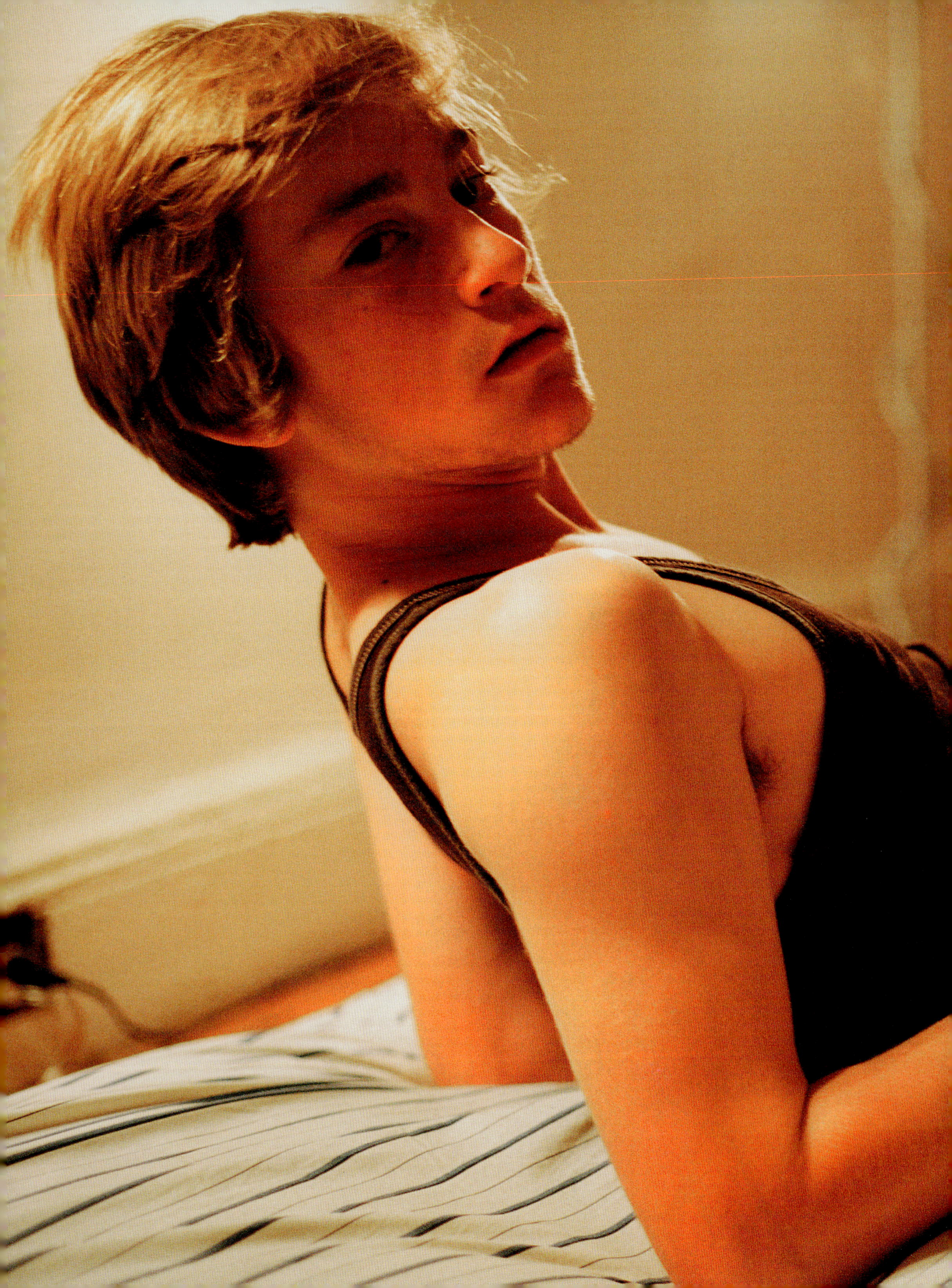

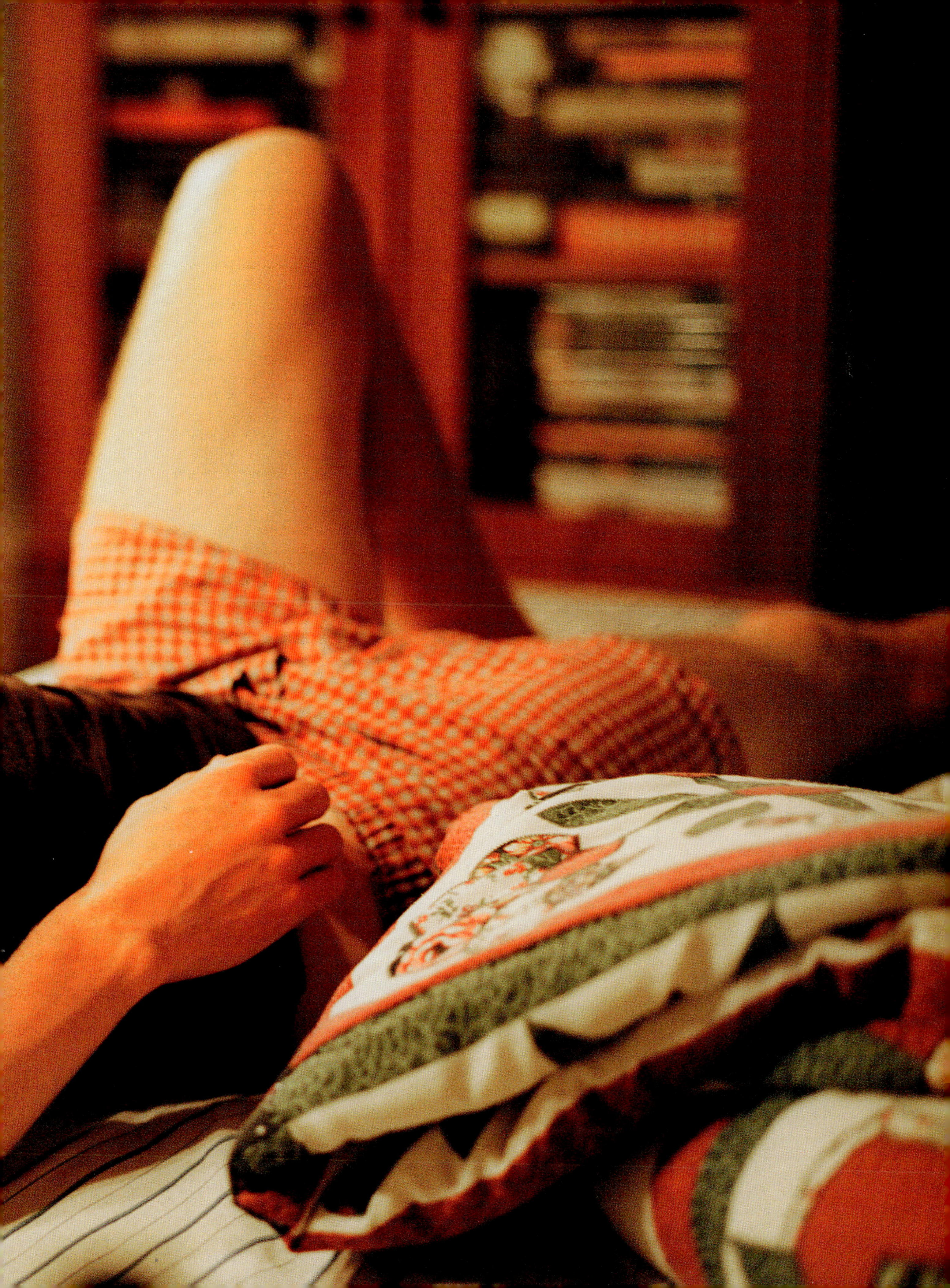

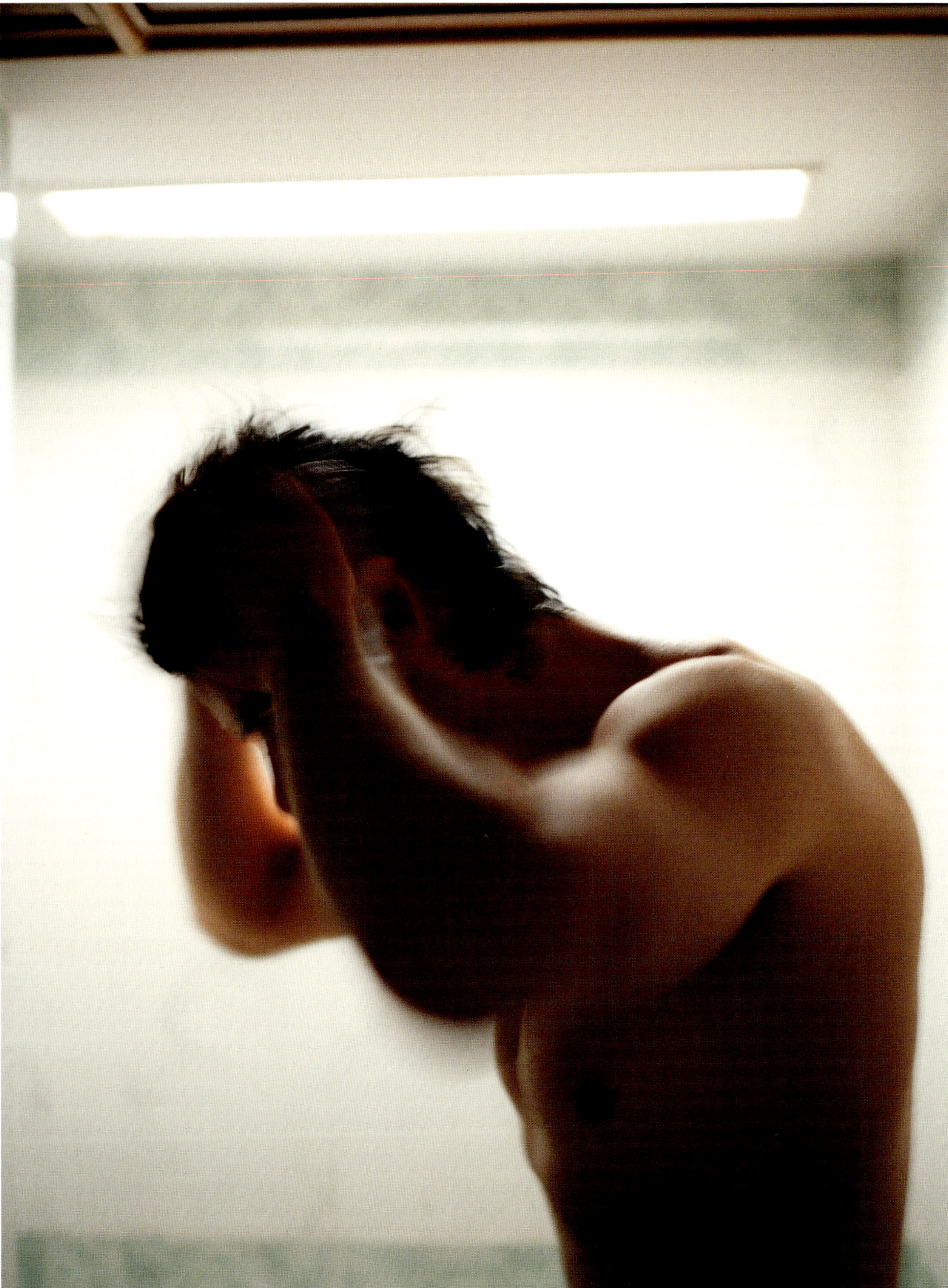

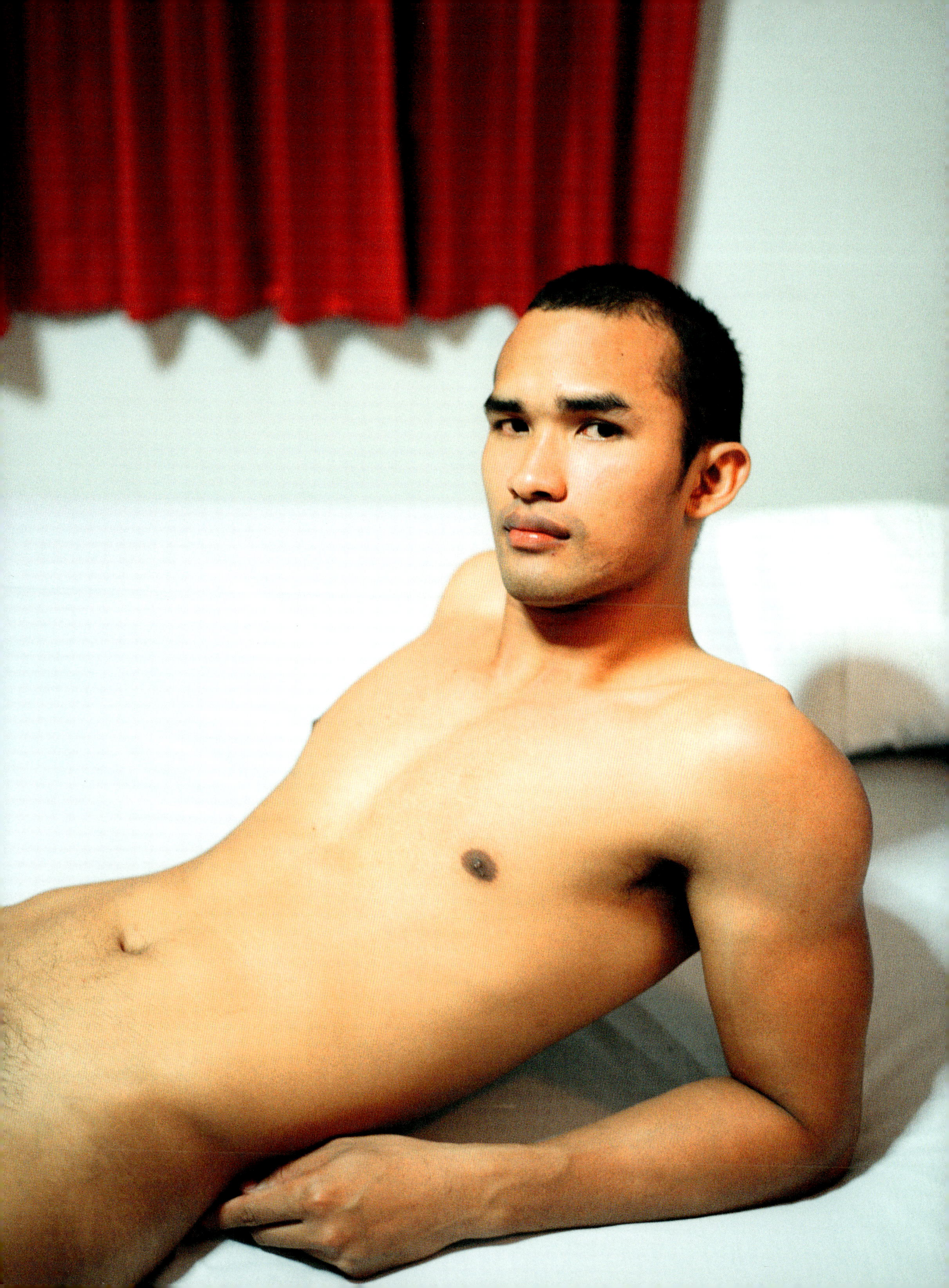

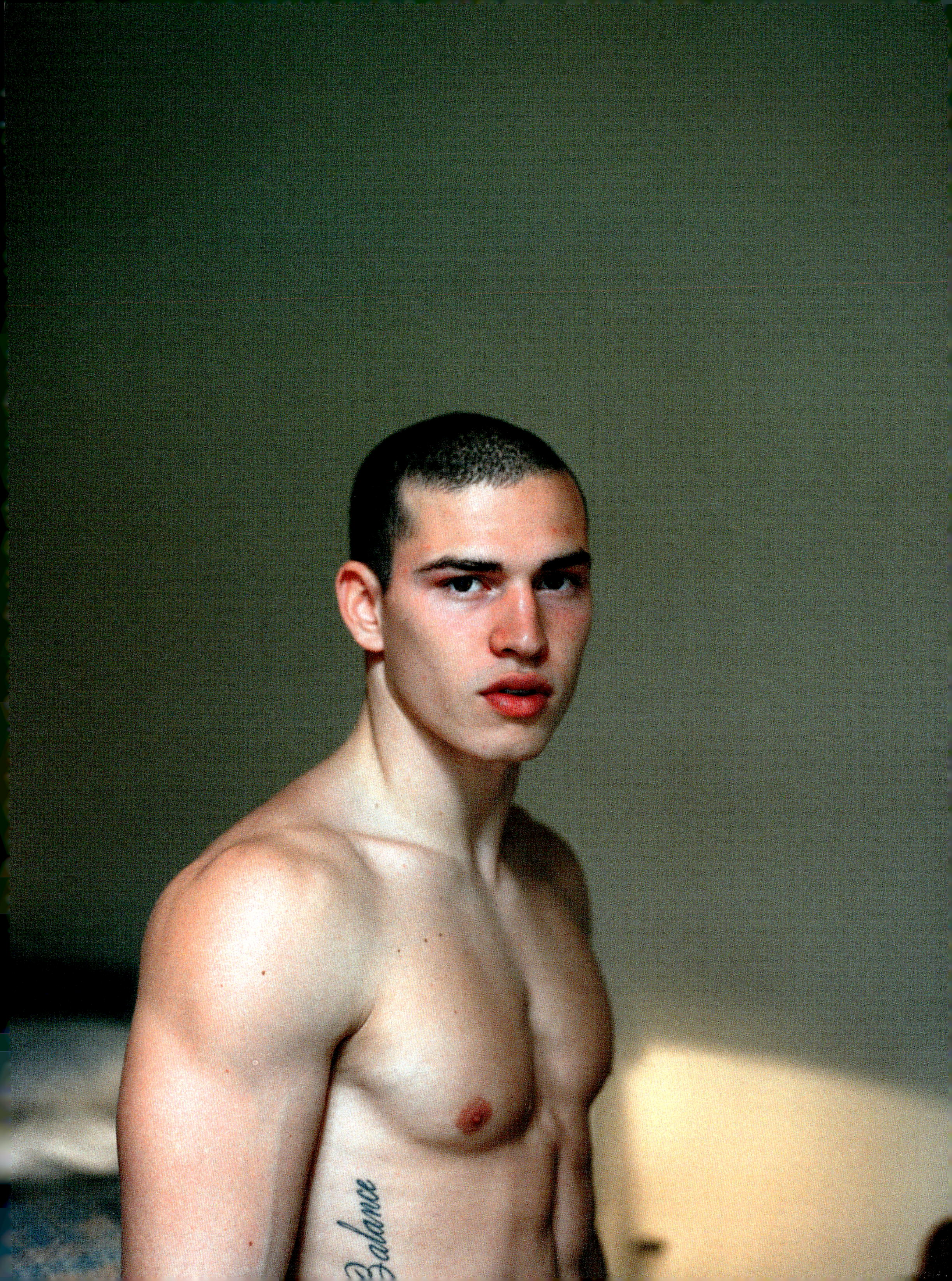

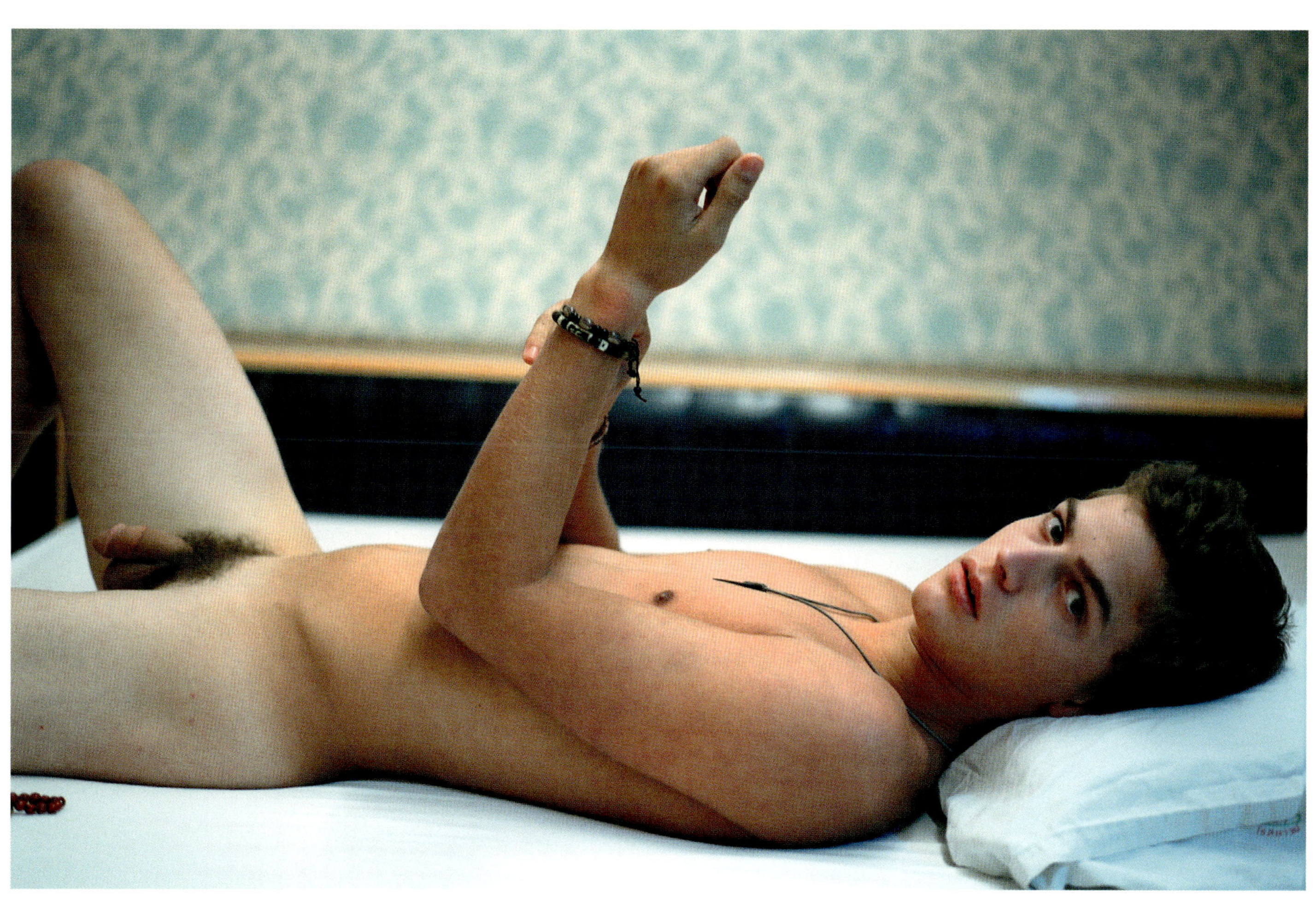

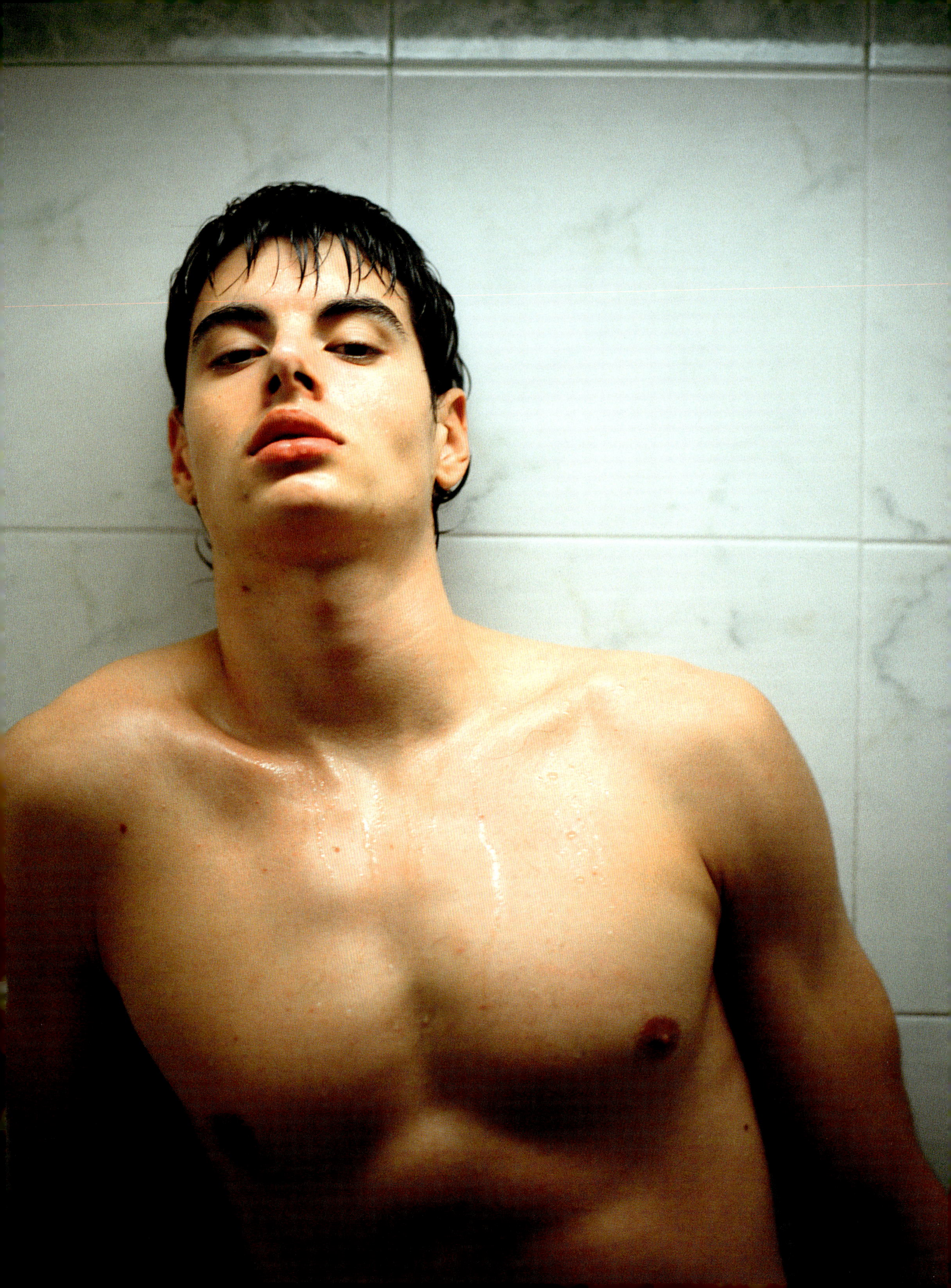

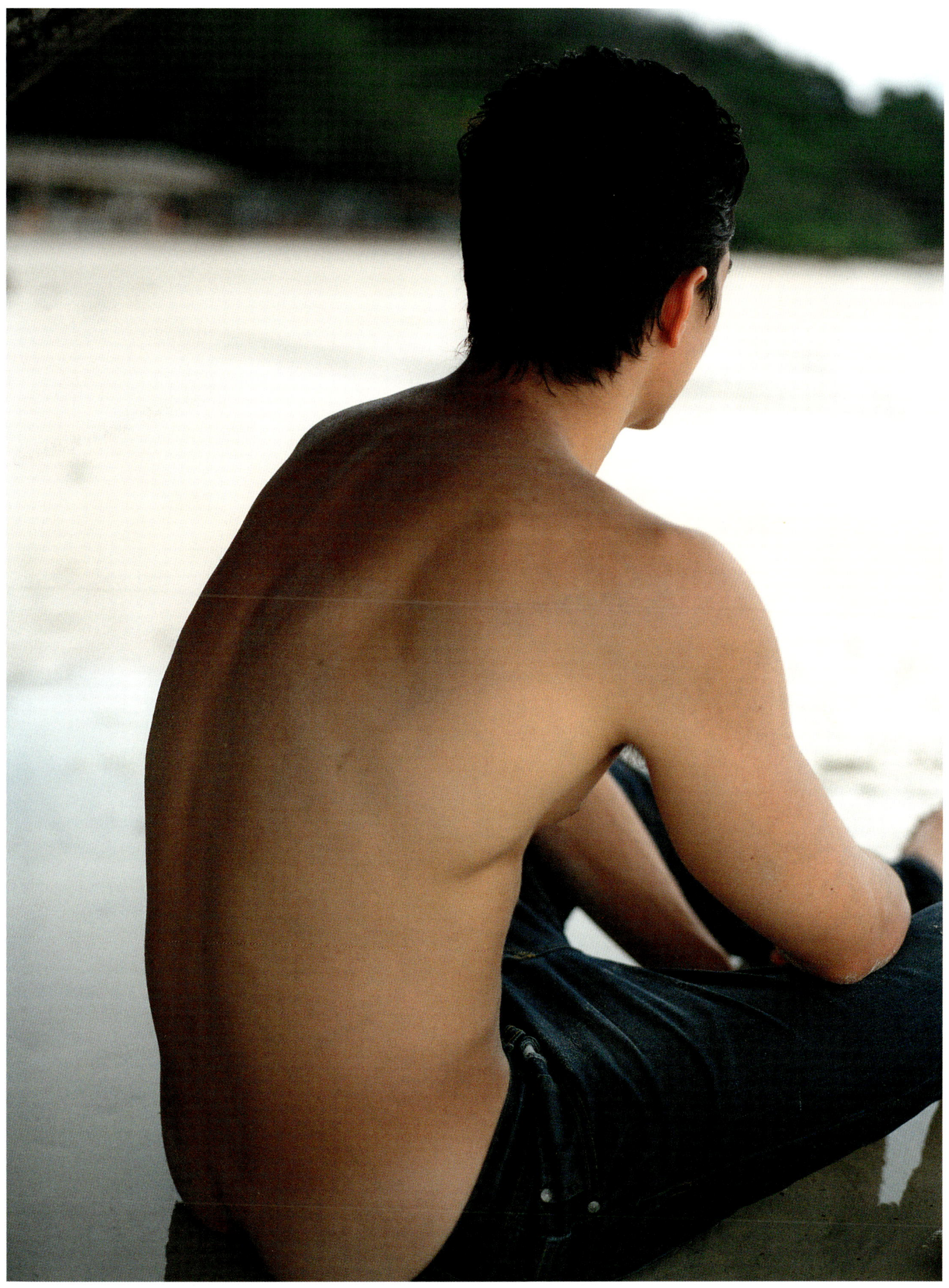

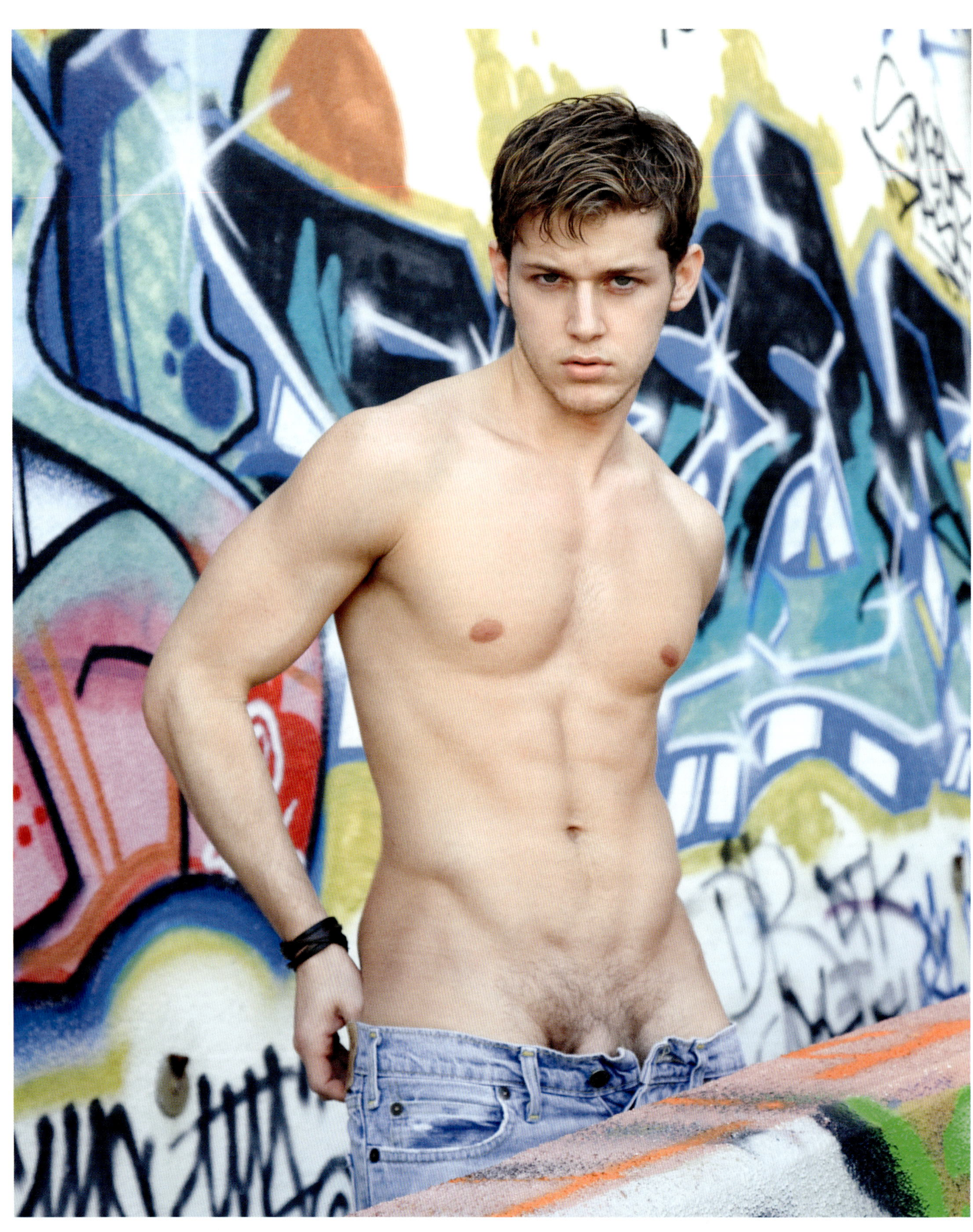

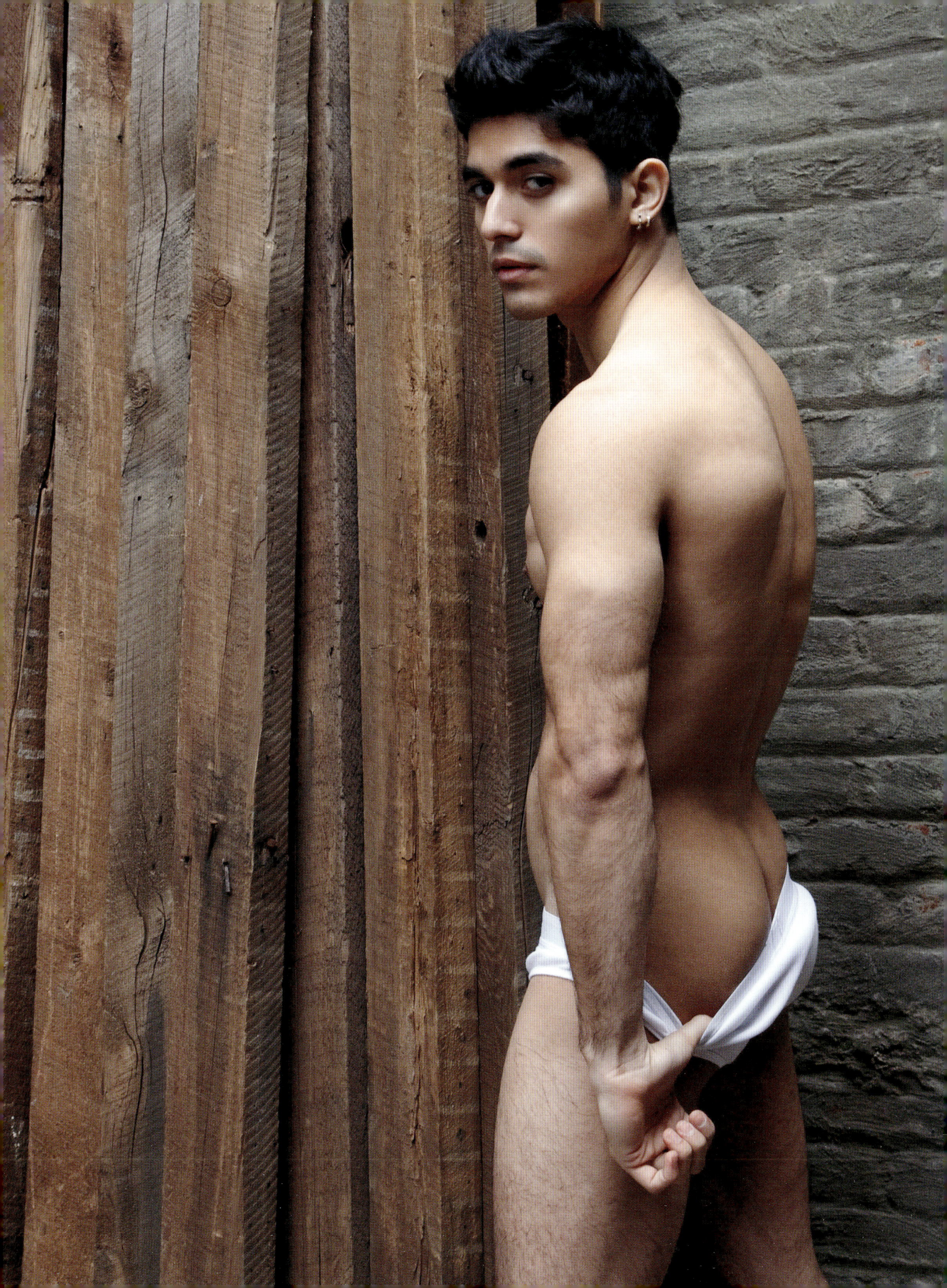

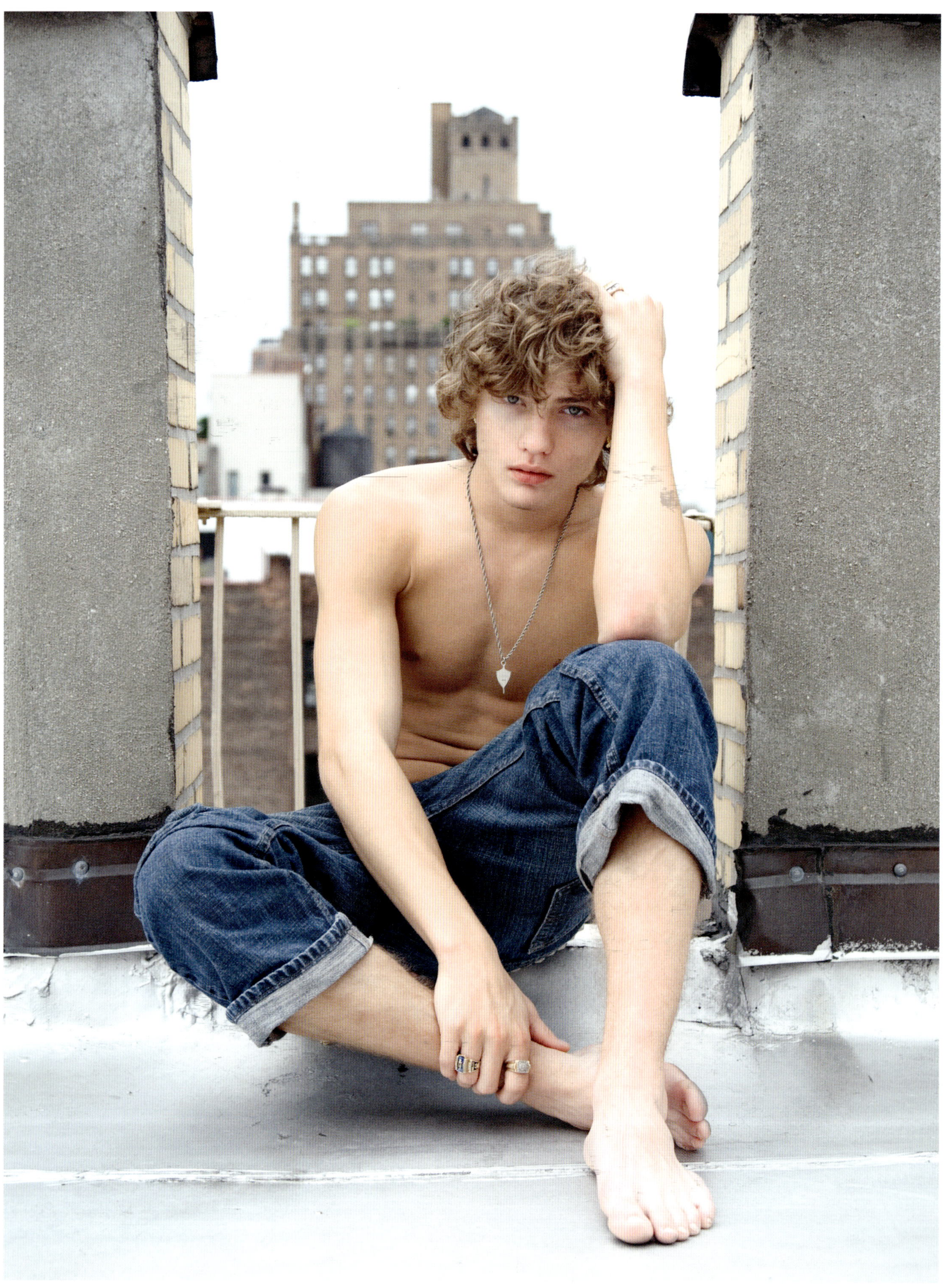

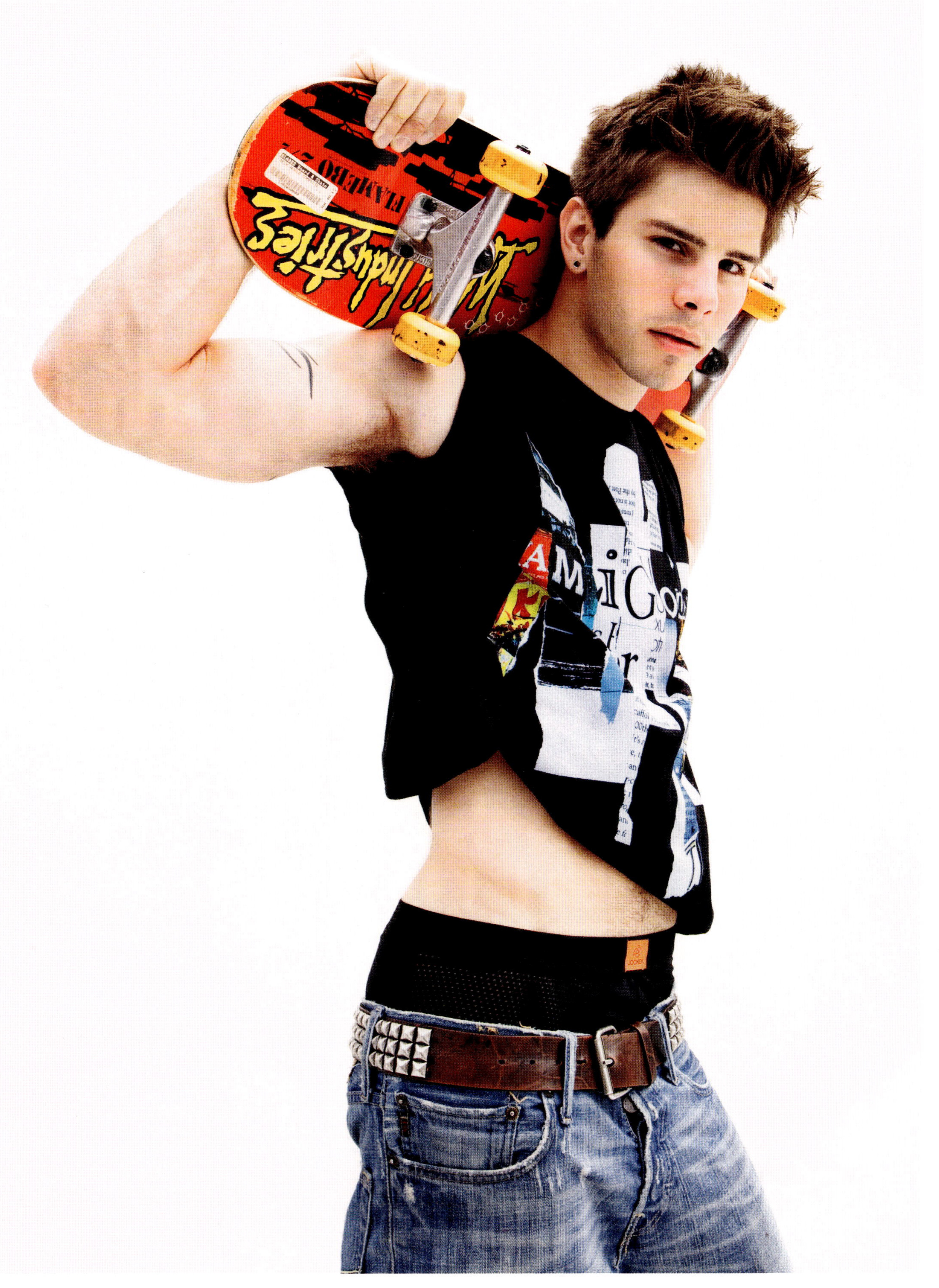
Blind Industries
FLAMENCO

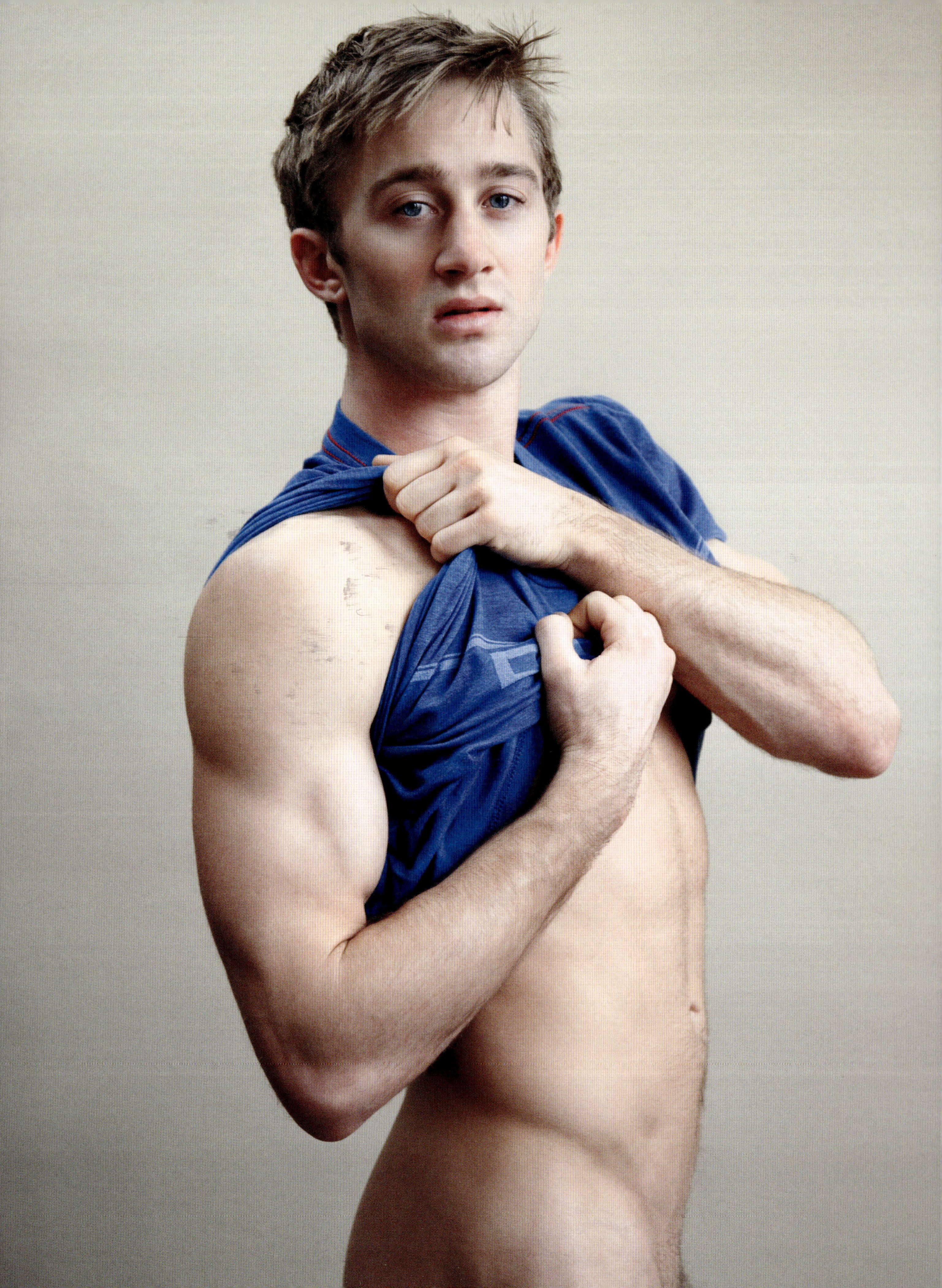

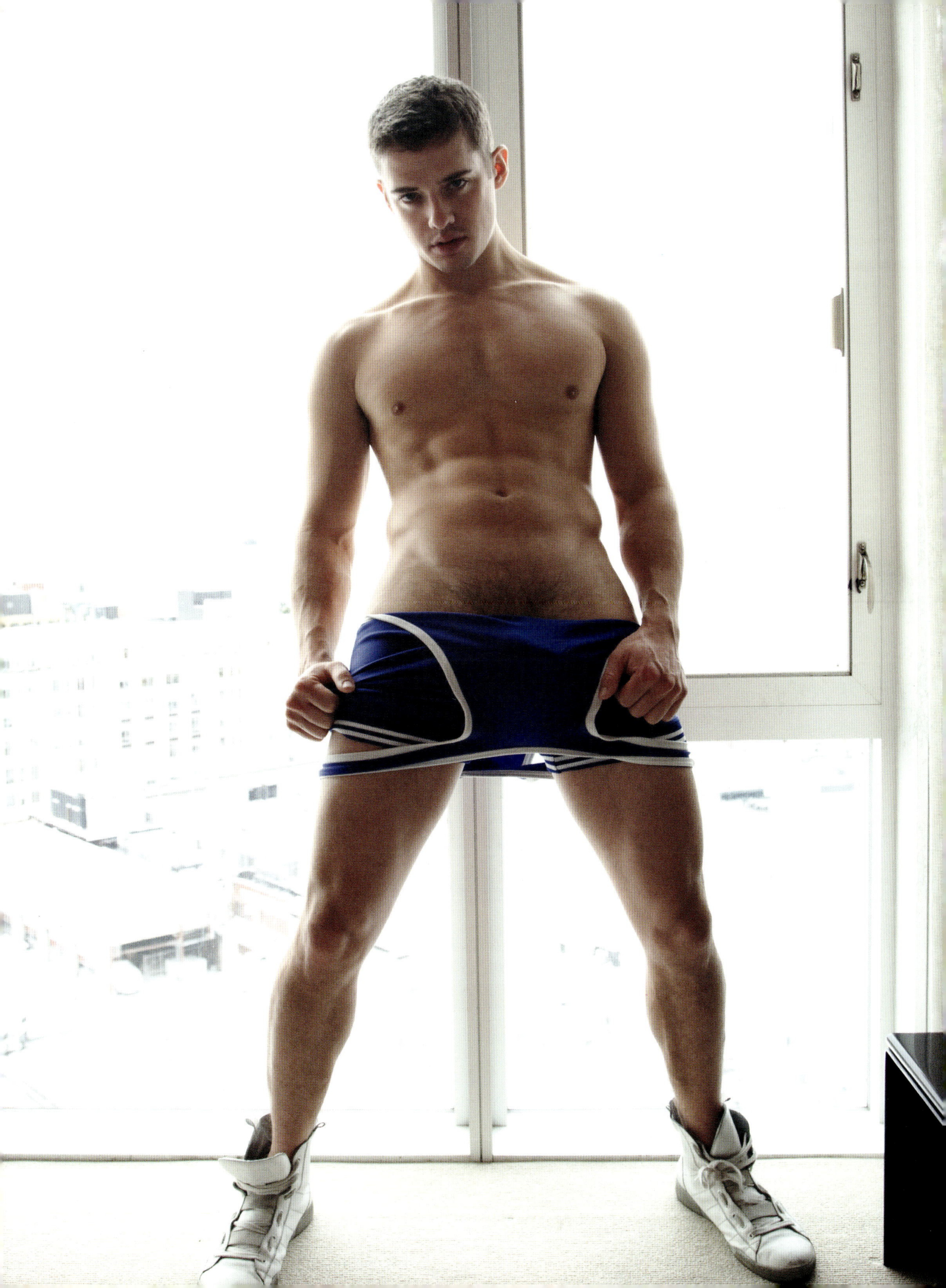

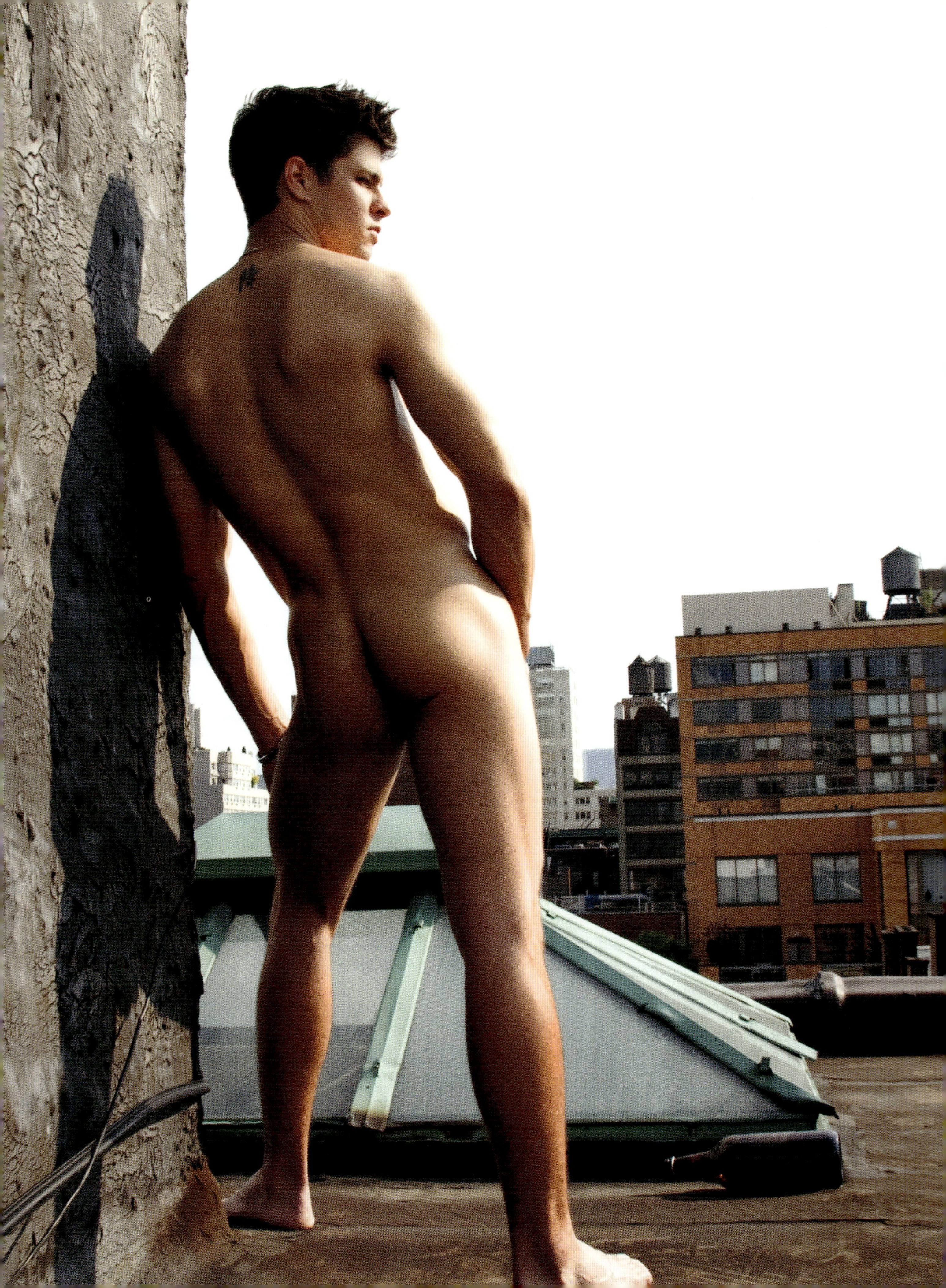

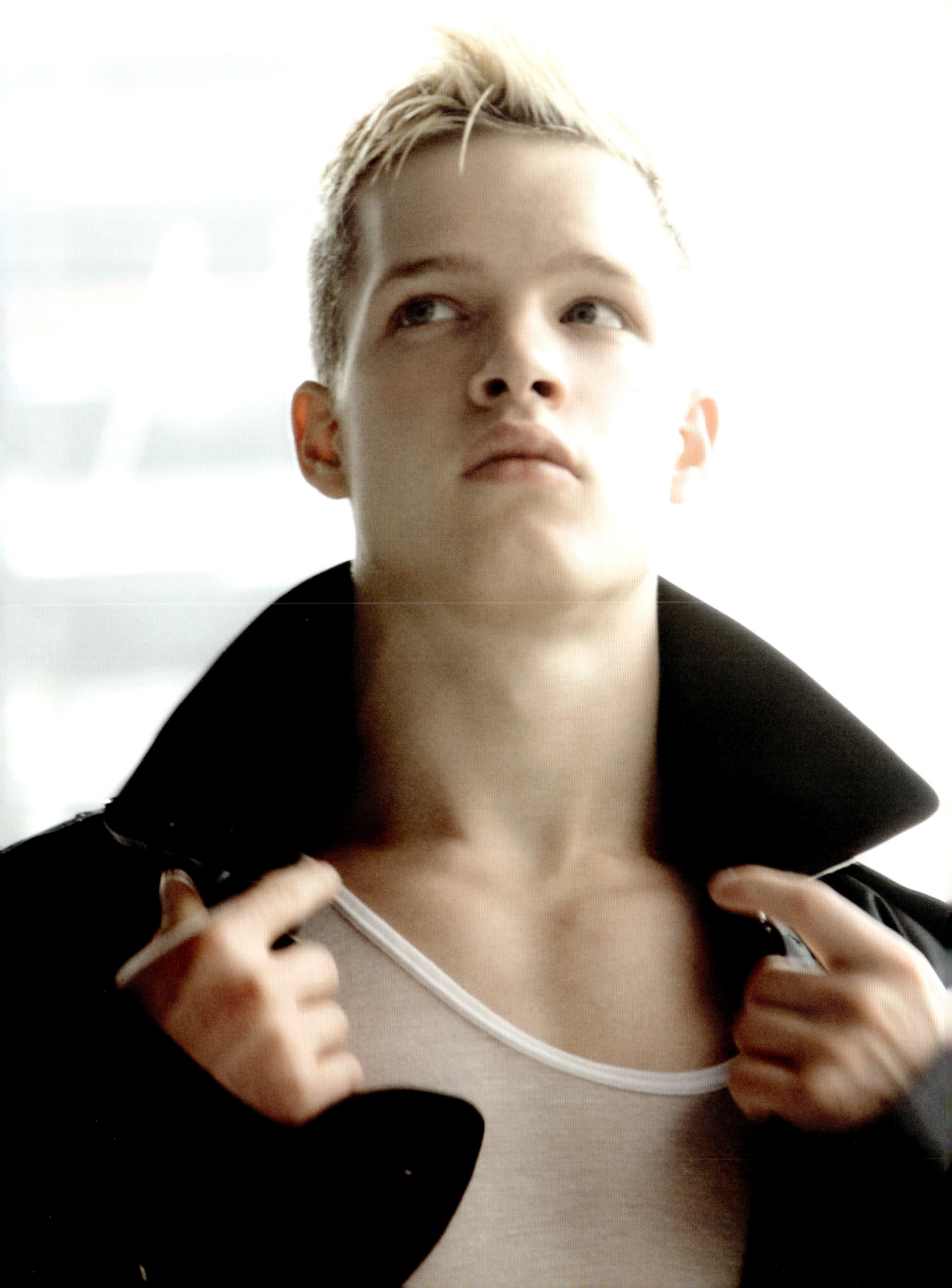

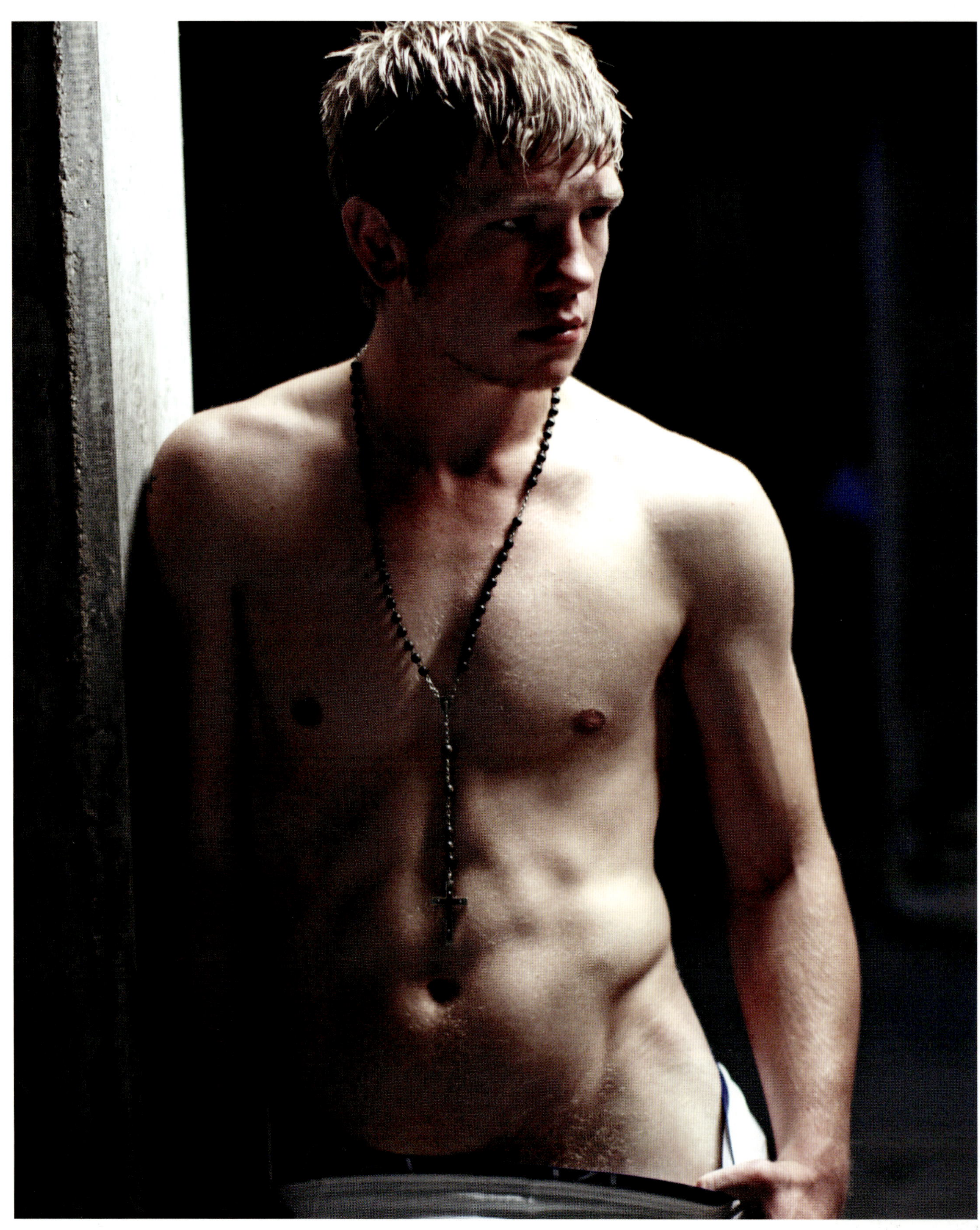

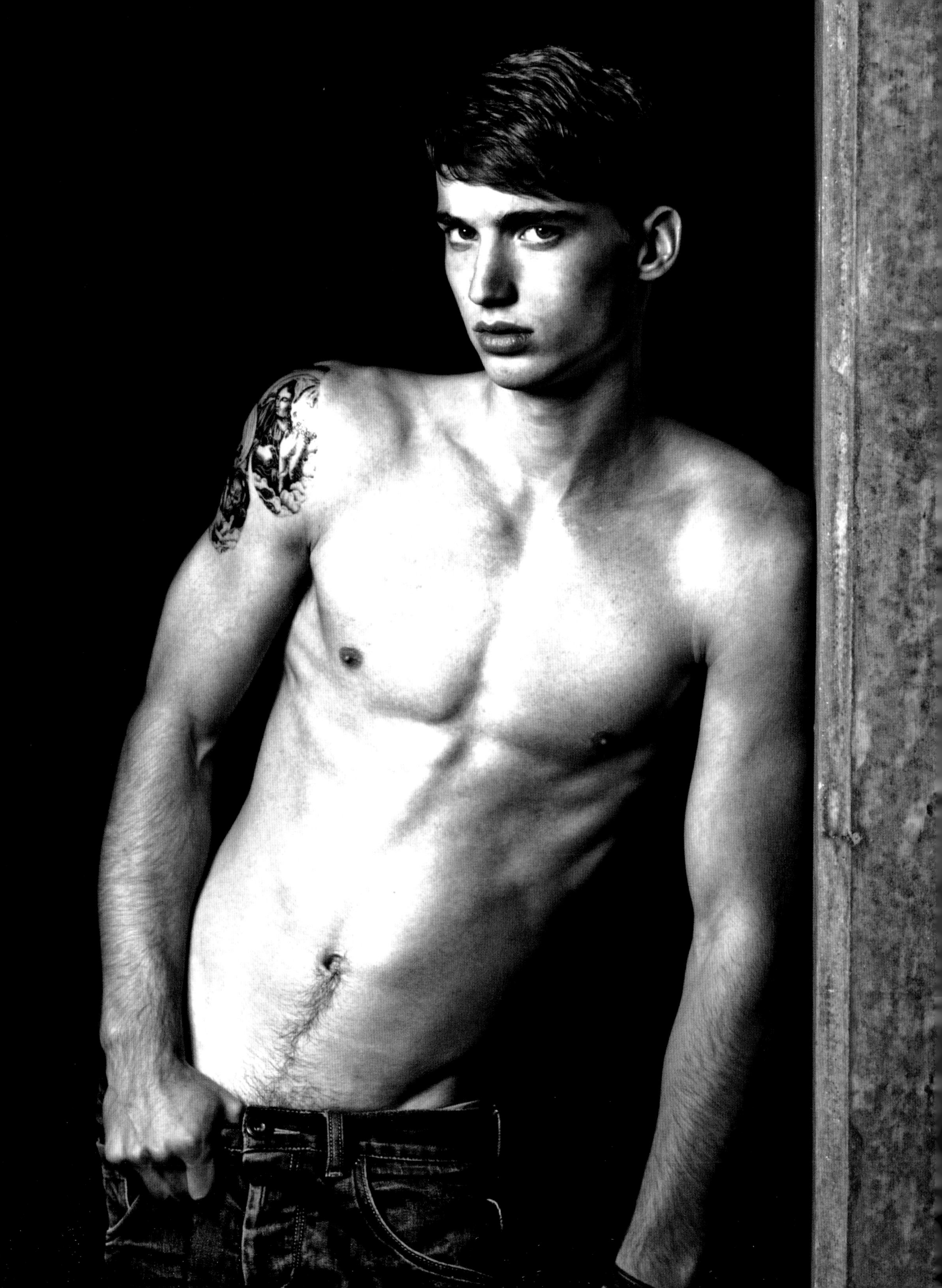

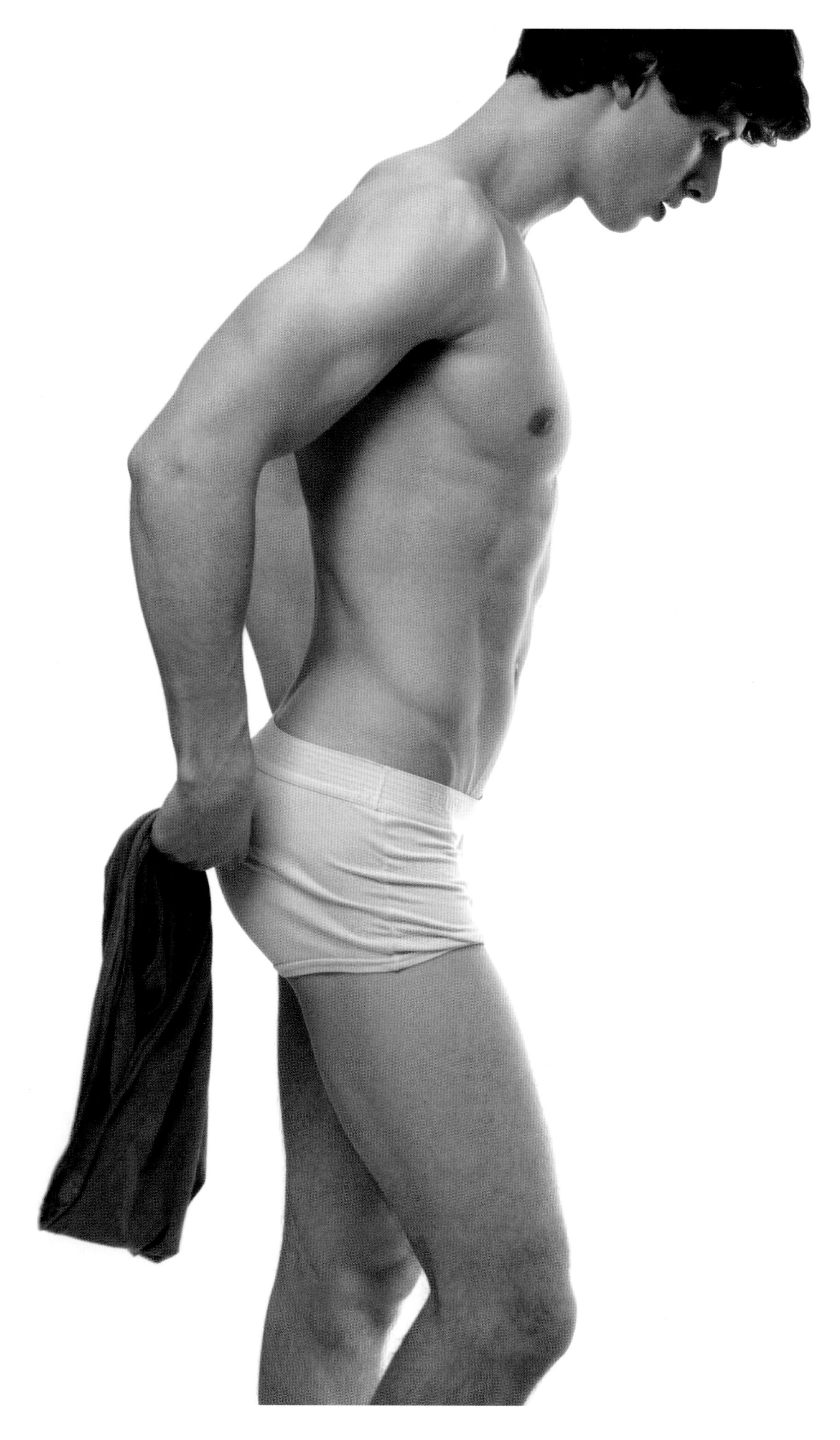

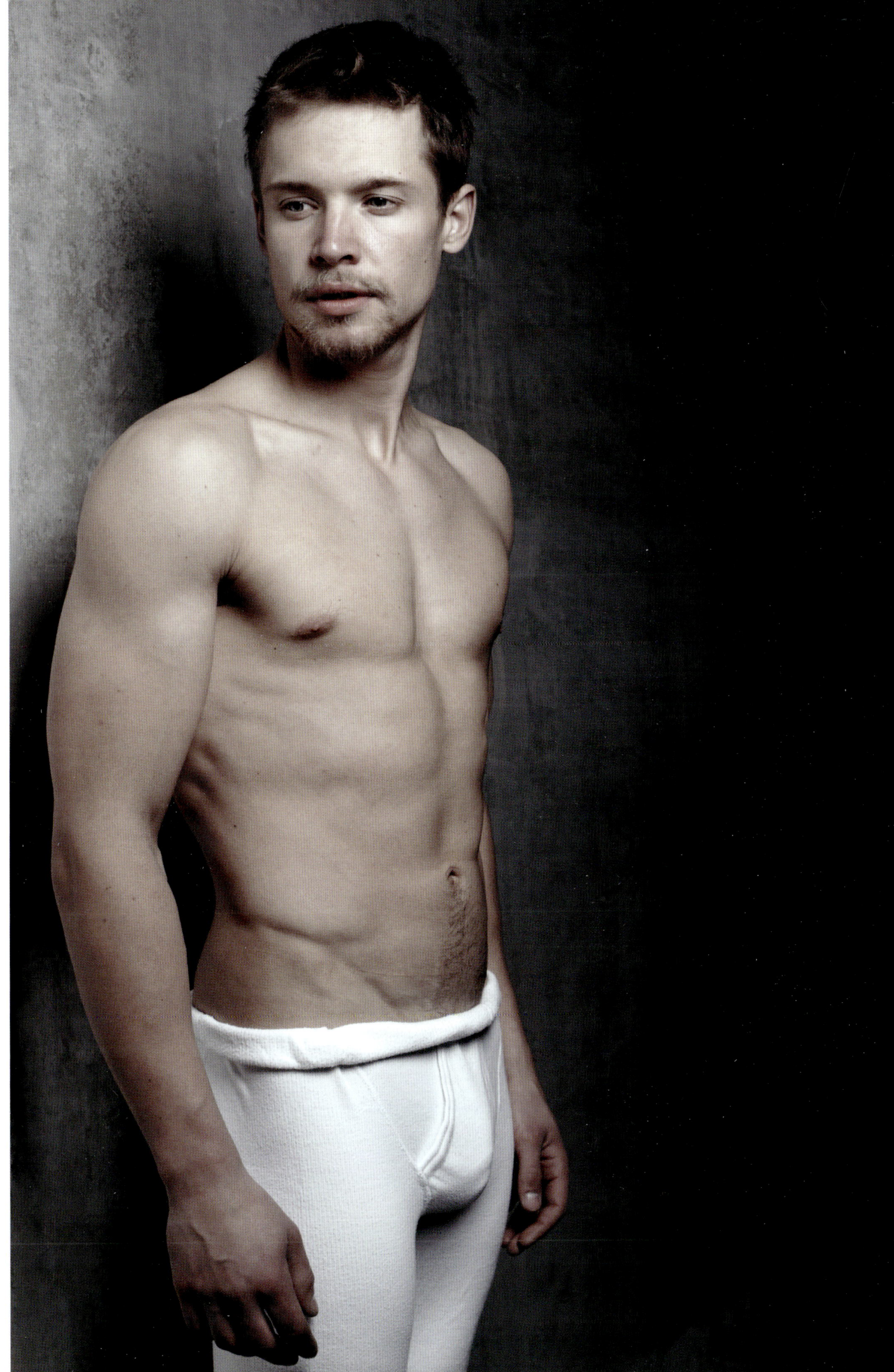

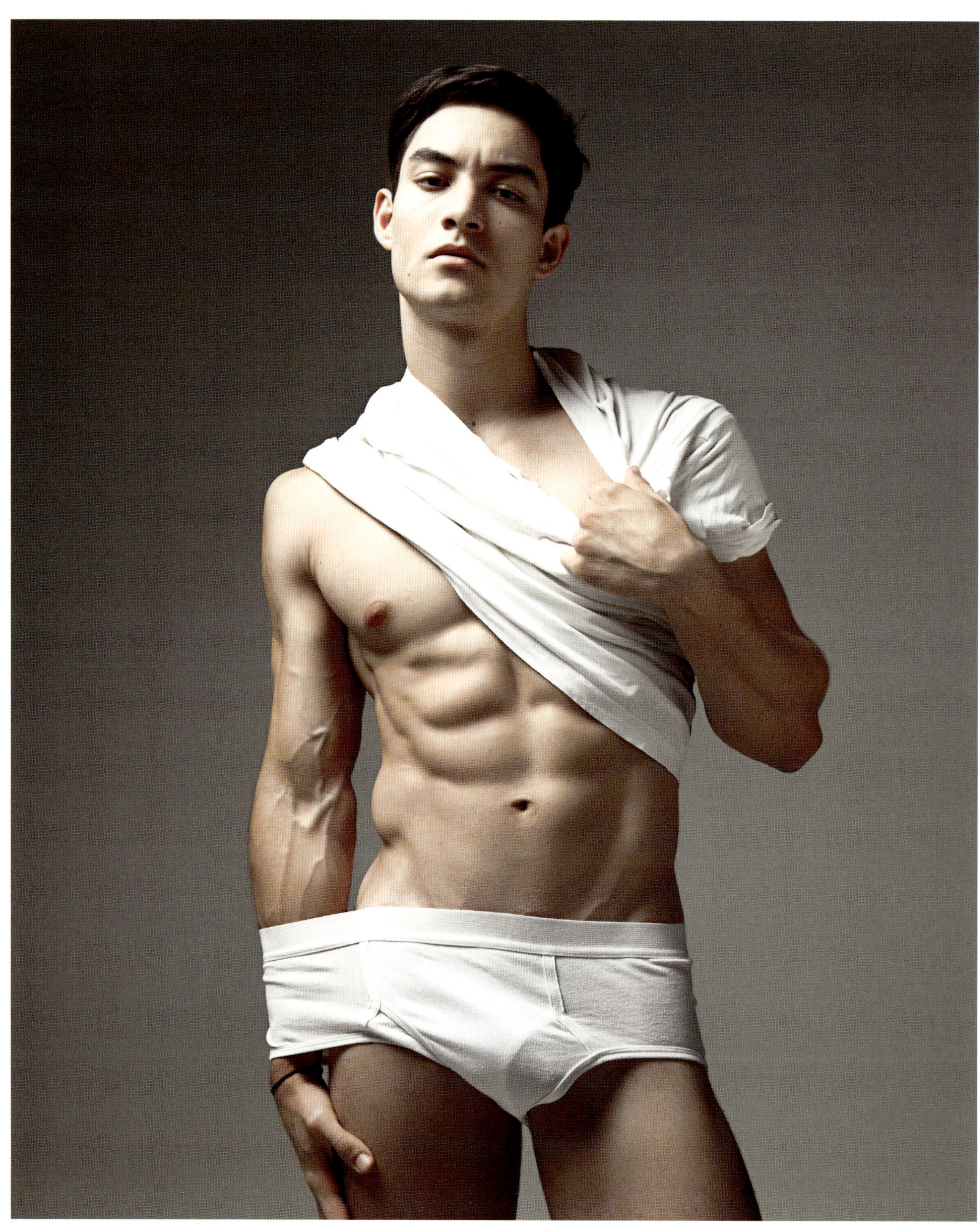

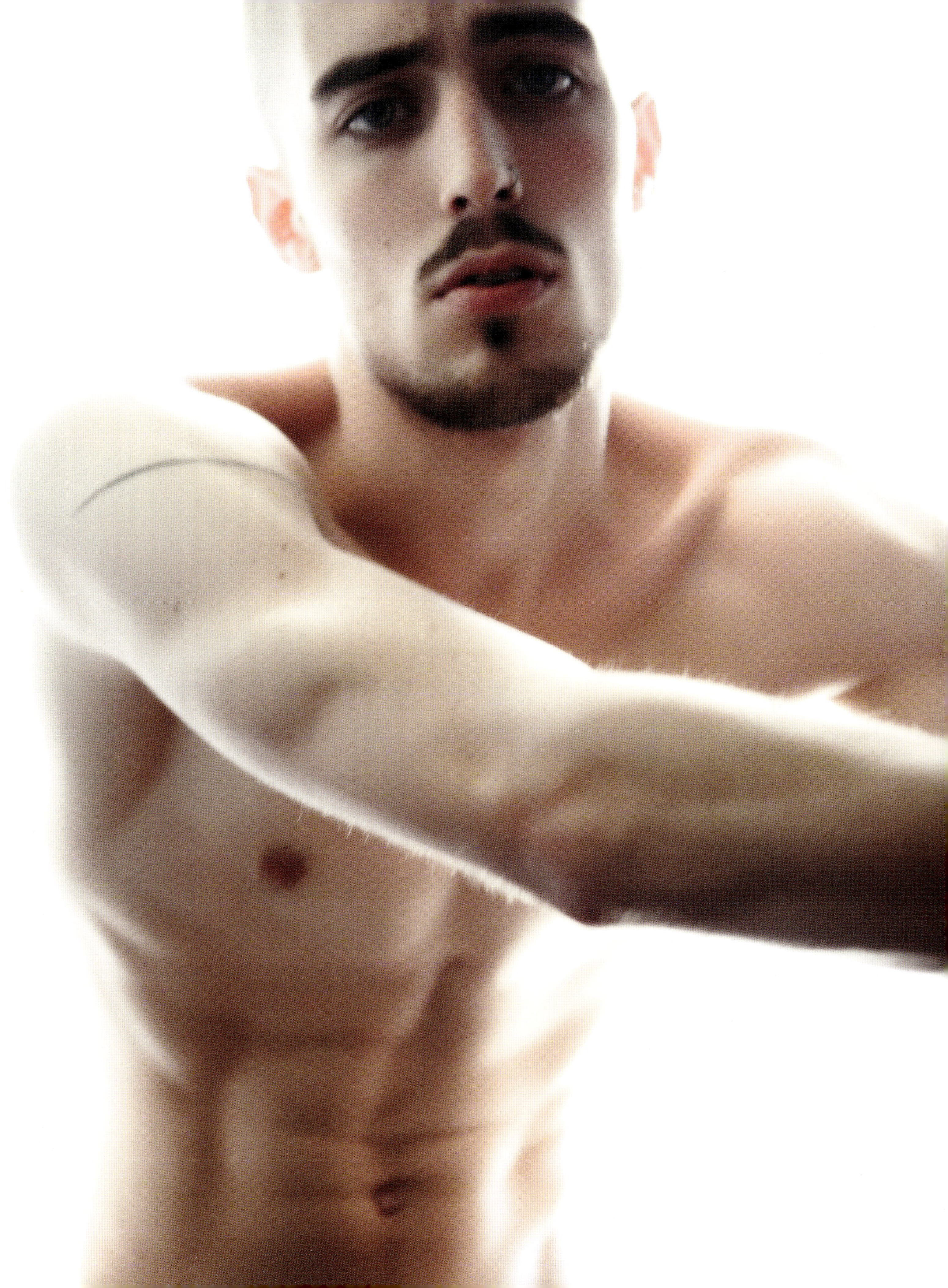

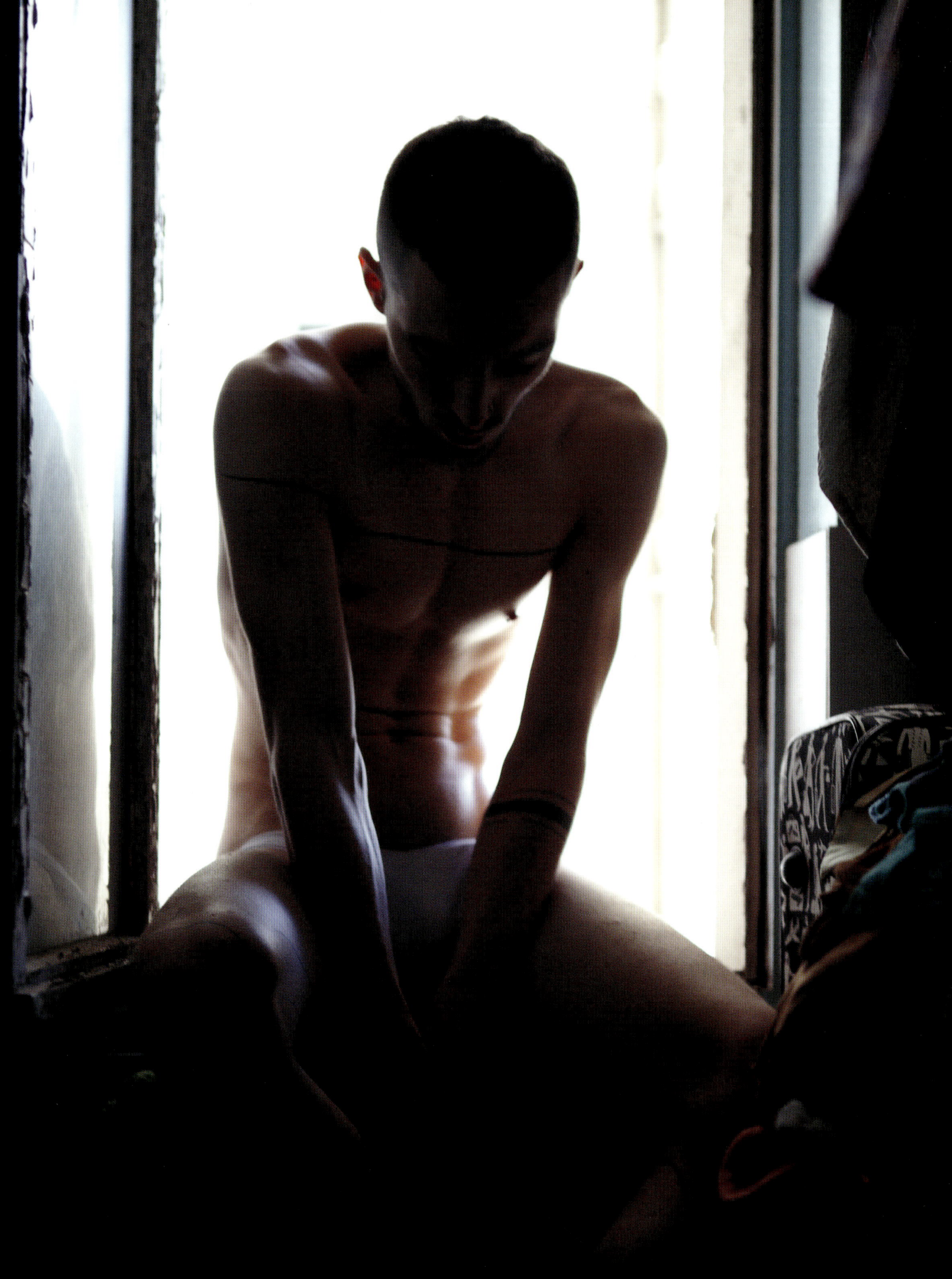

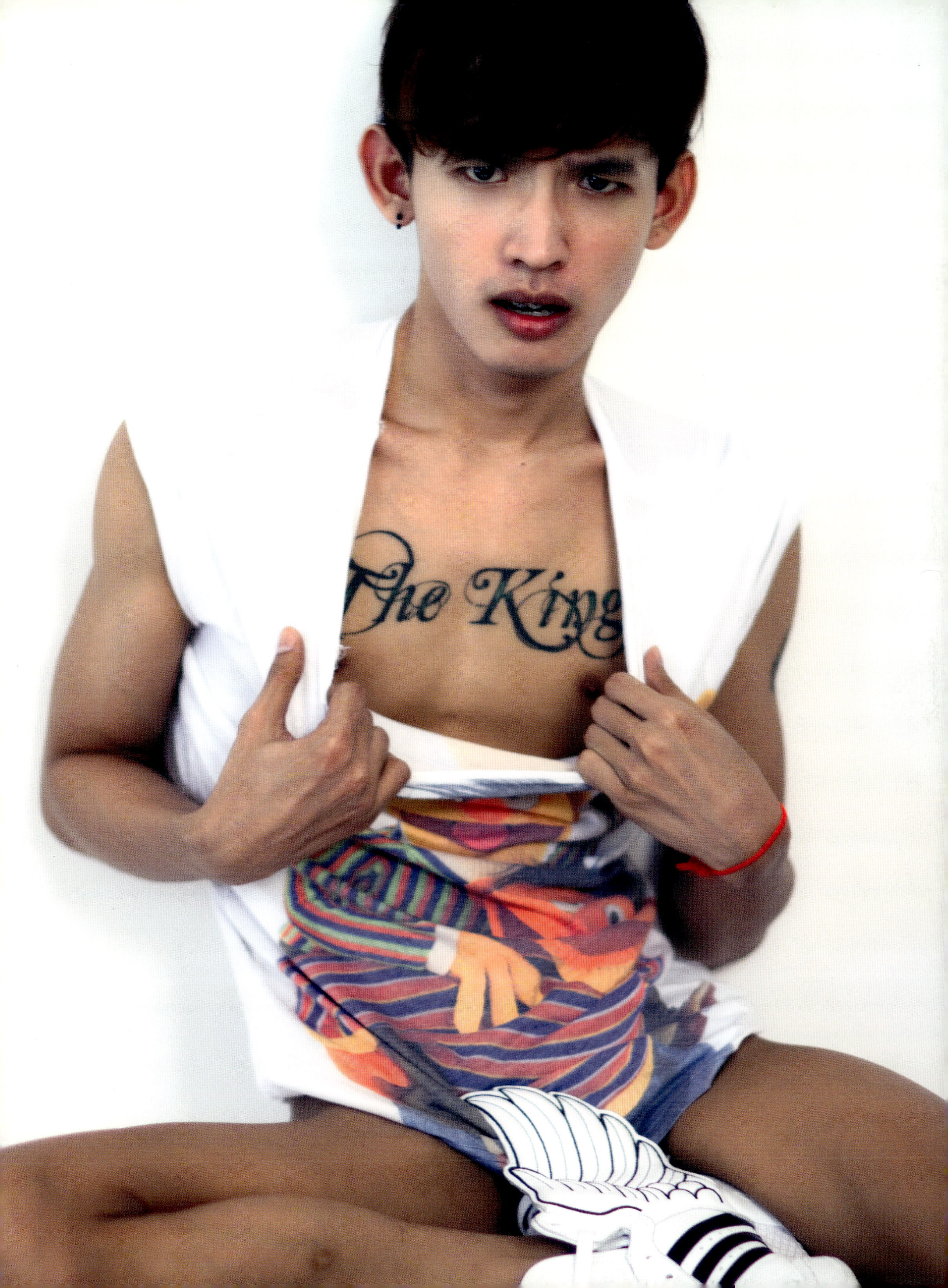
The King

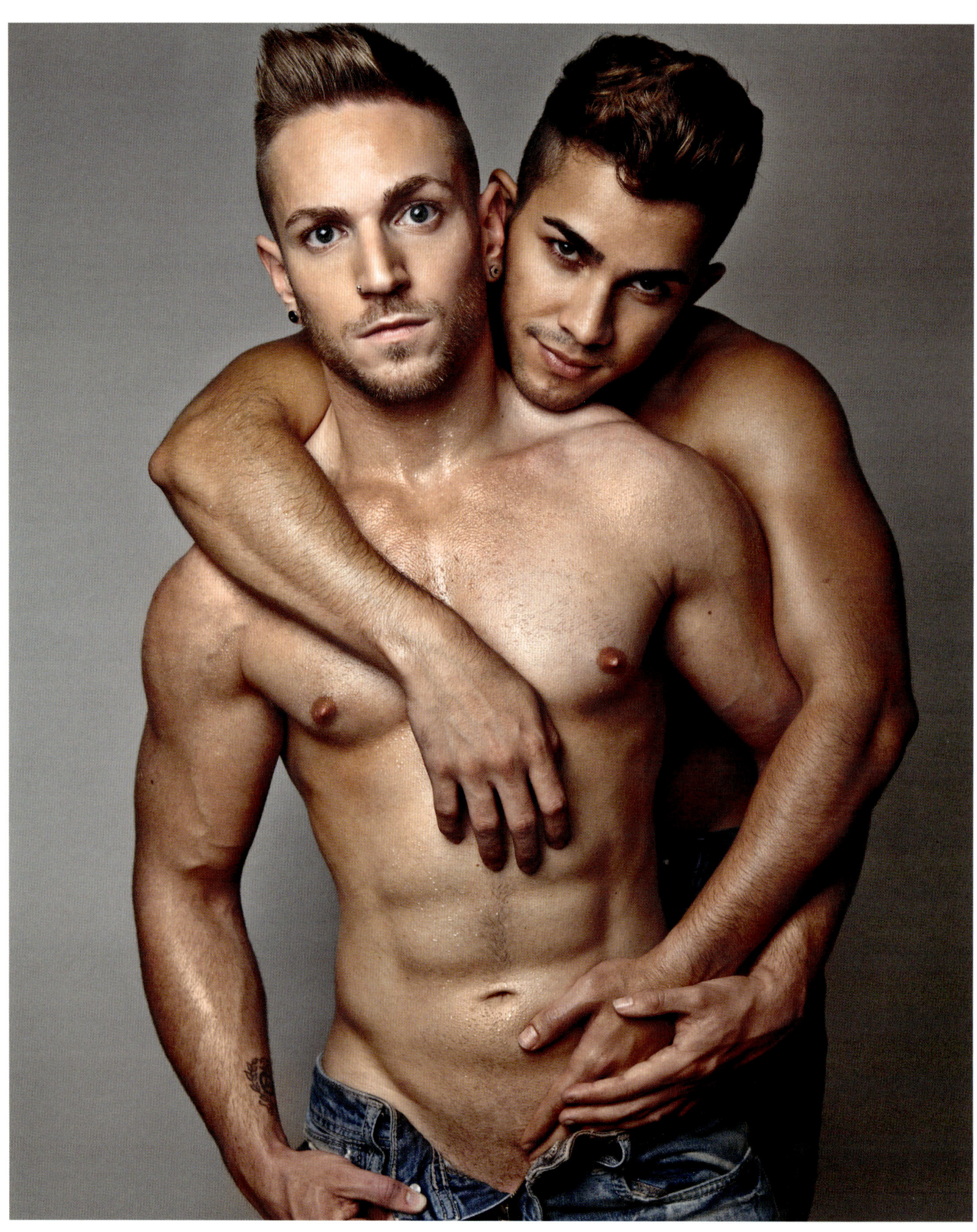

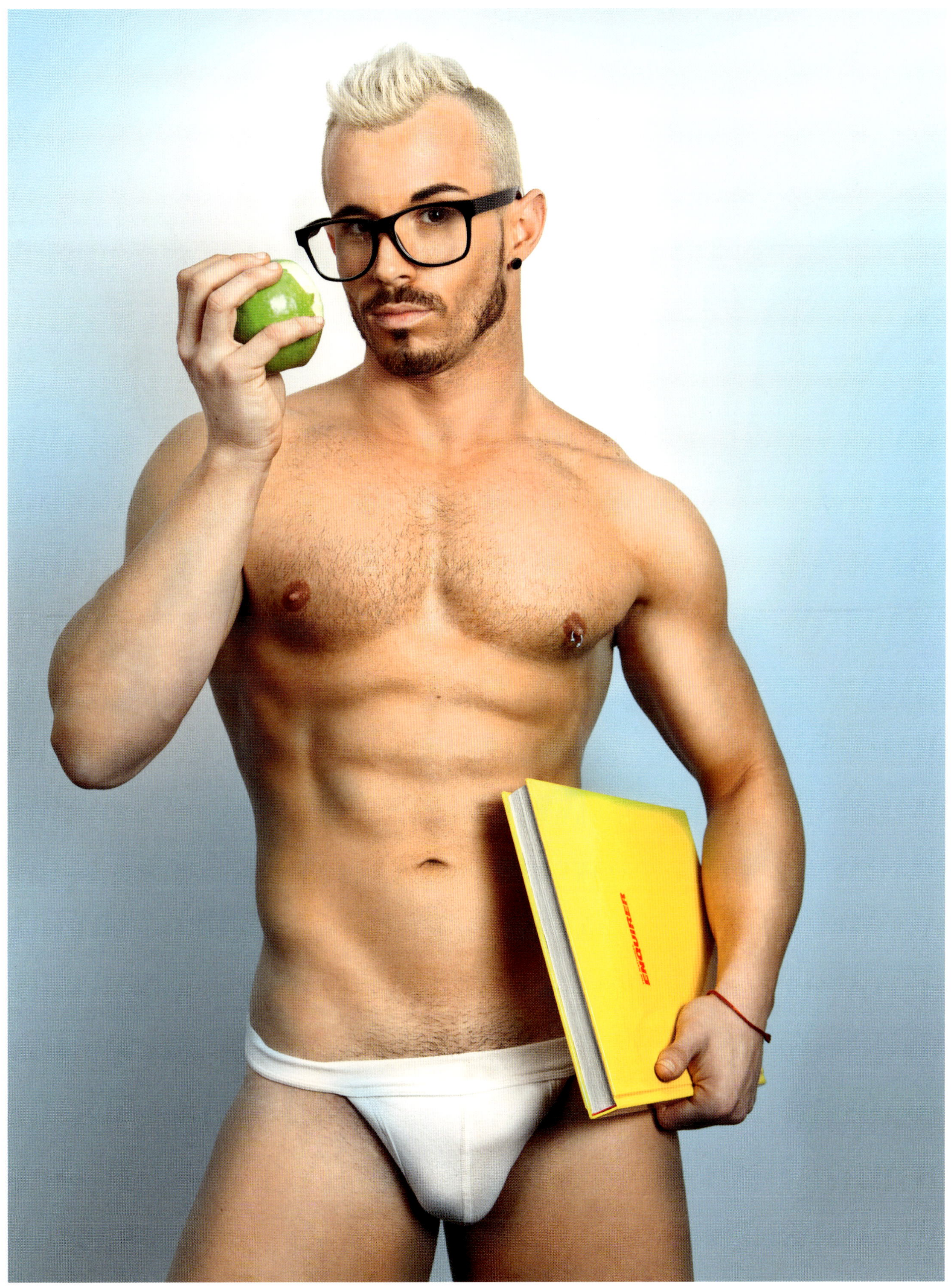
ENGINEER

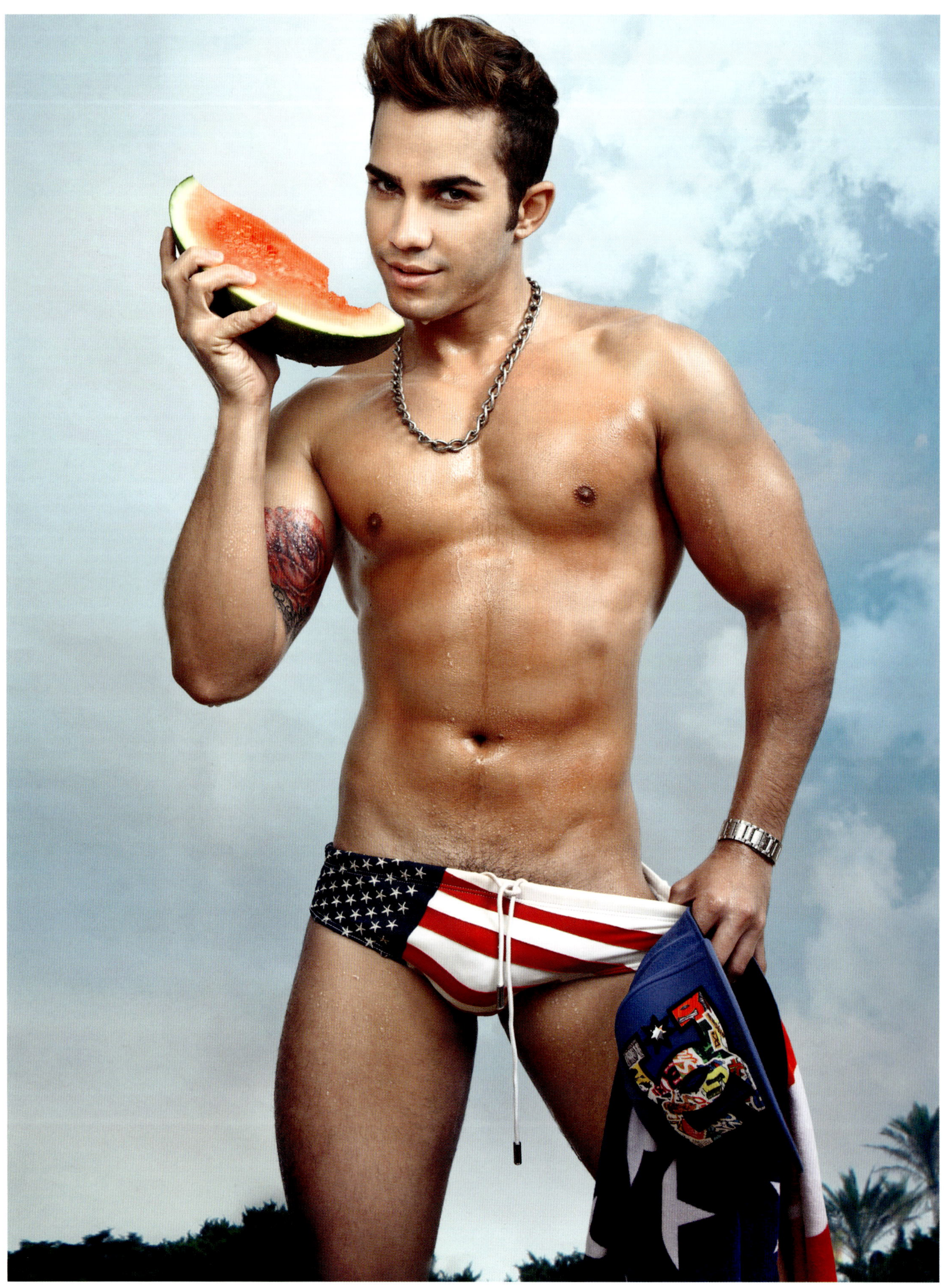

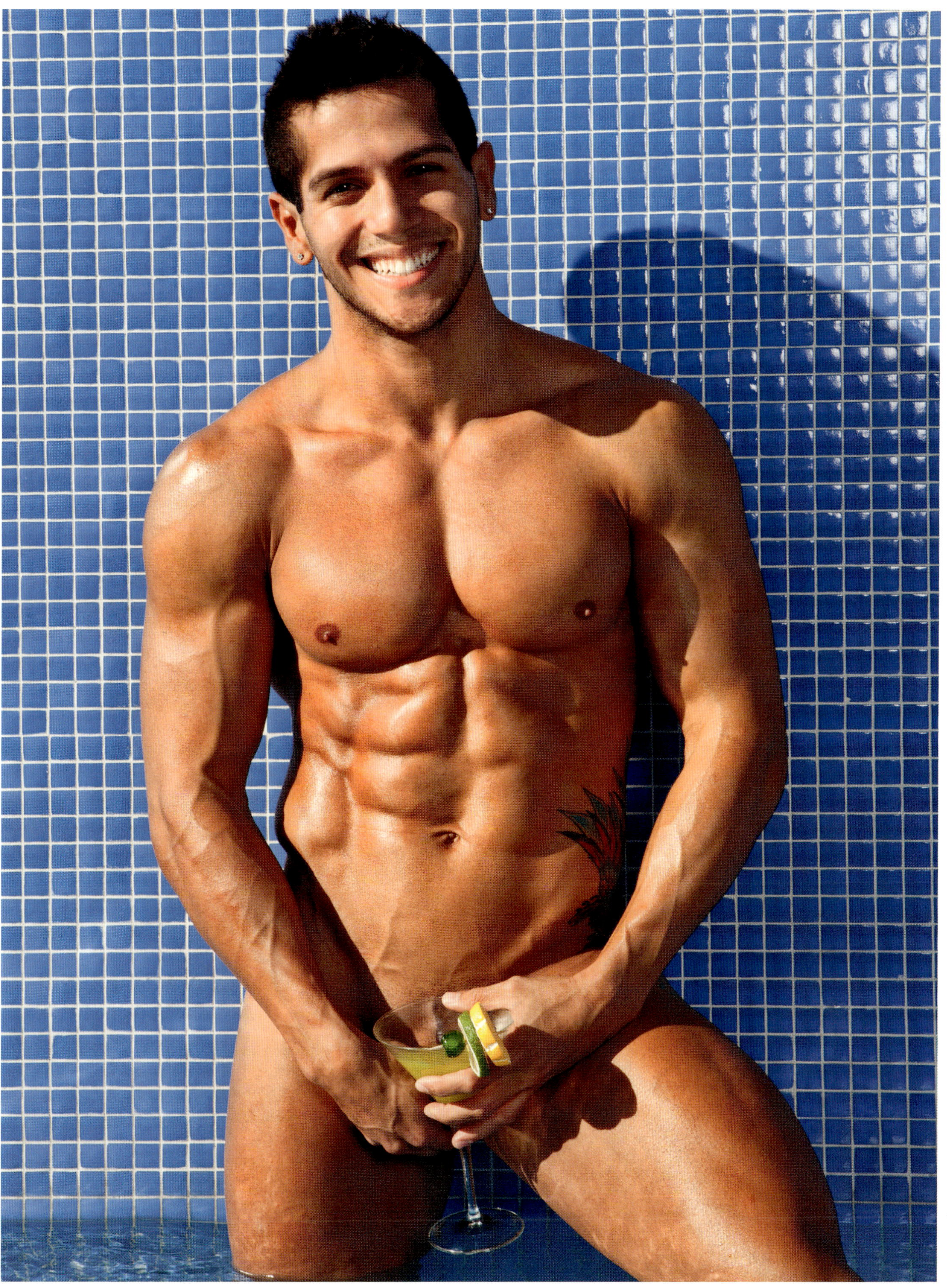

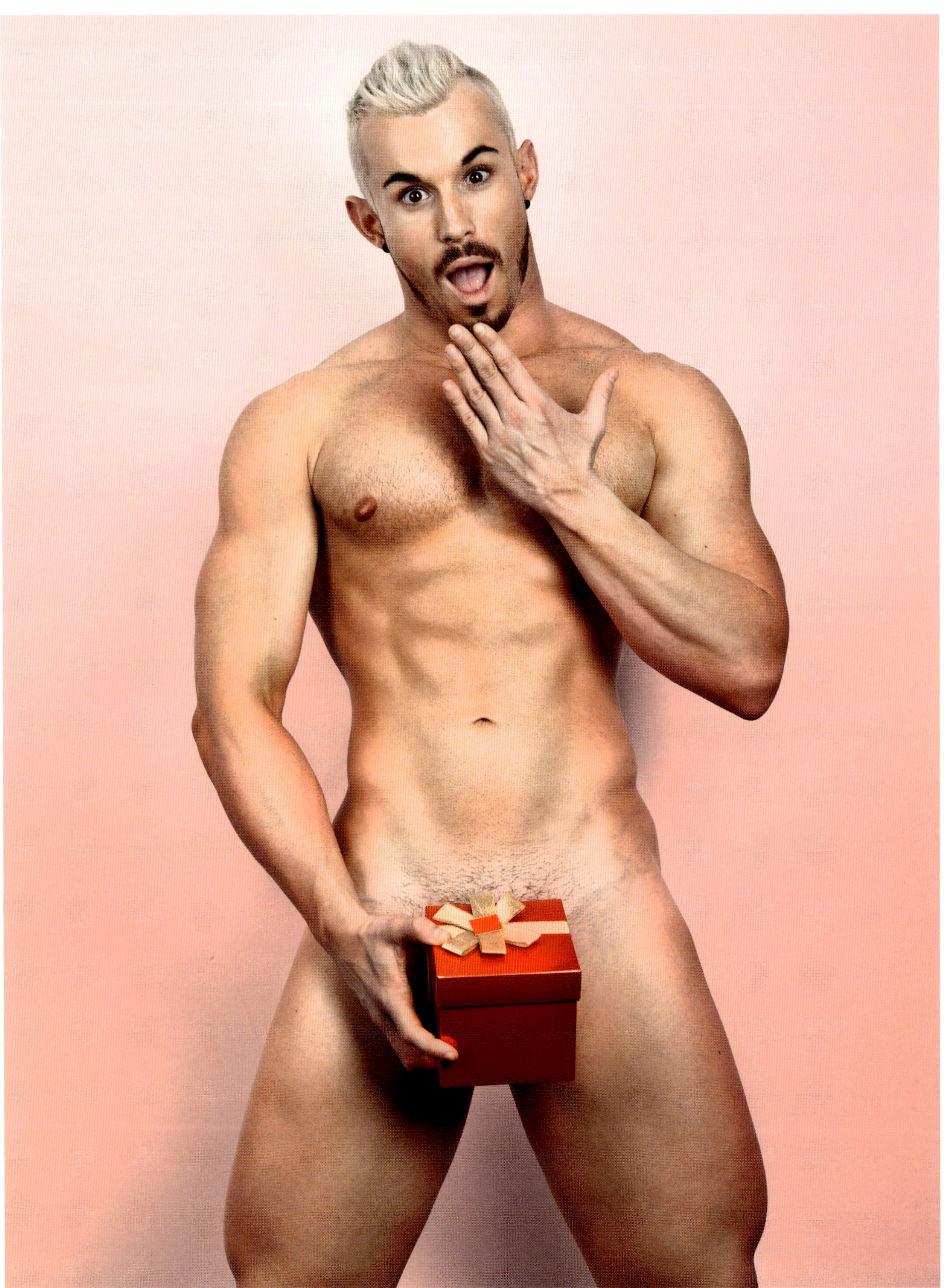

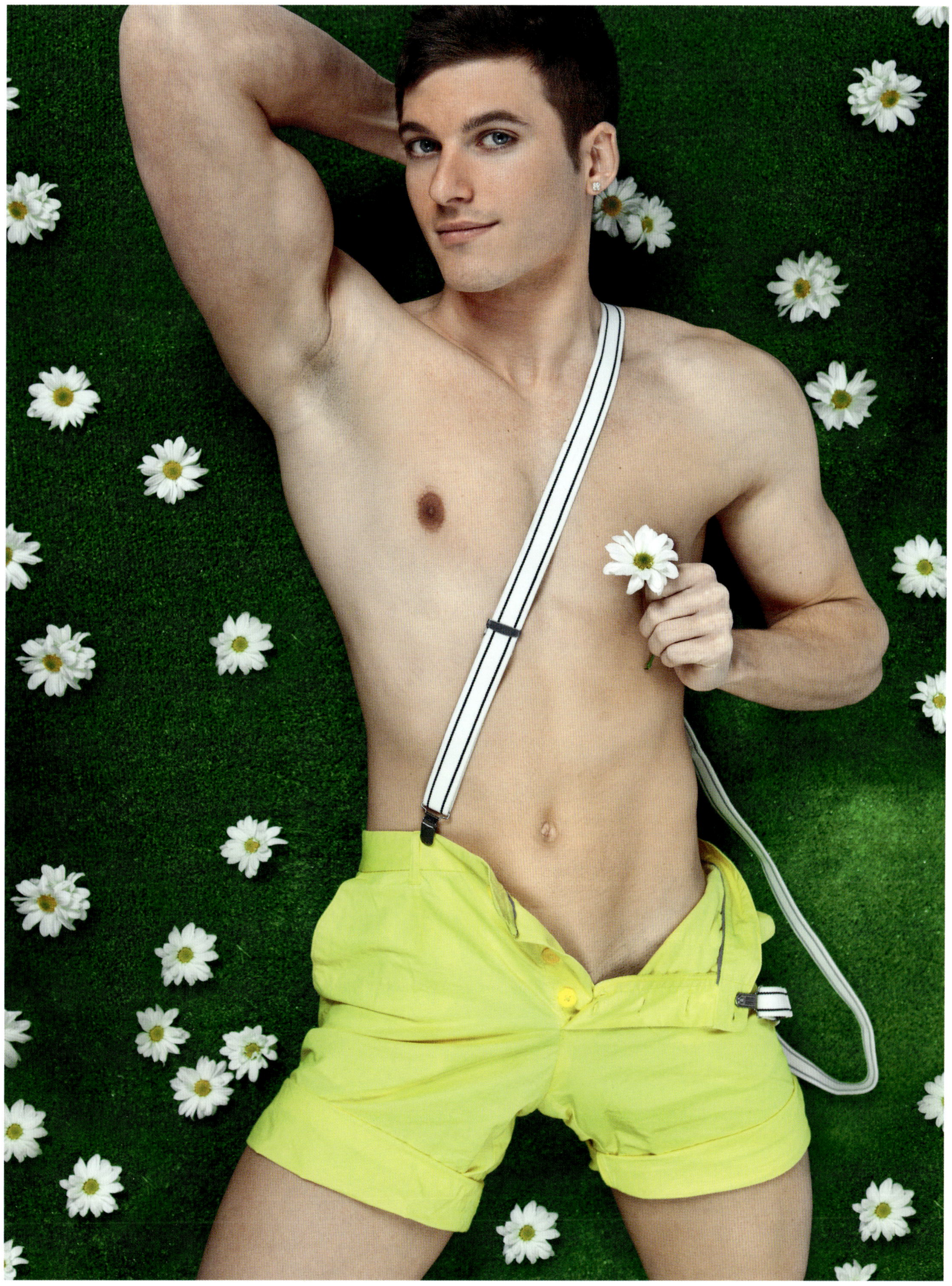

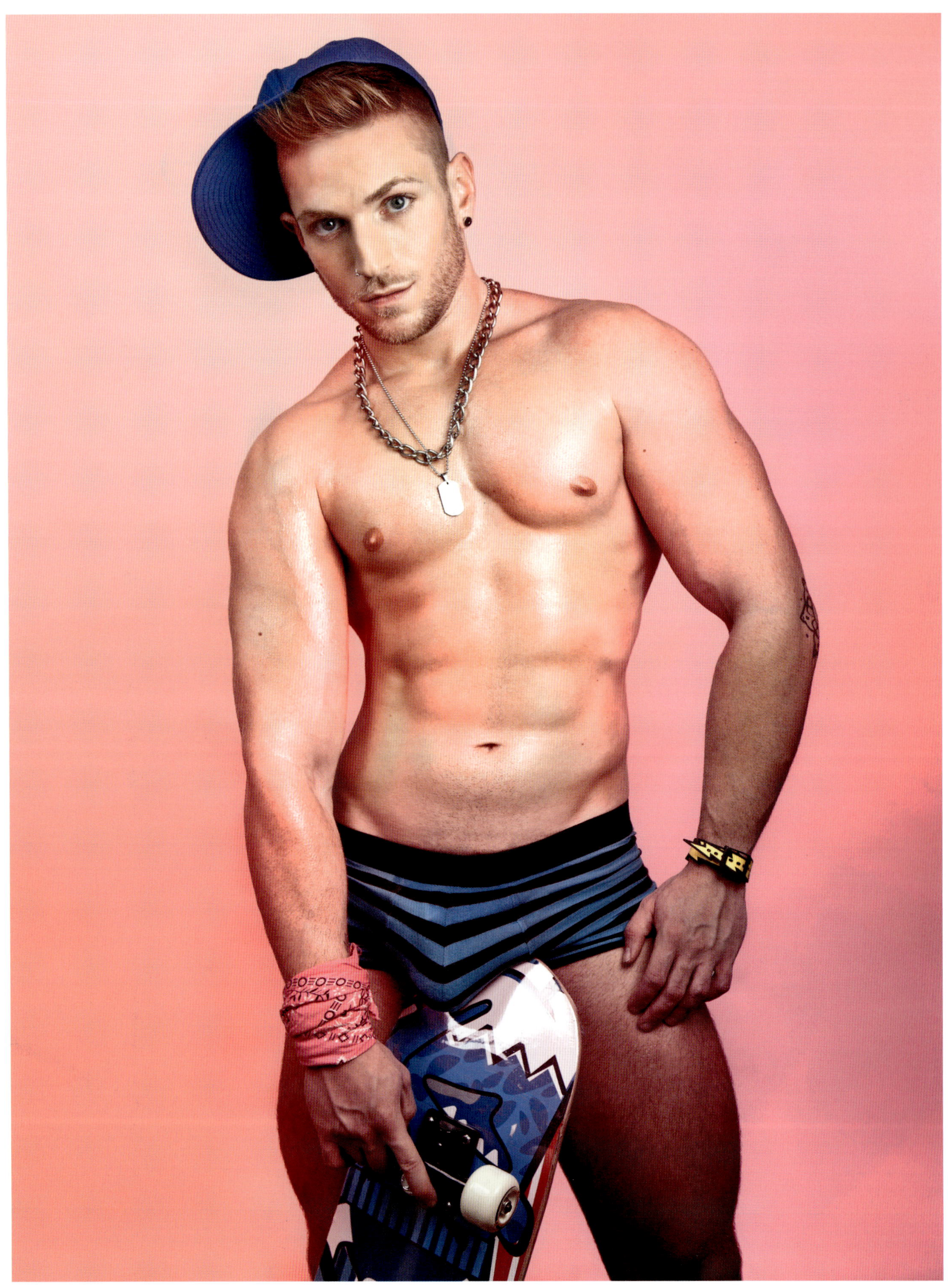

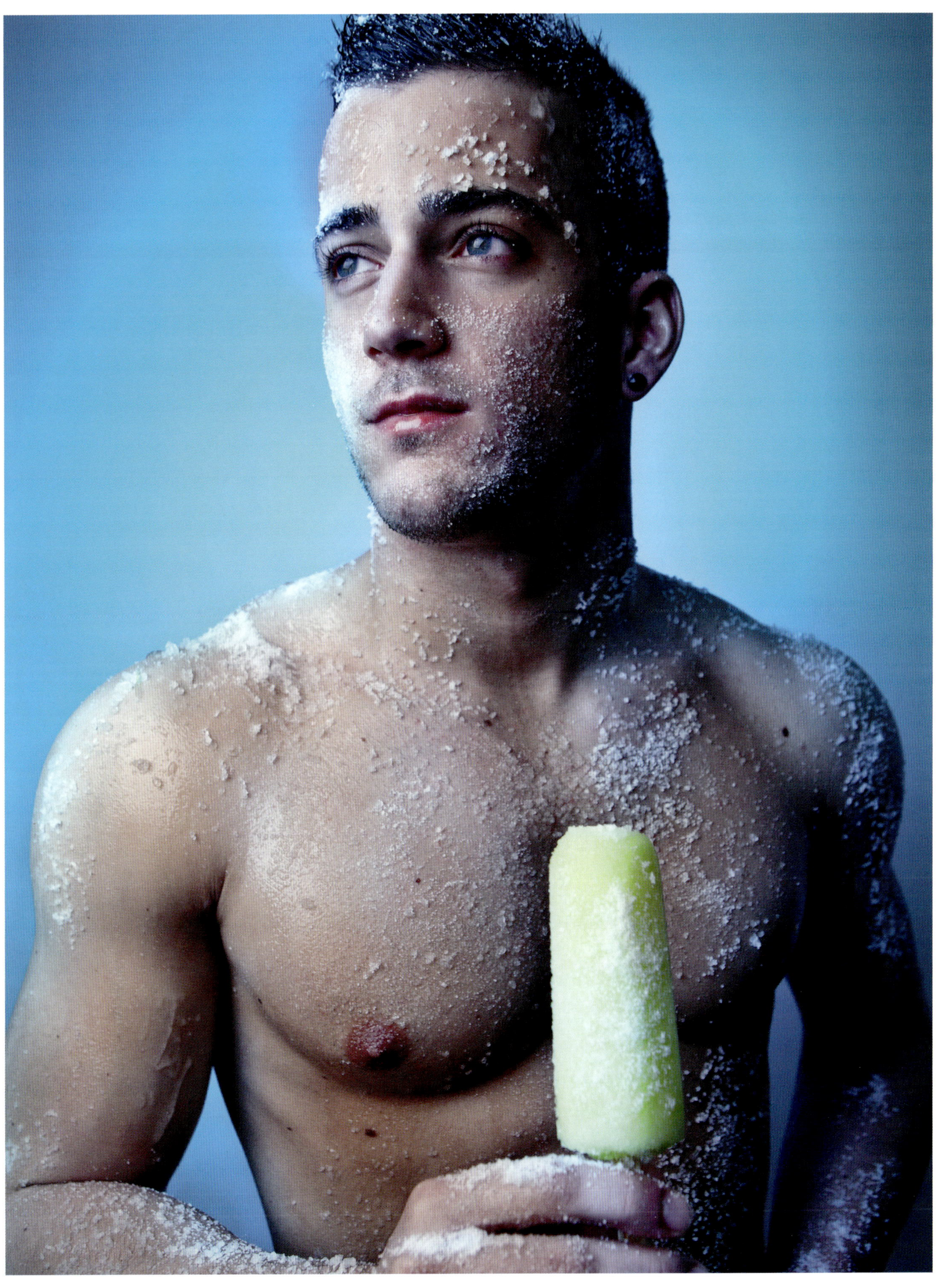

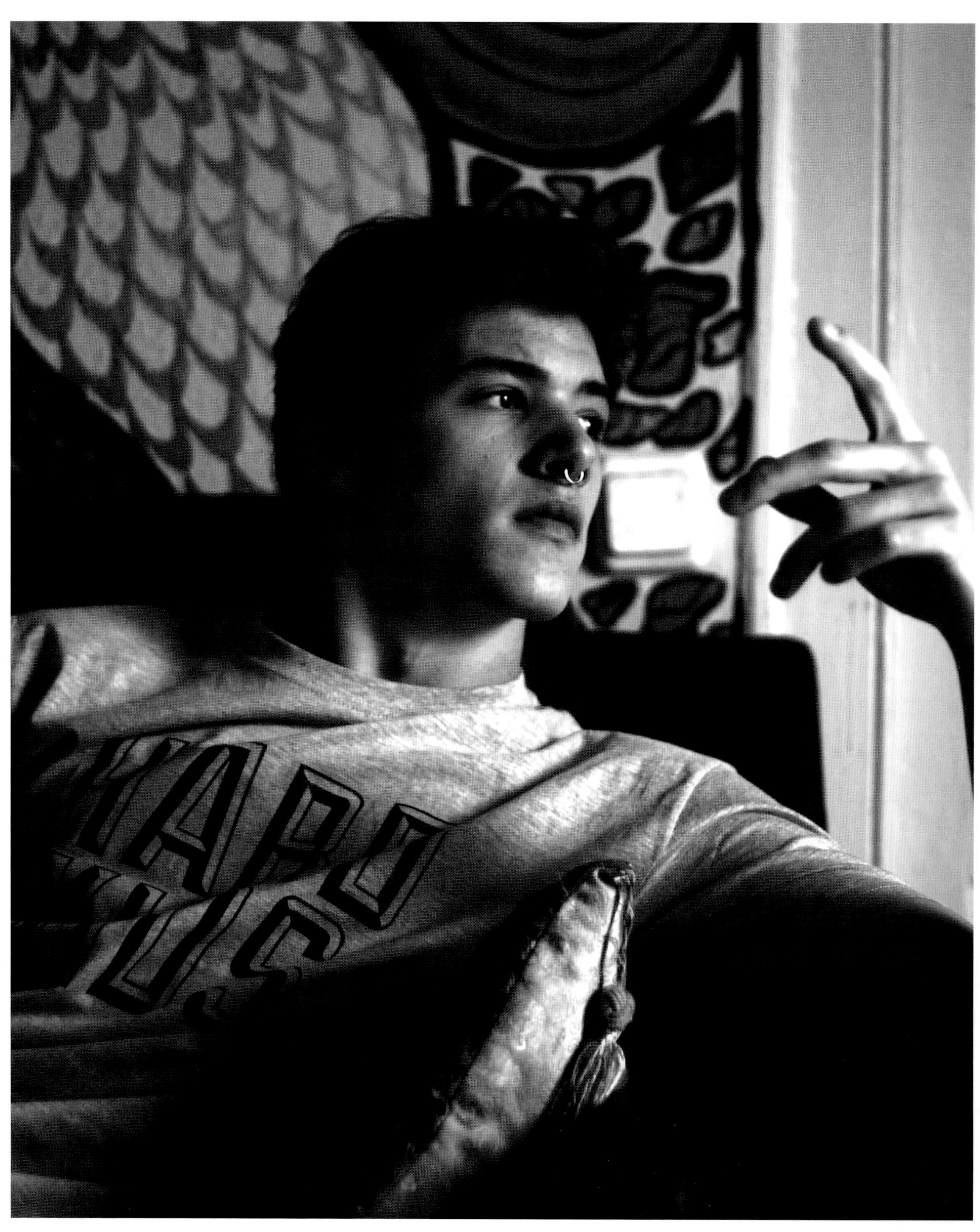

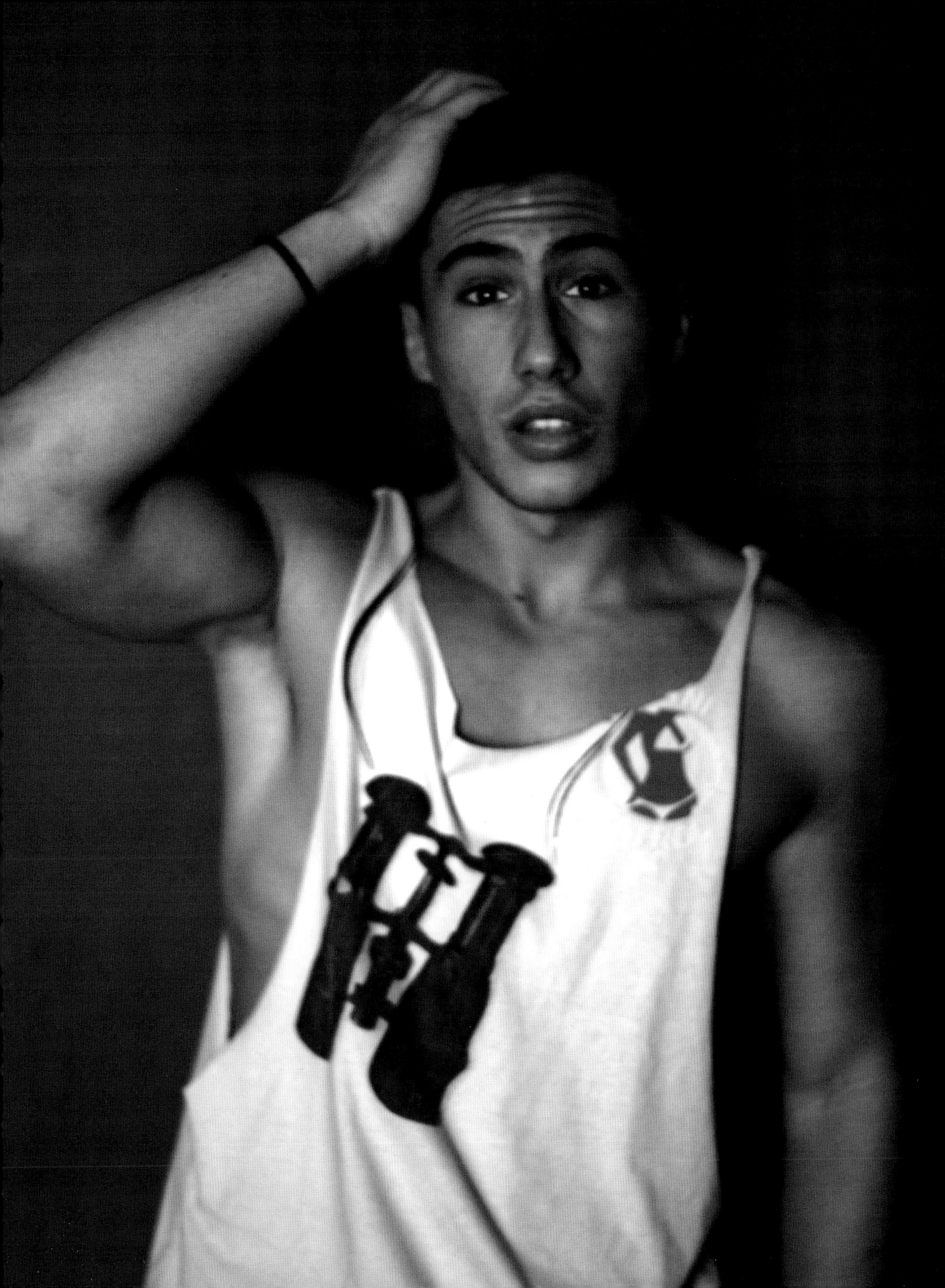

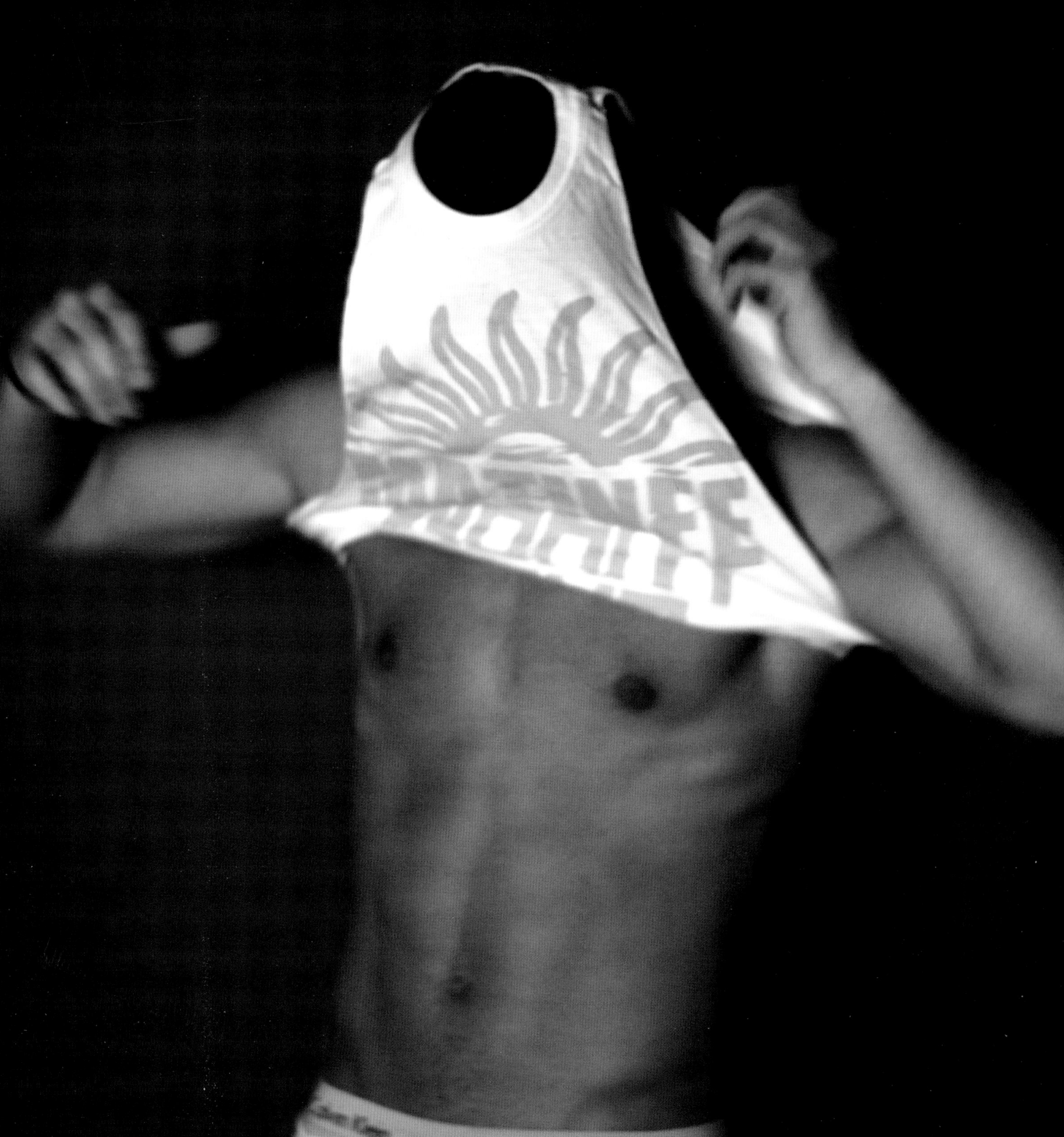

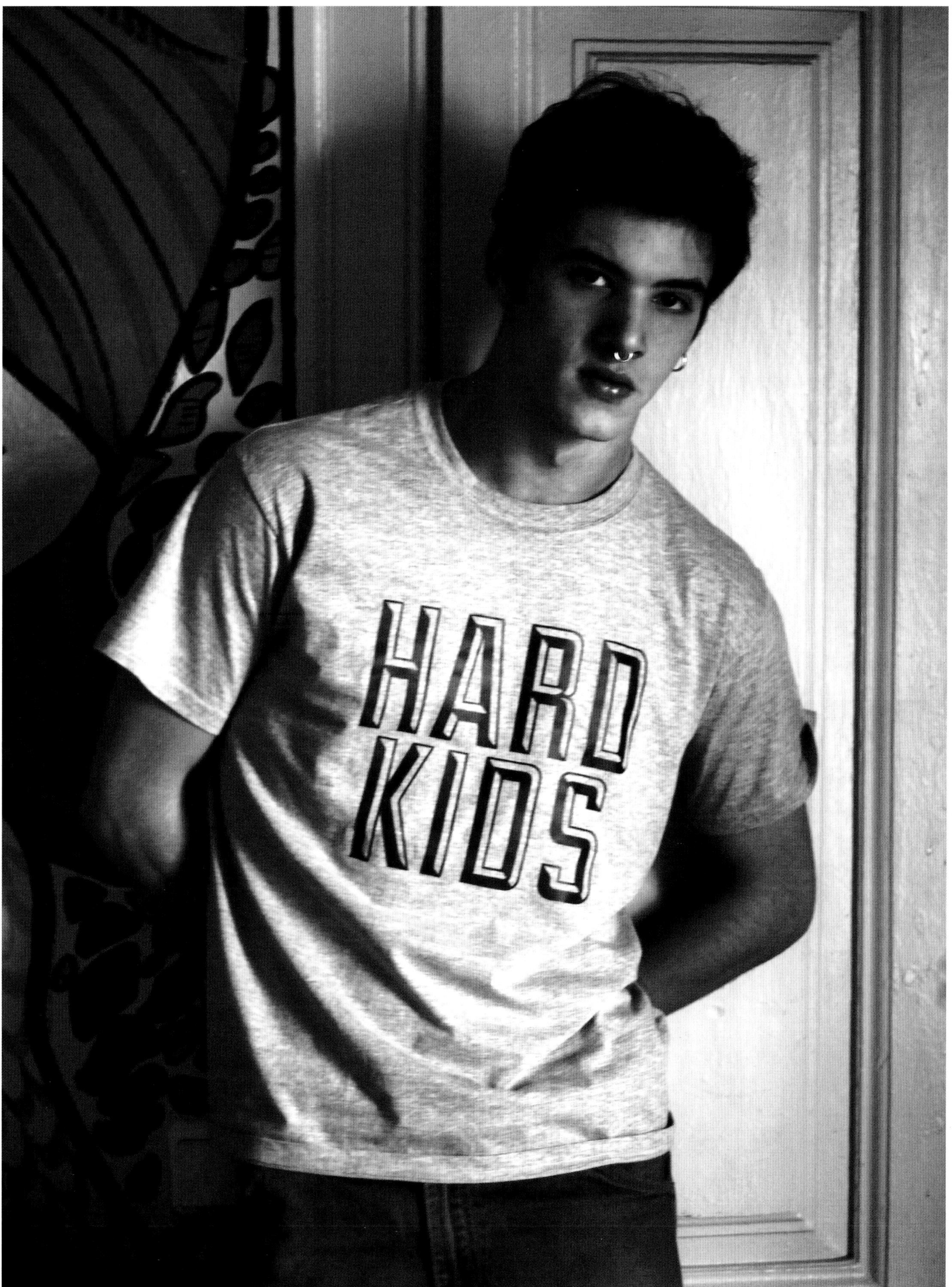

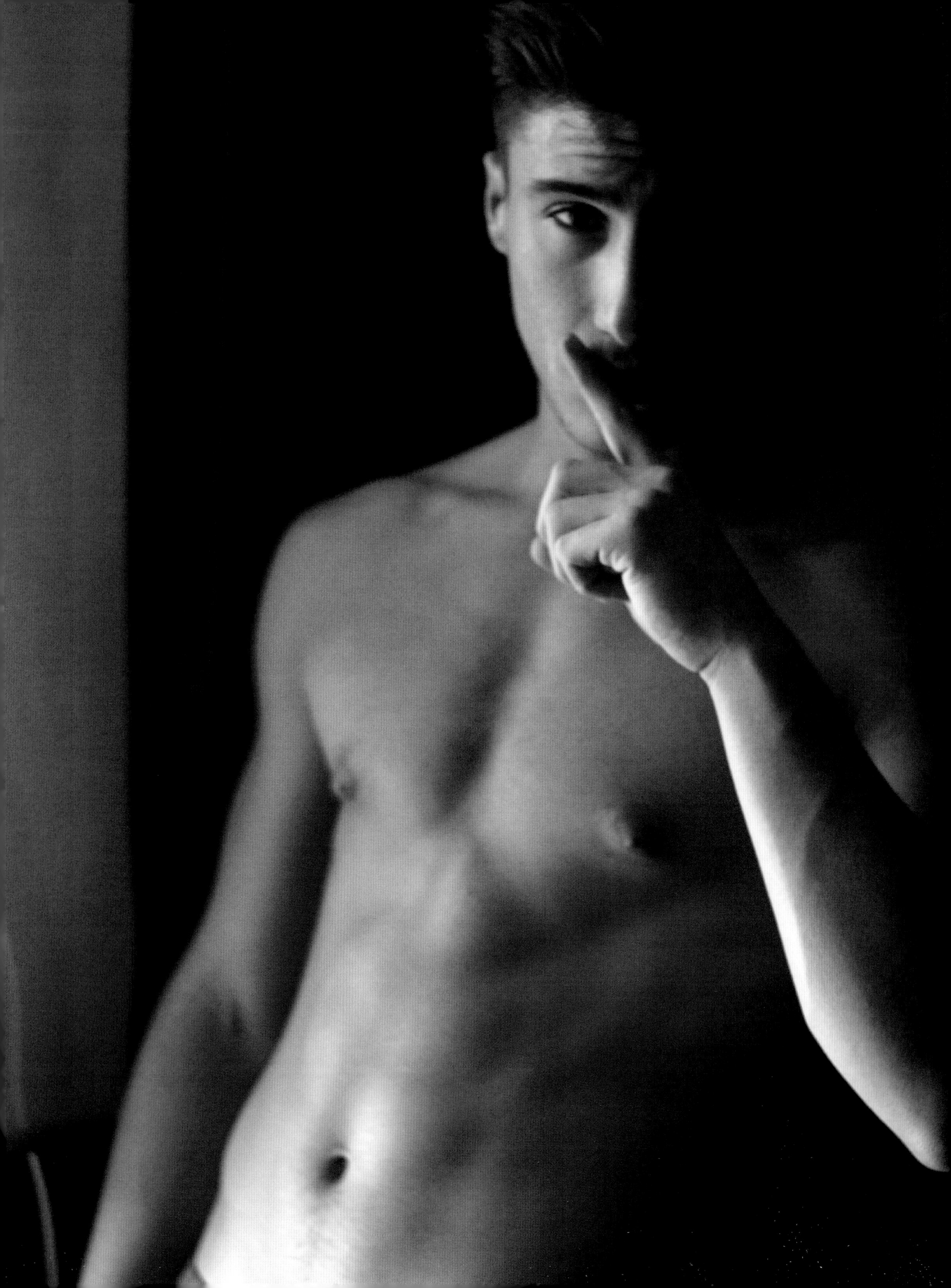

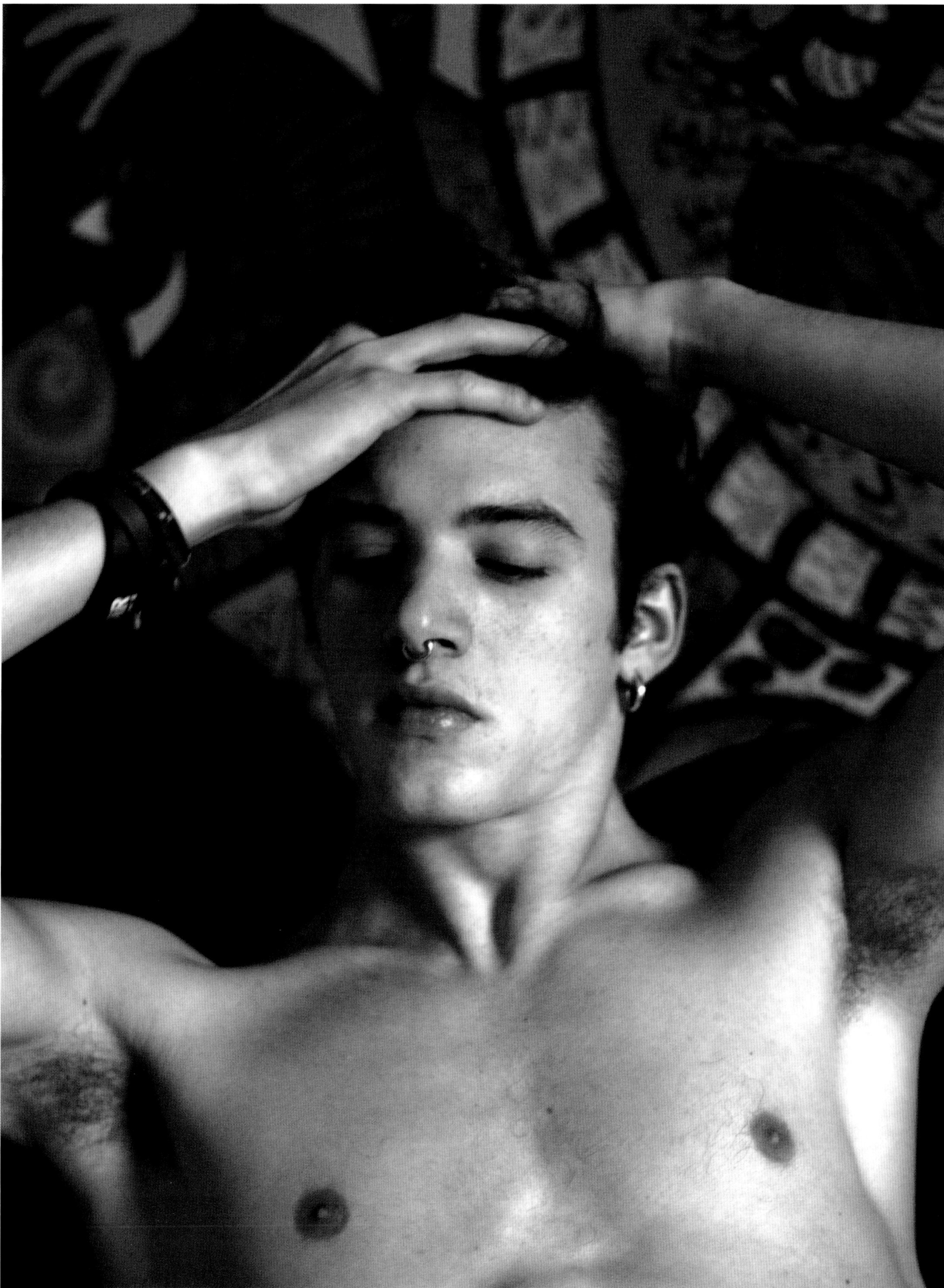

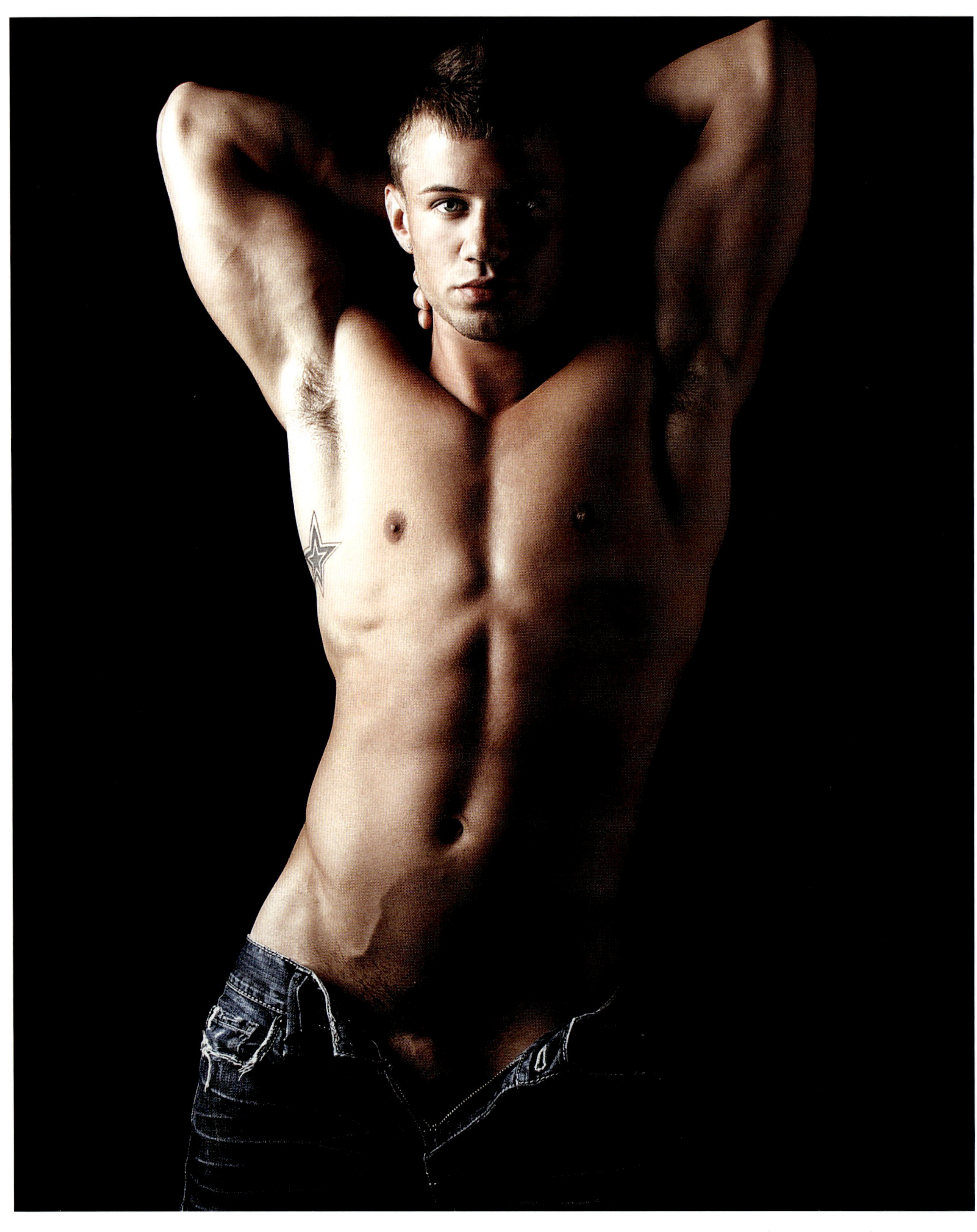

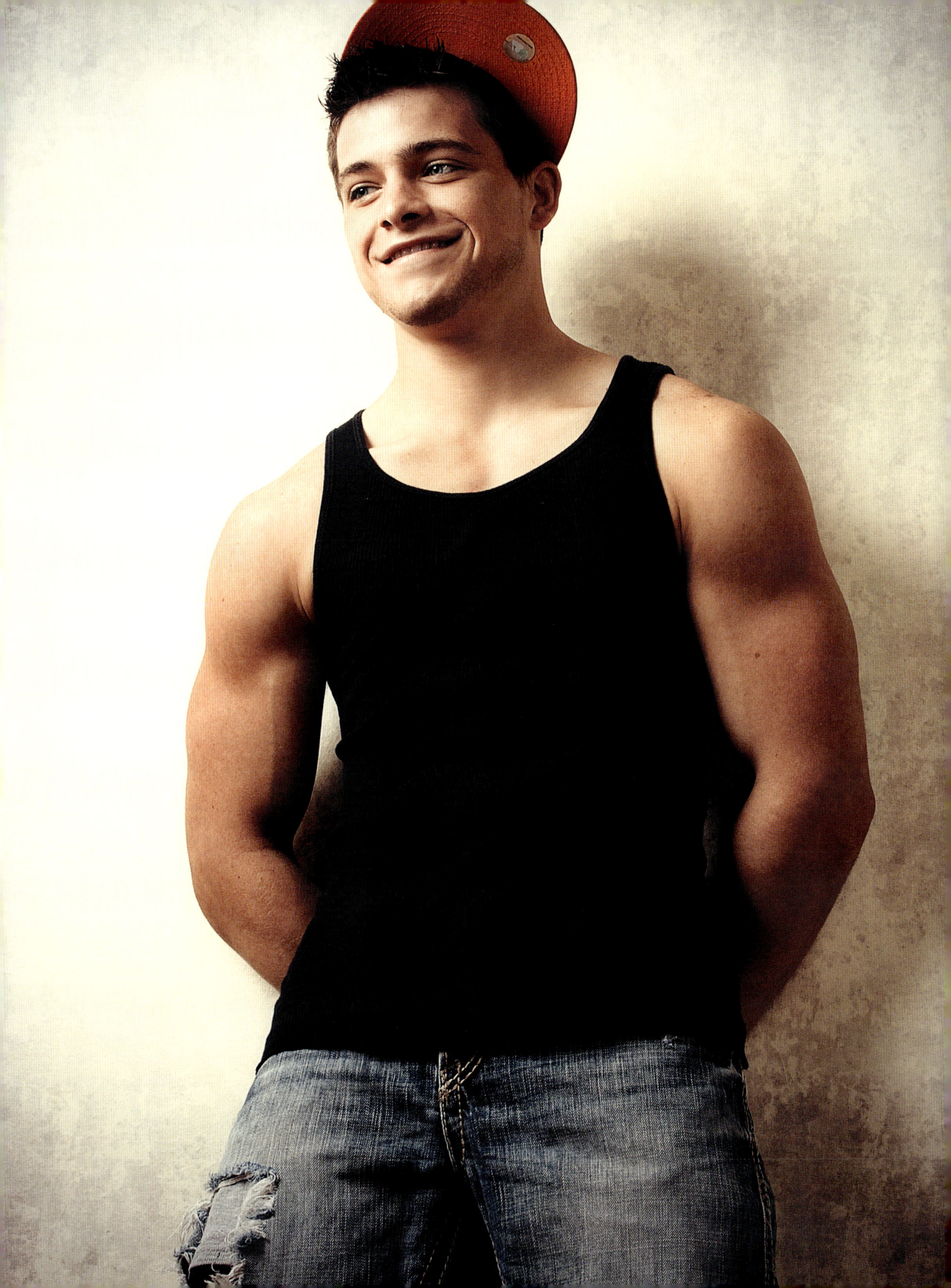

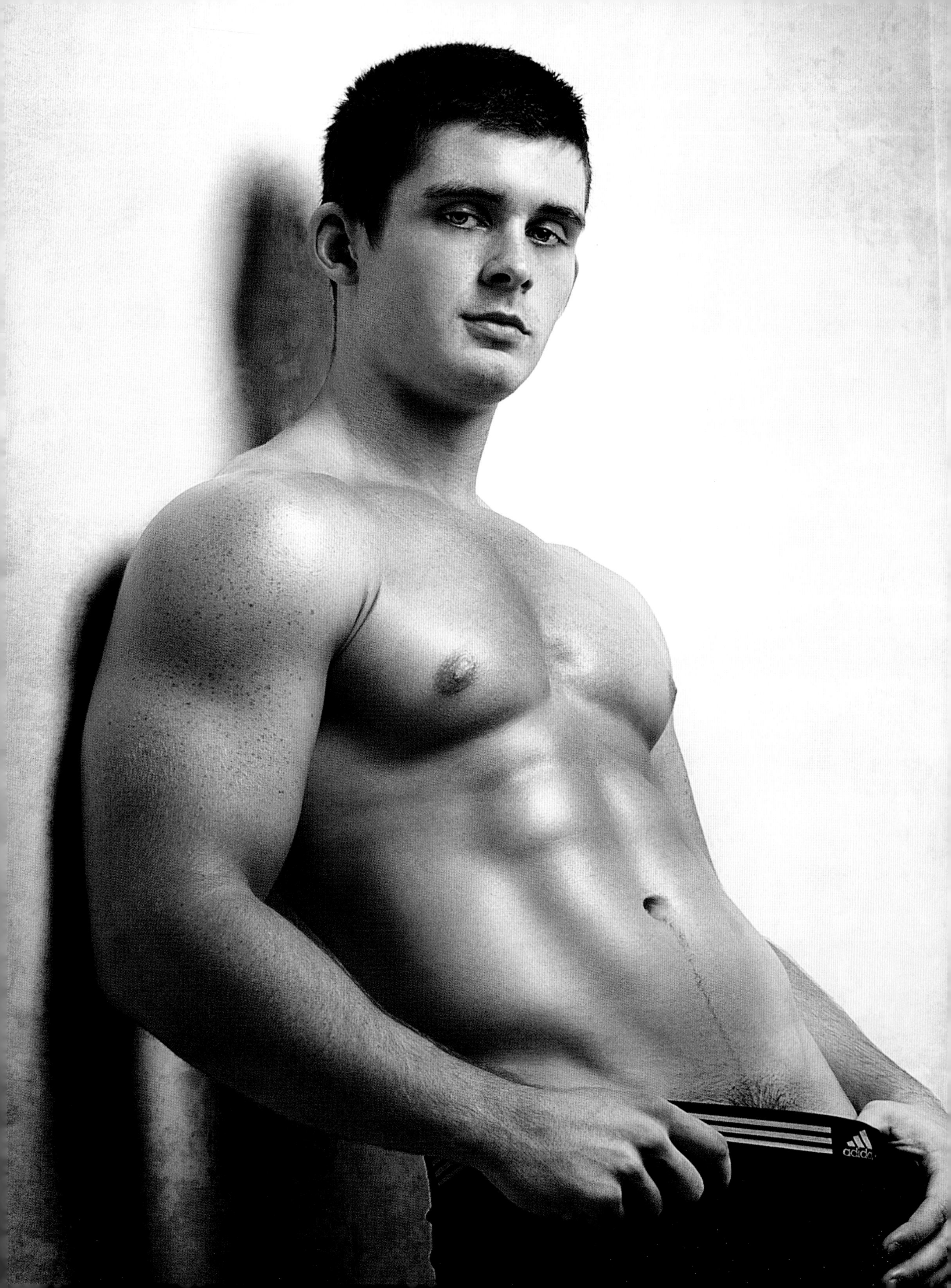

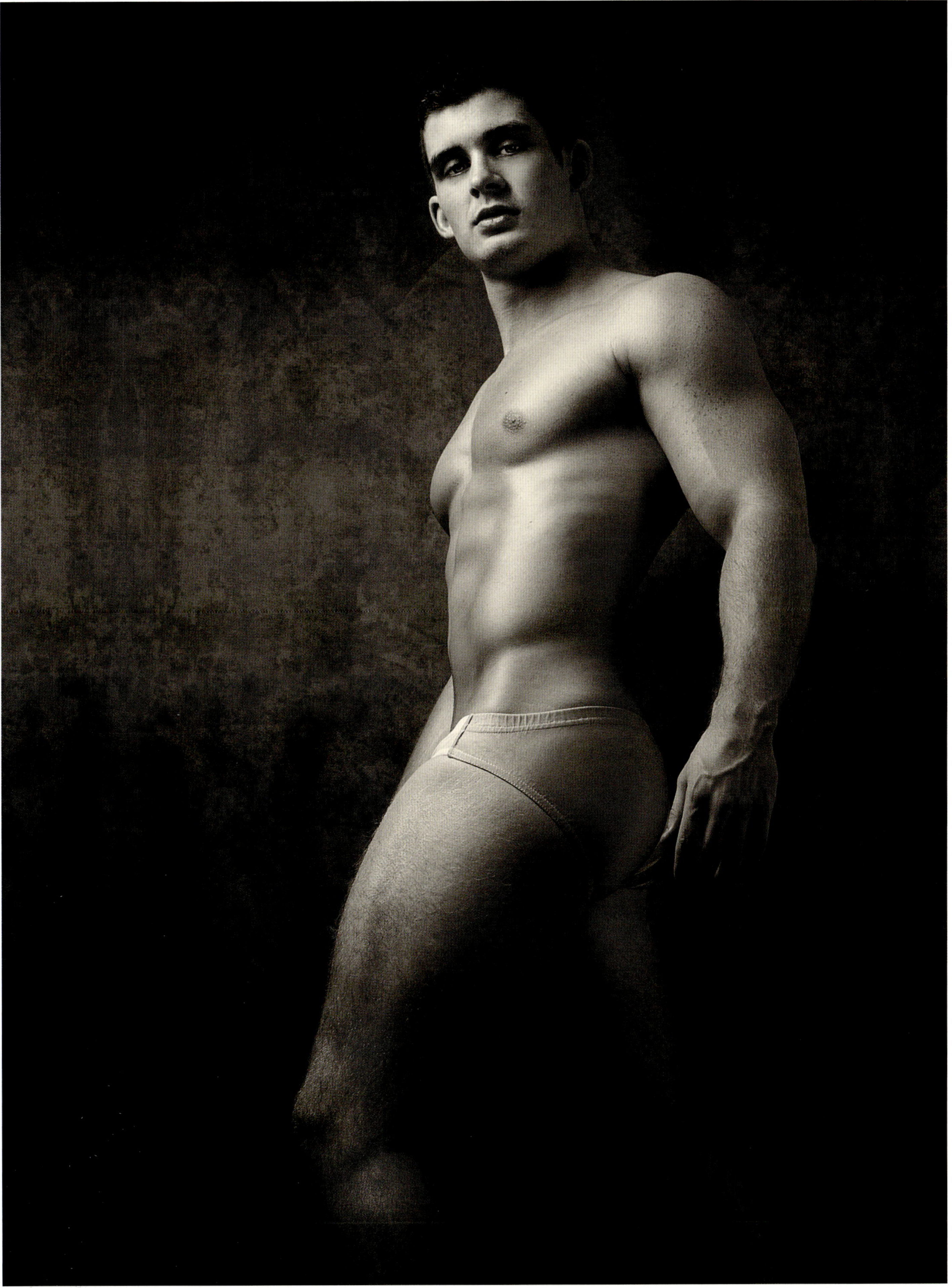

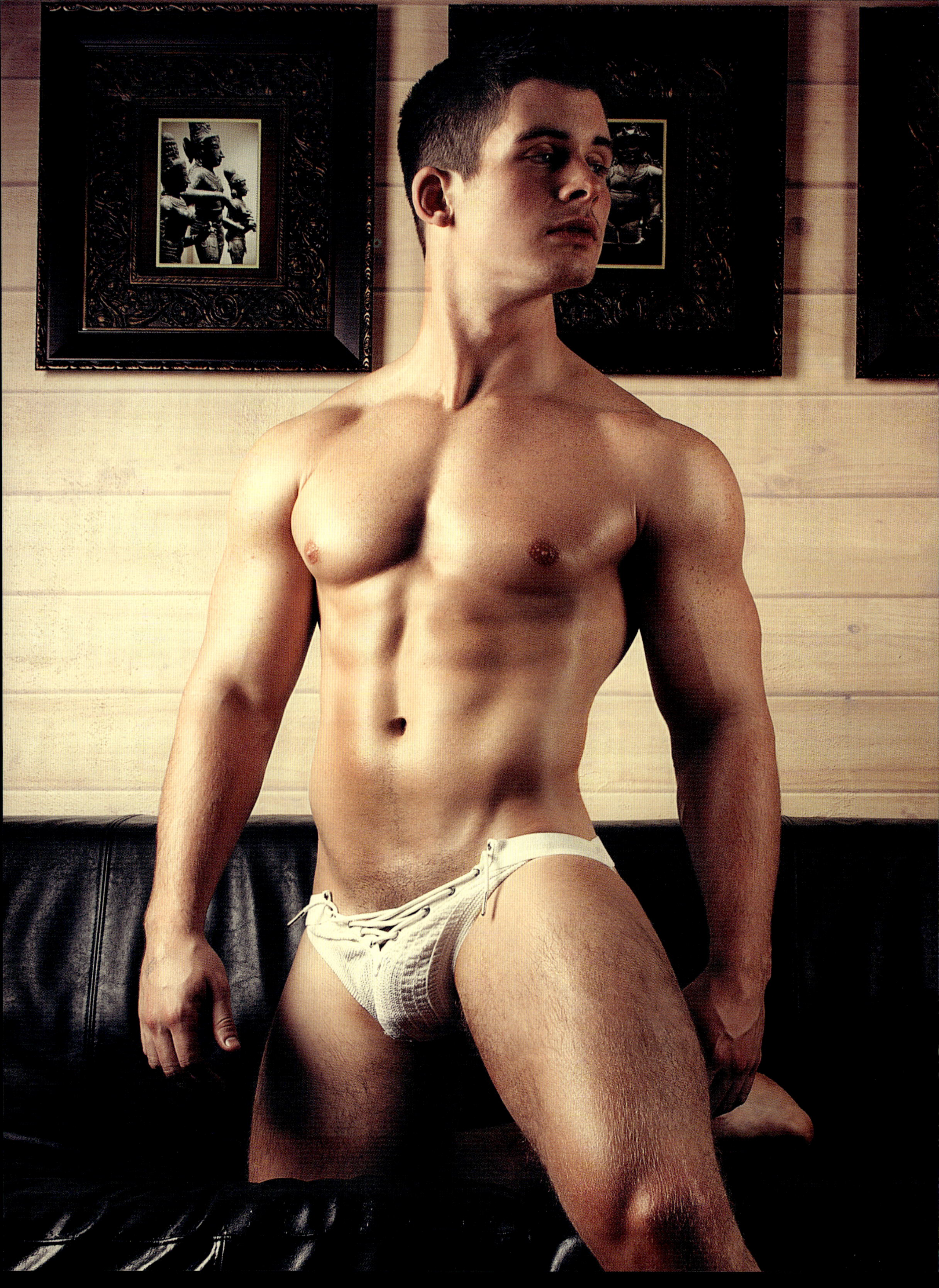

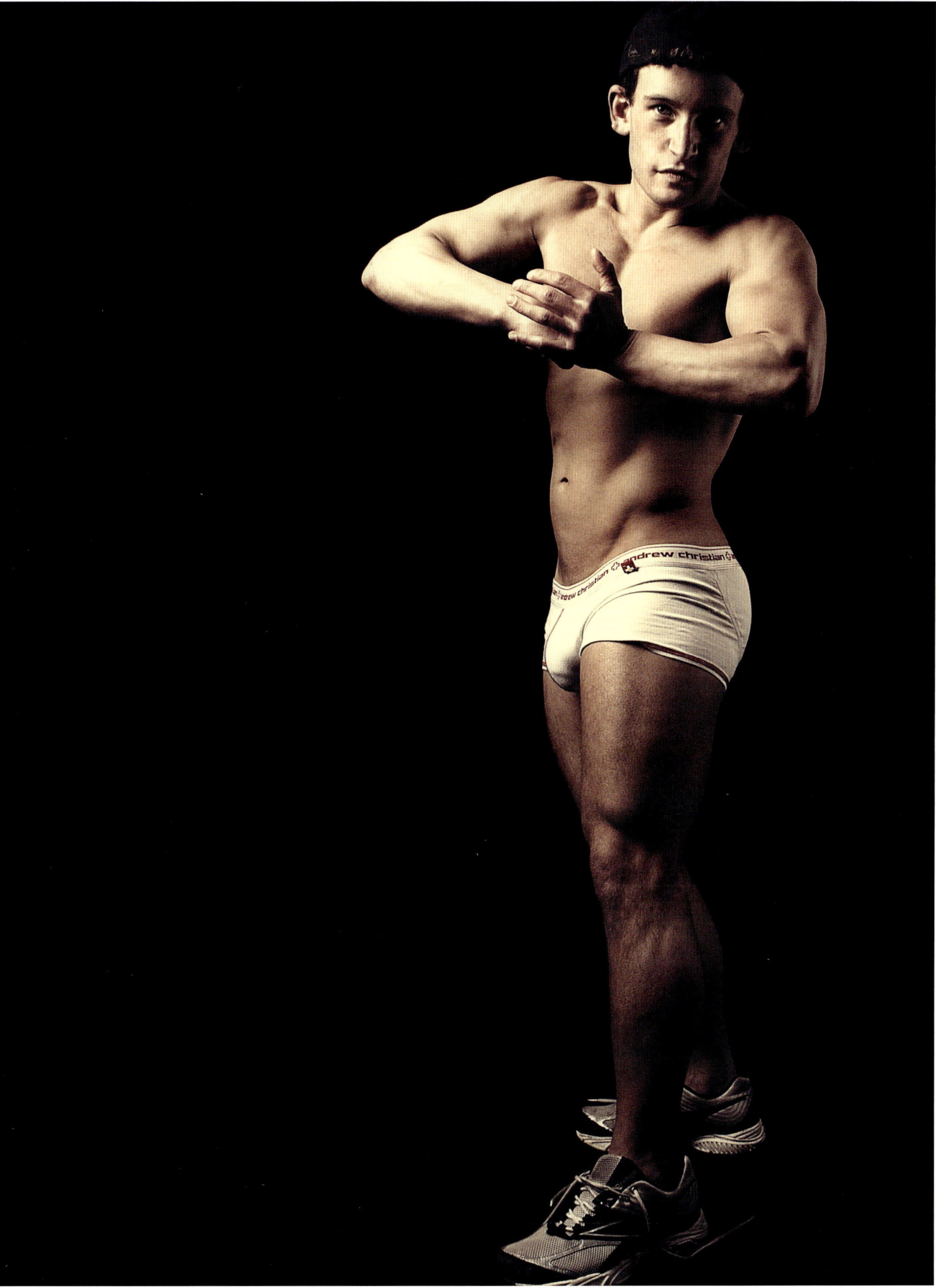

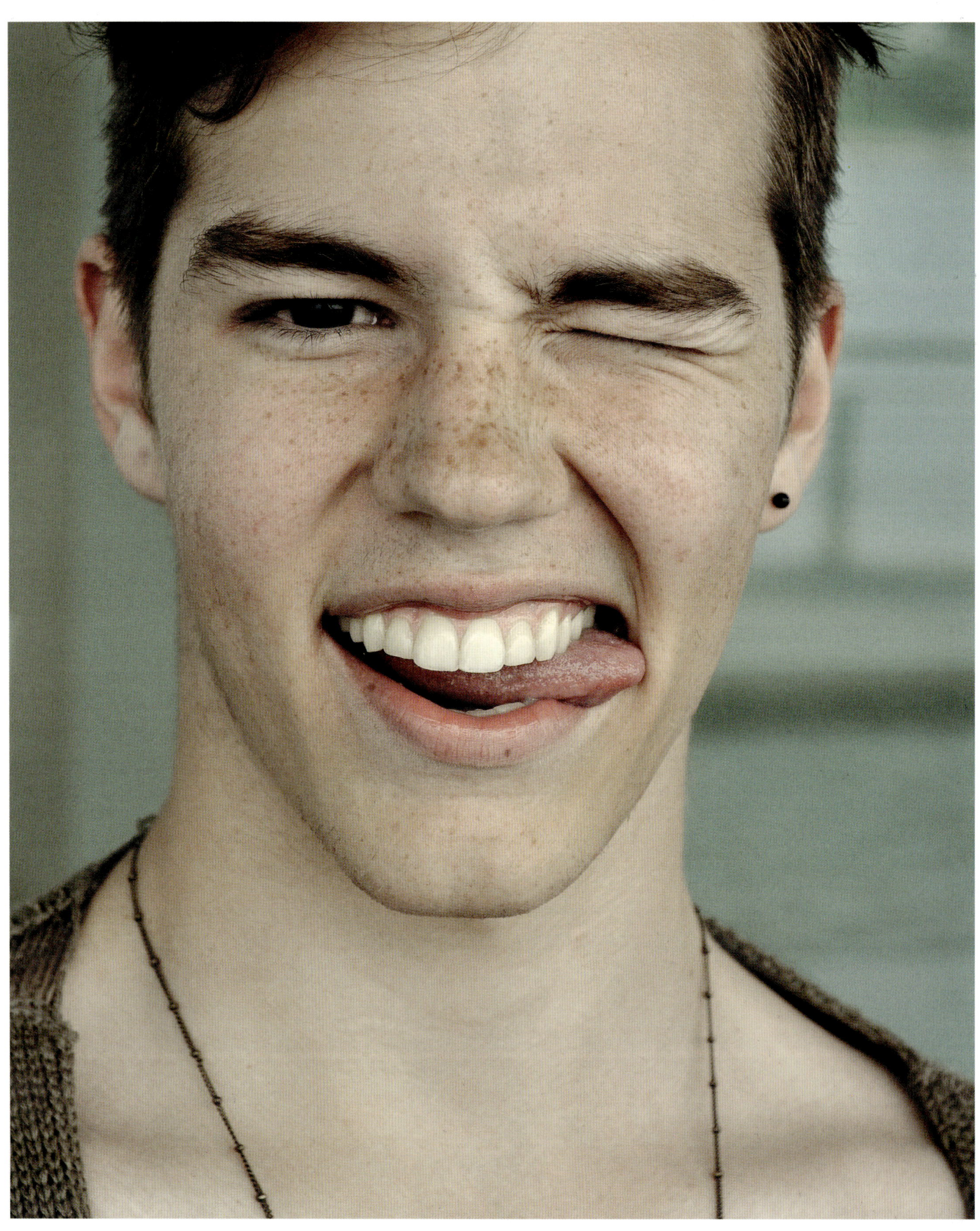

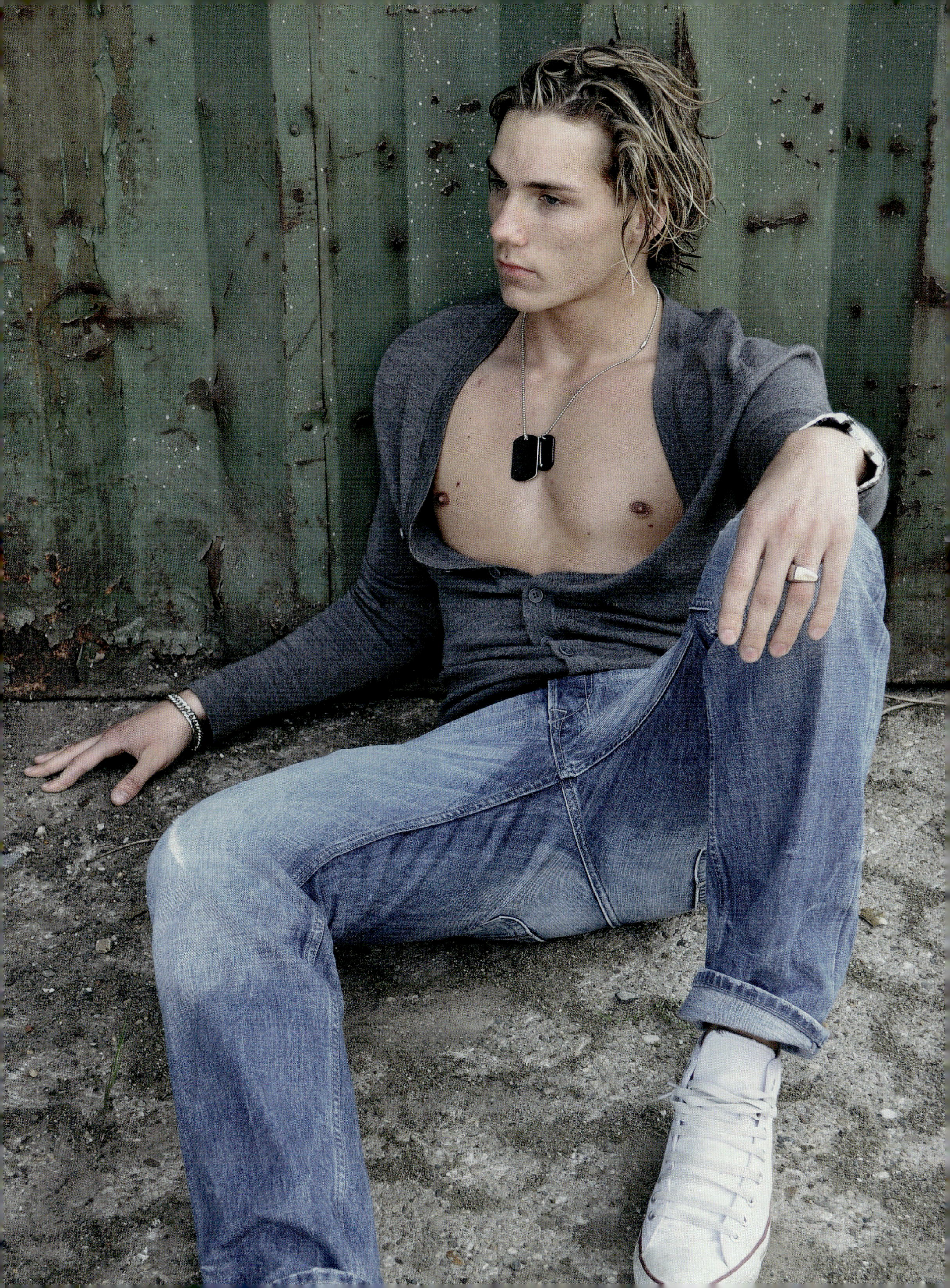

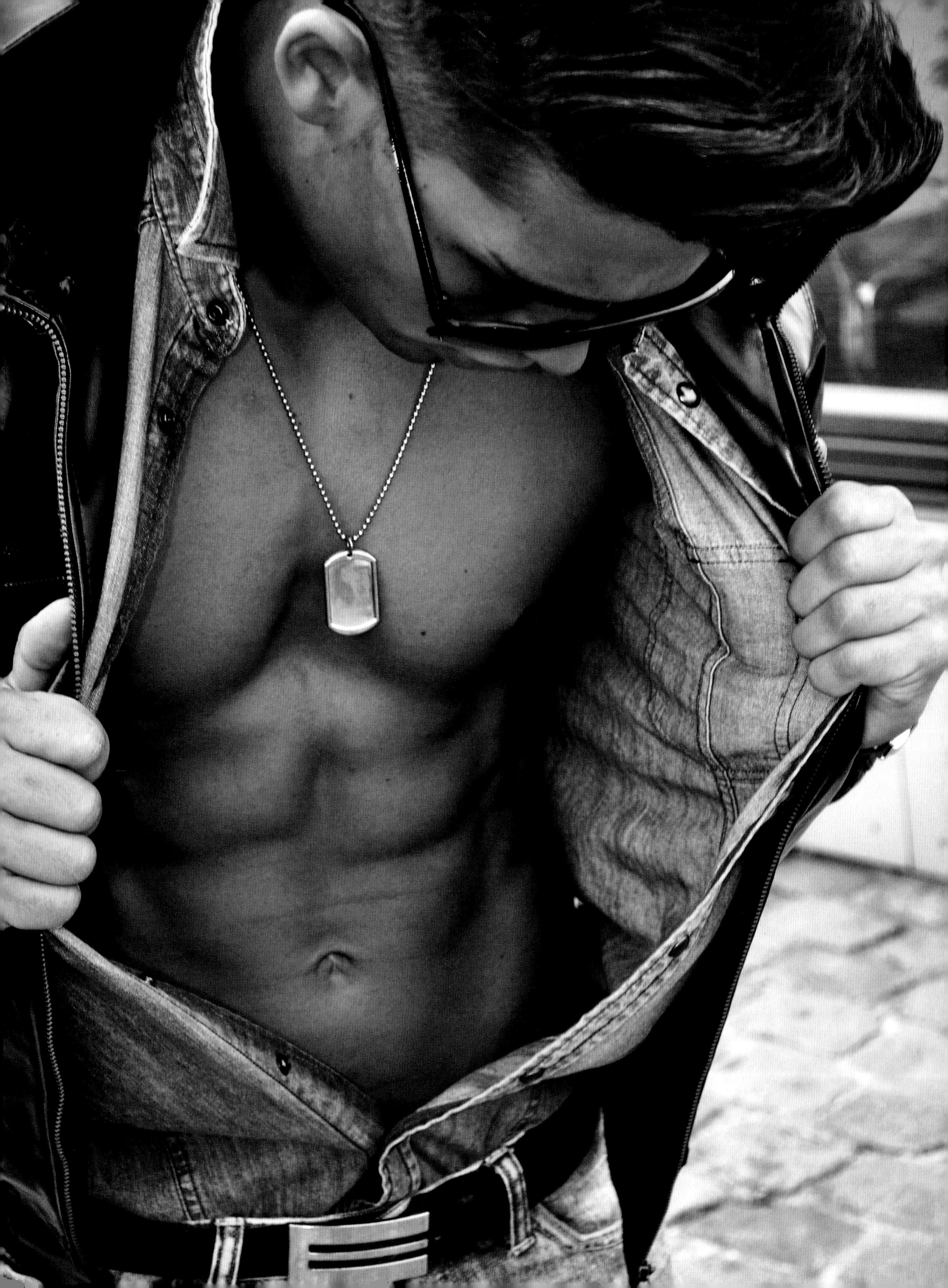

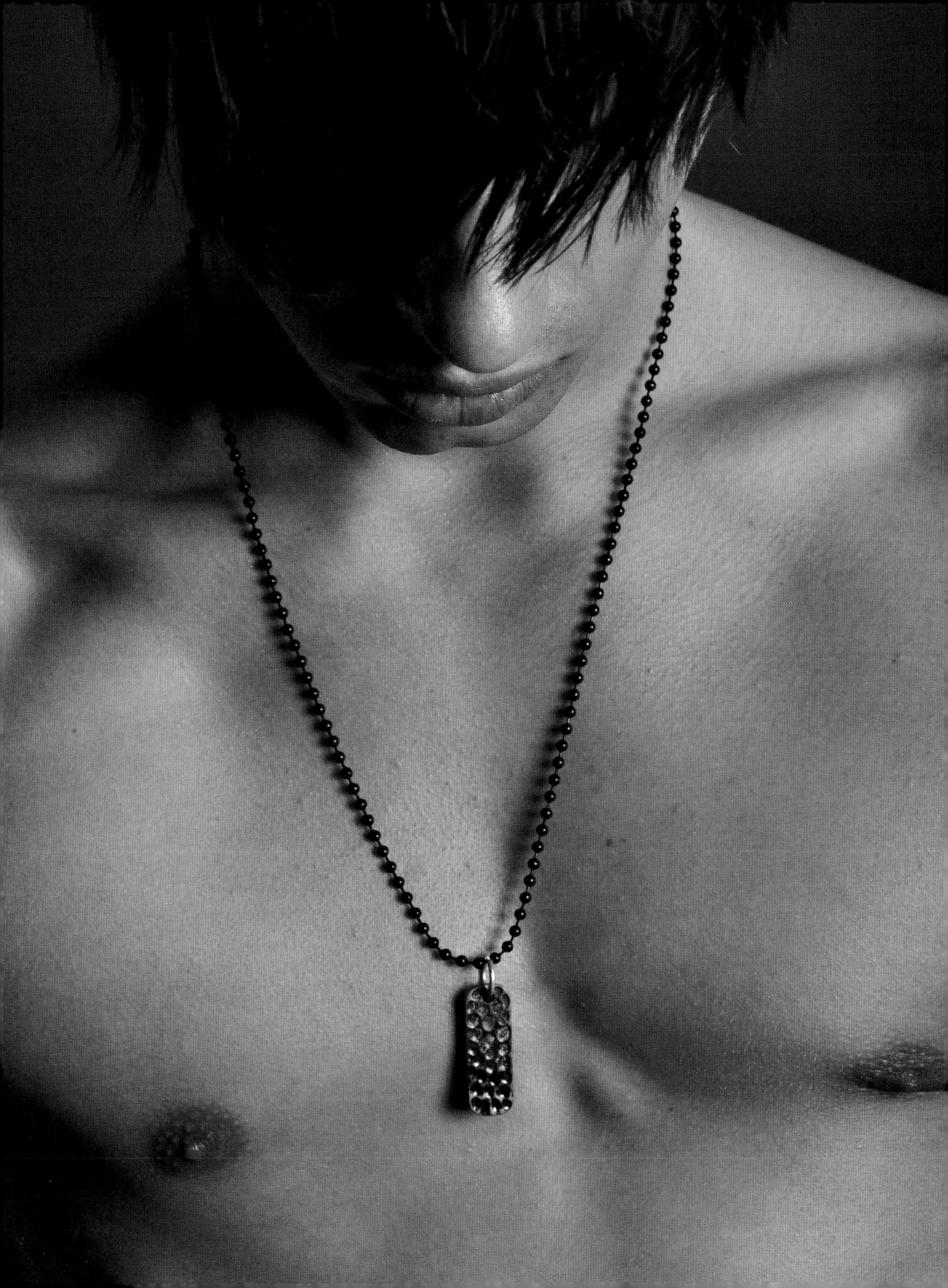

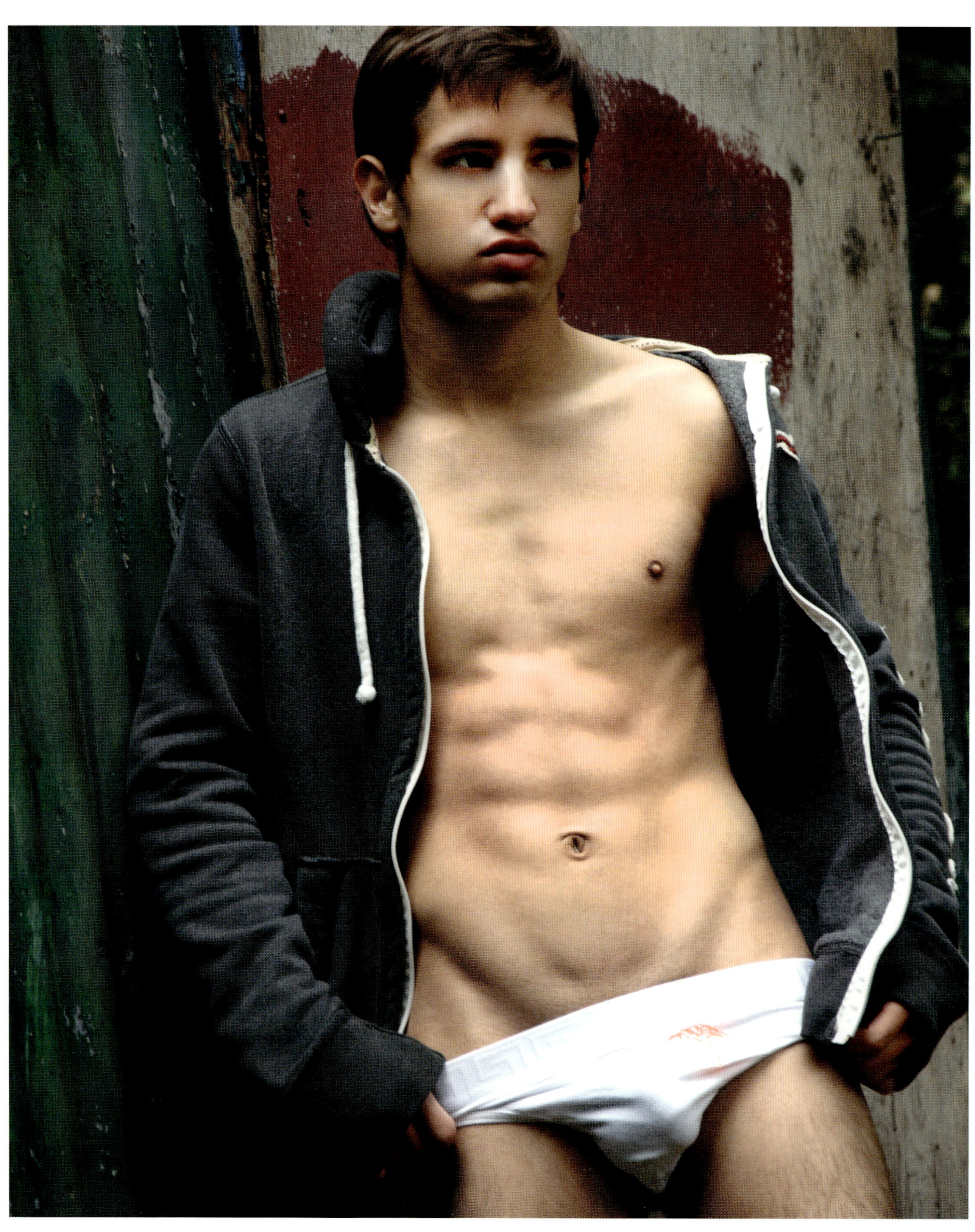

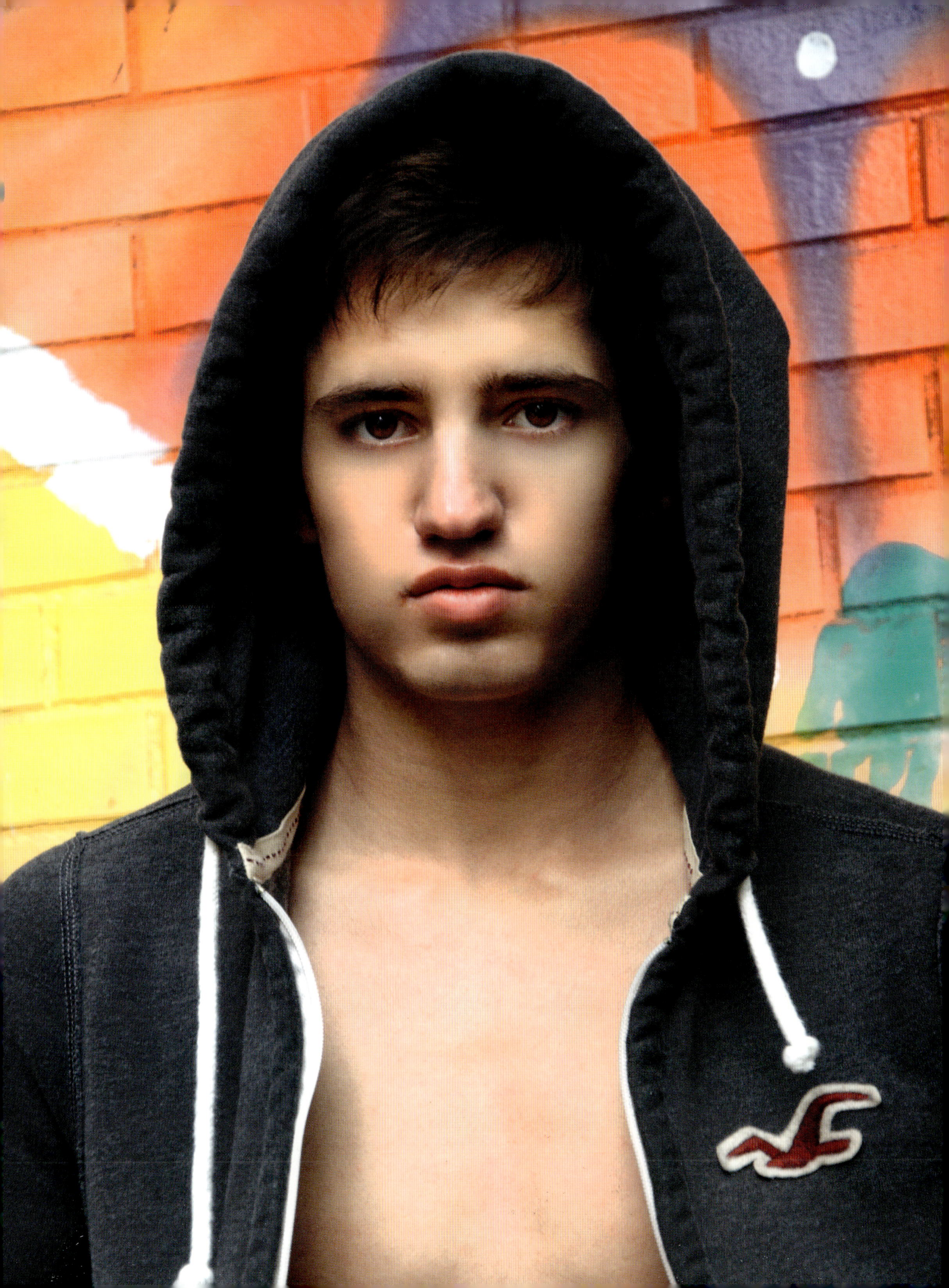

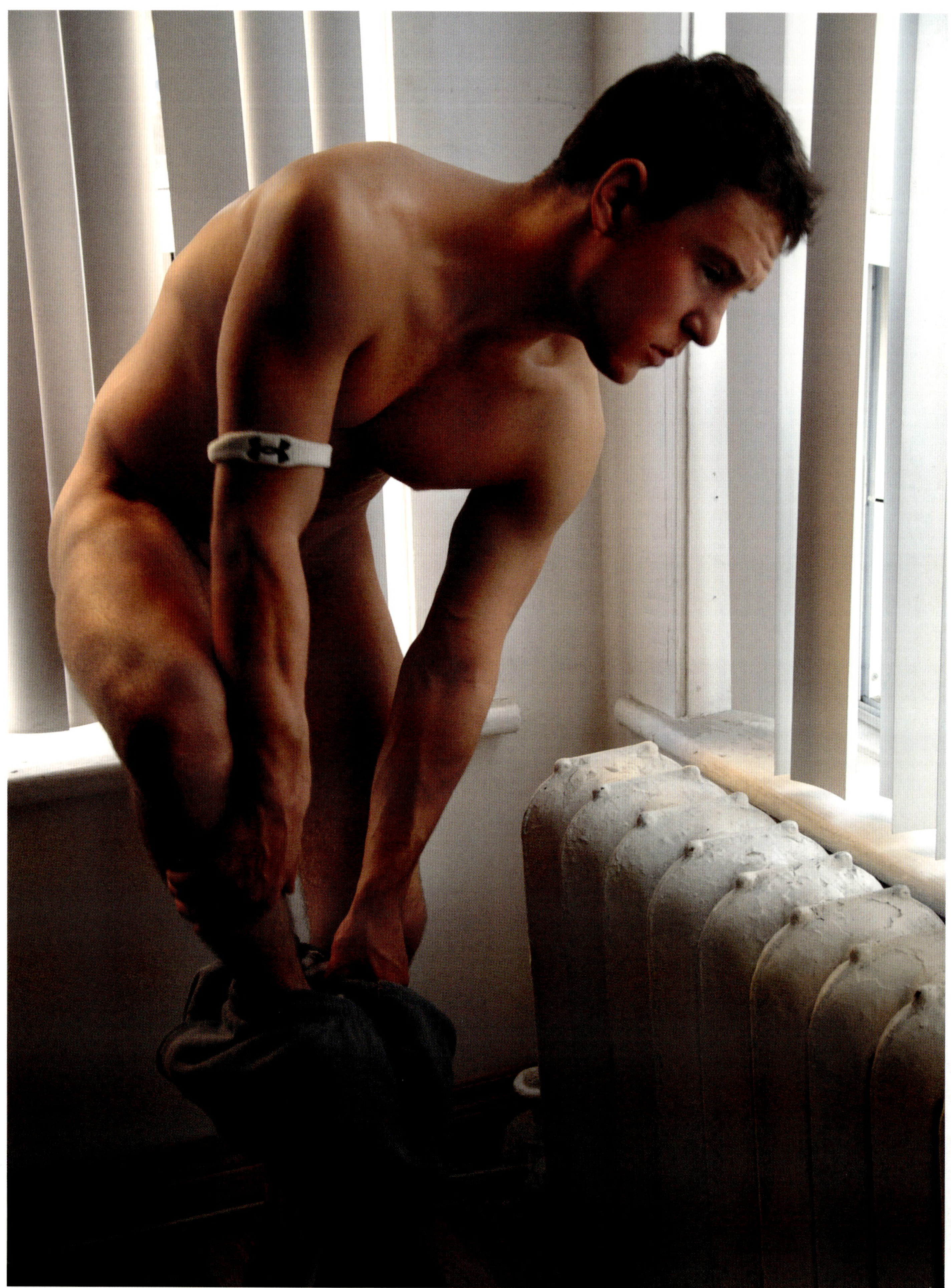

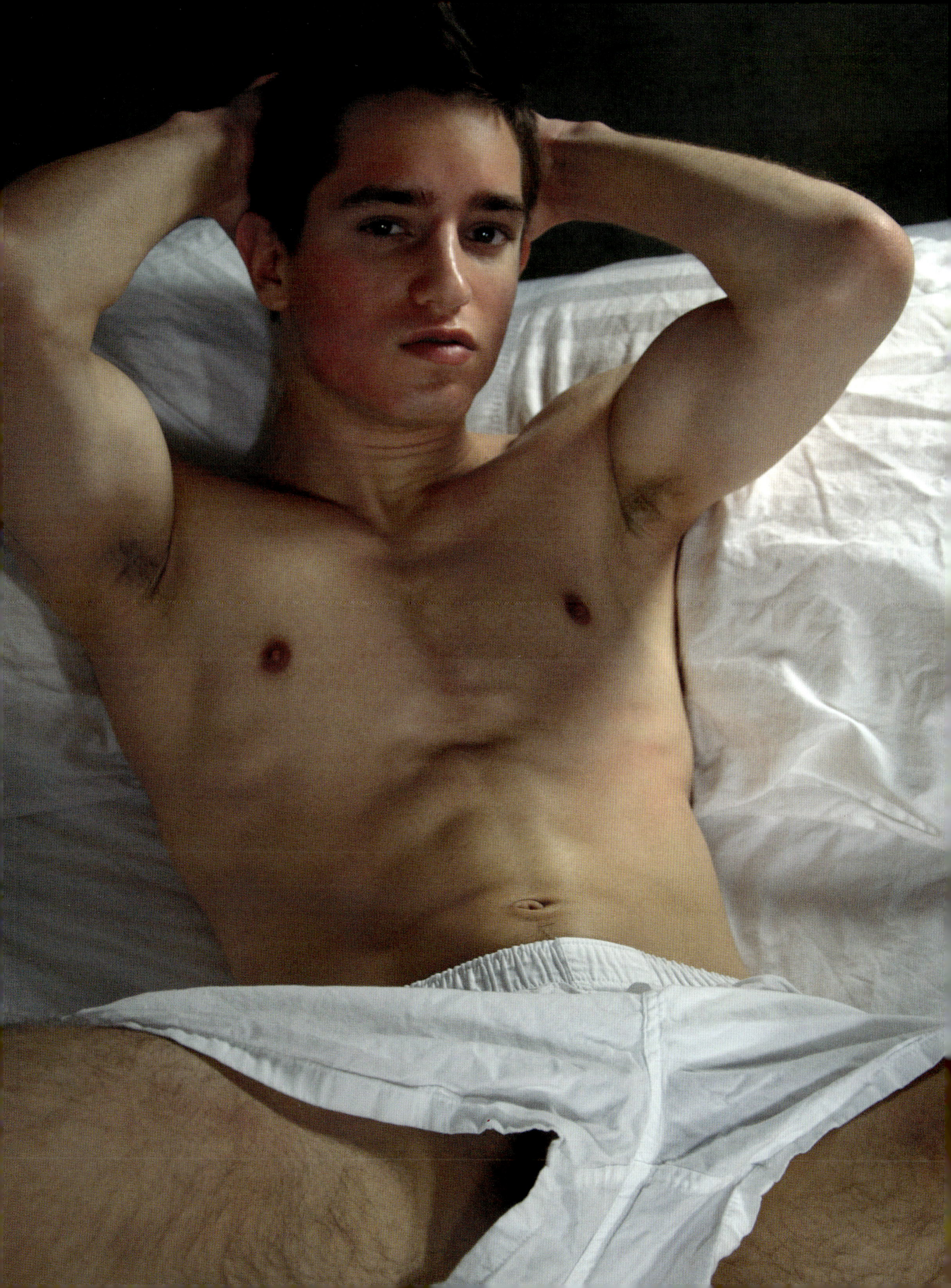

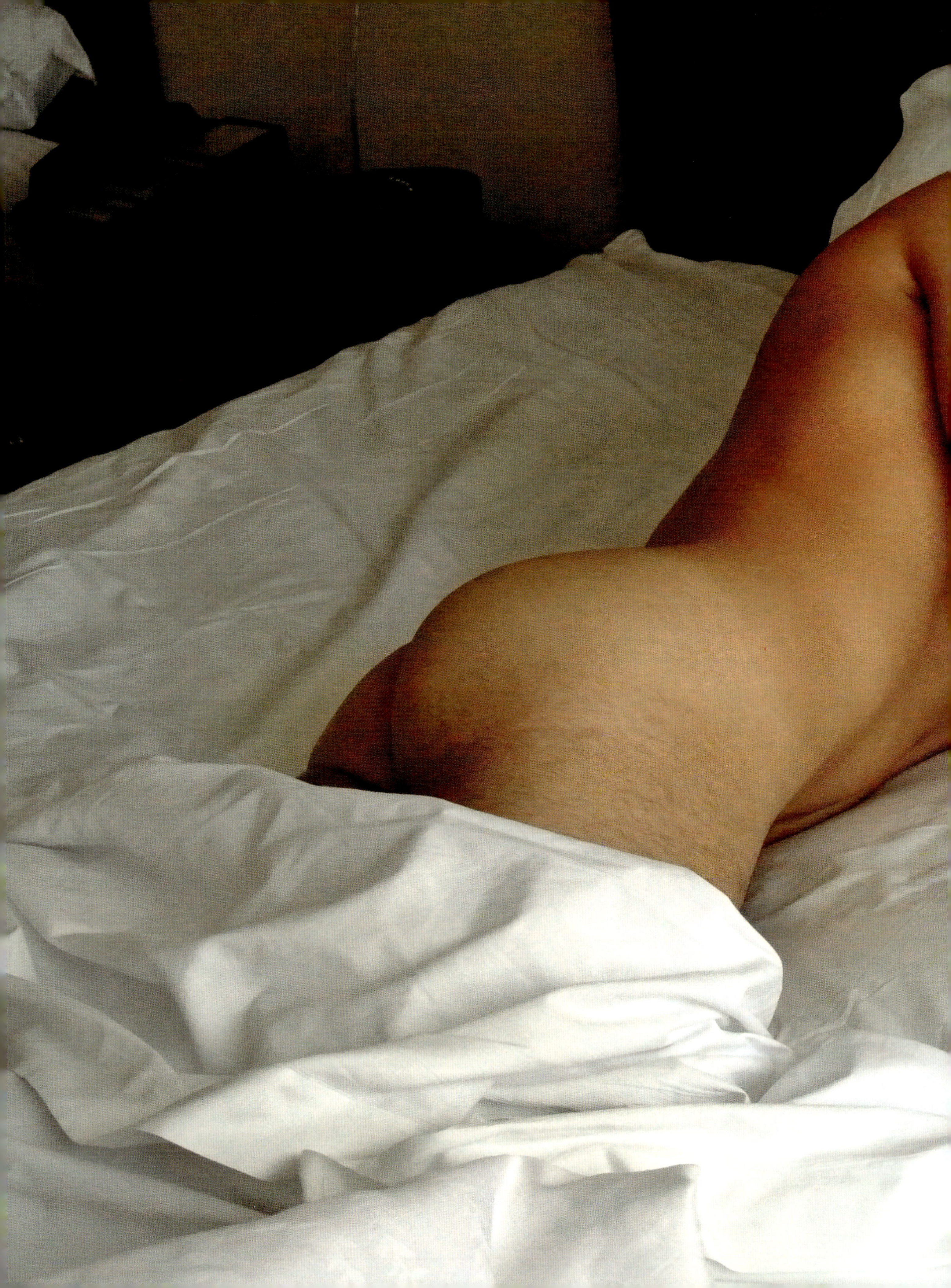

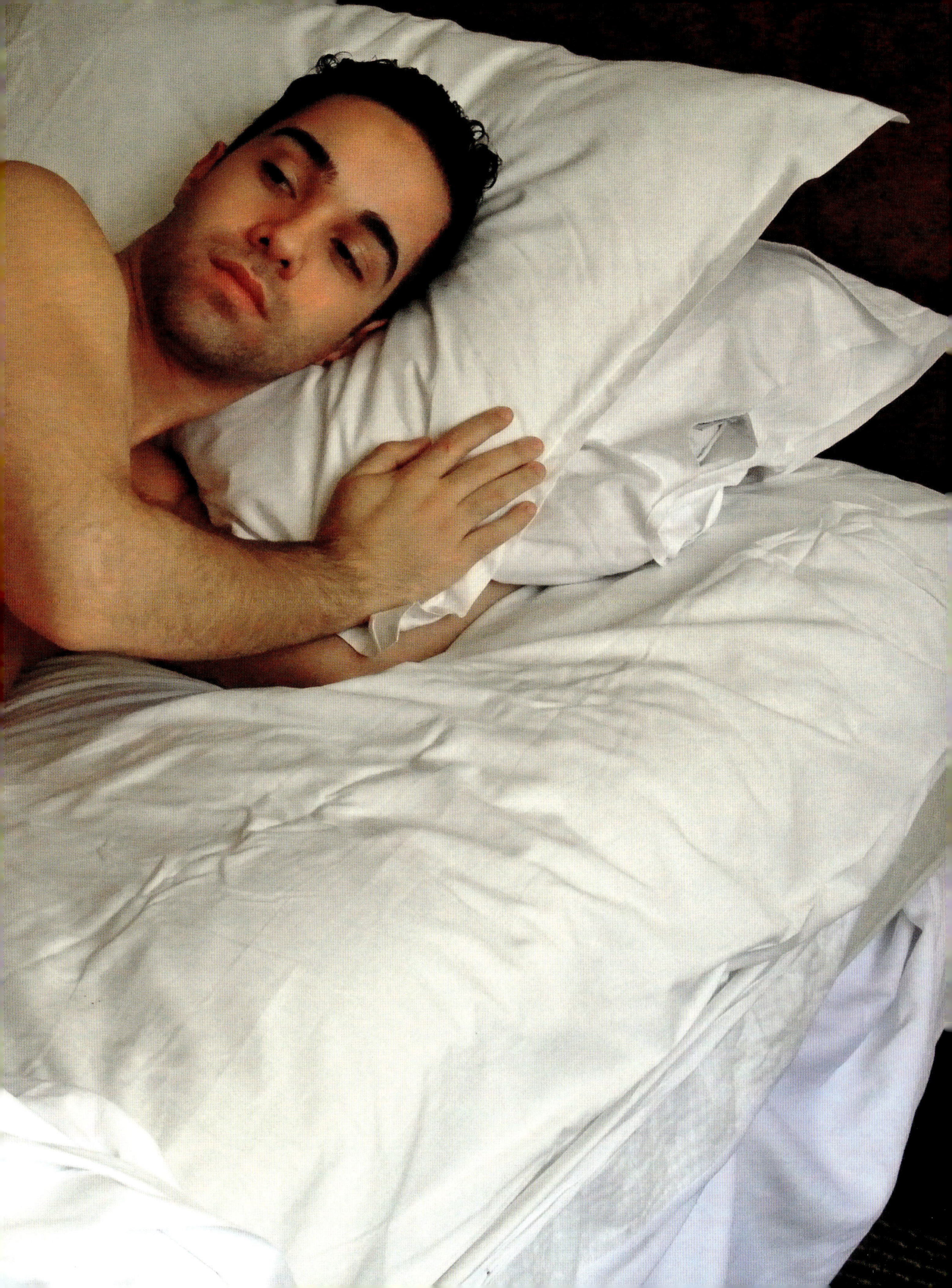

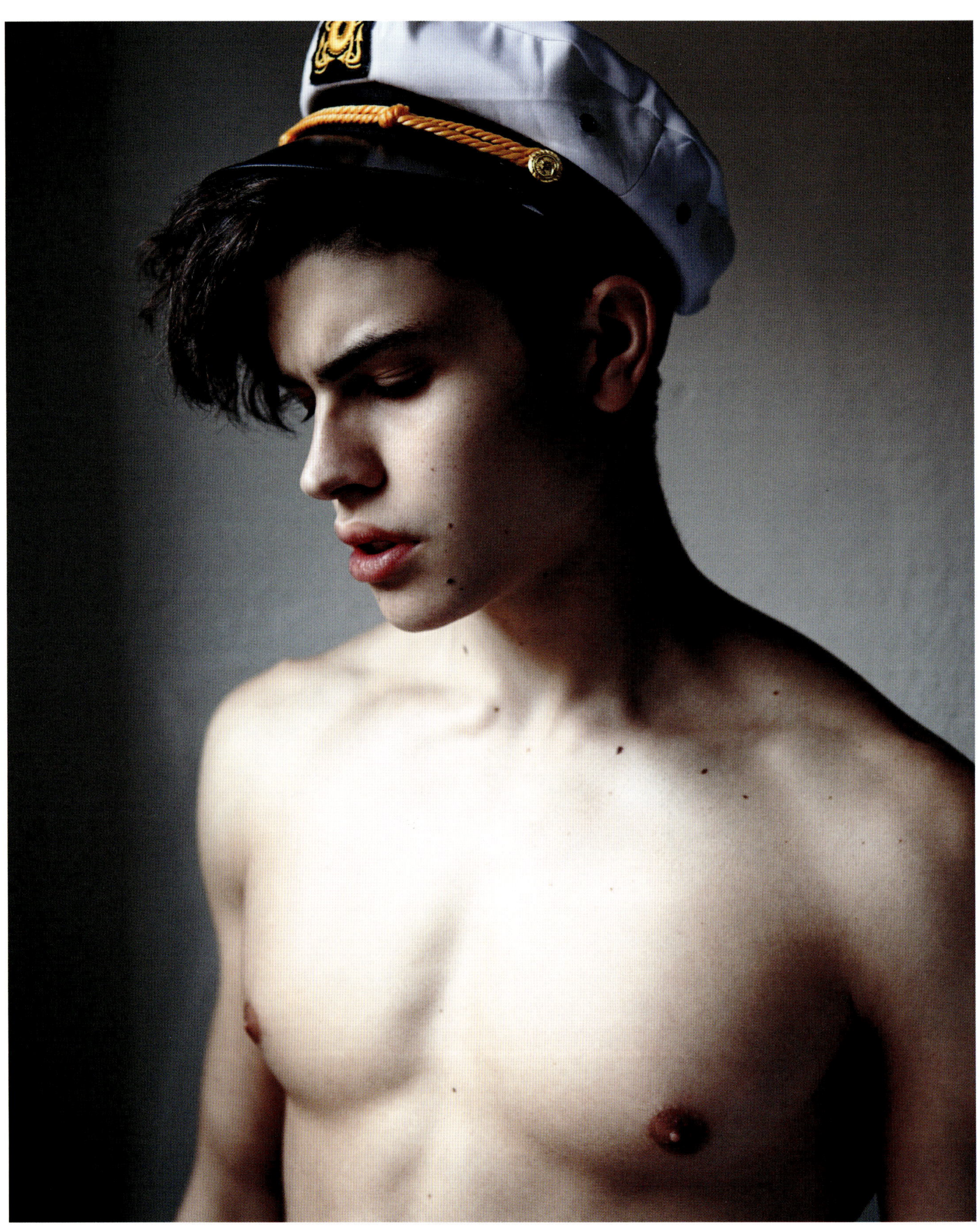

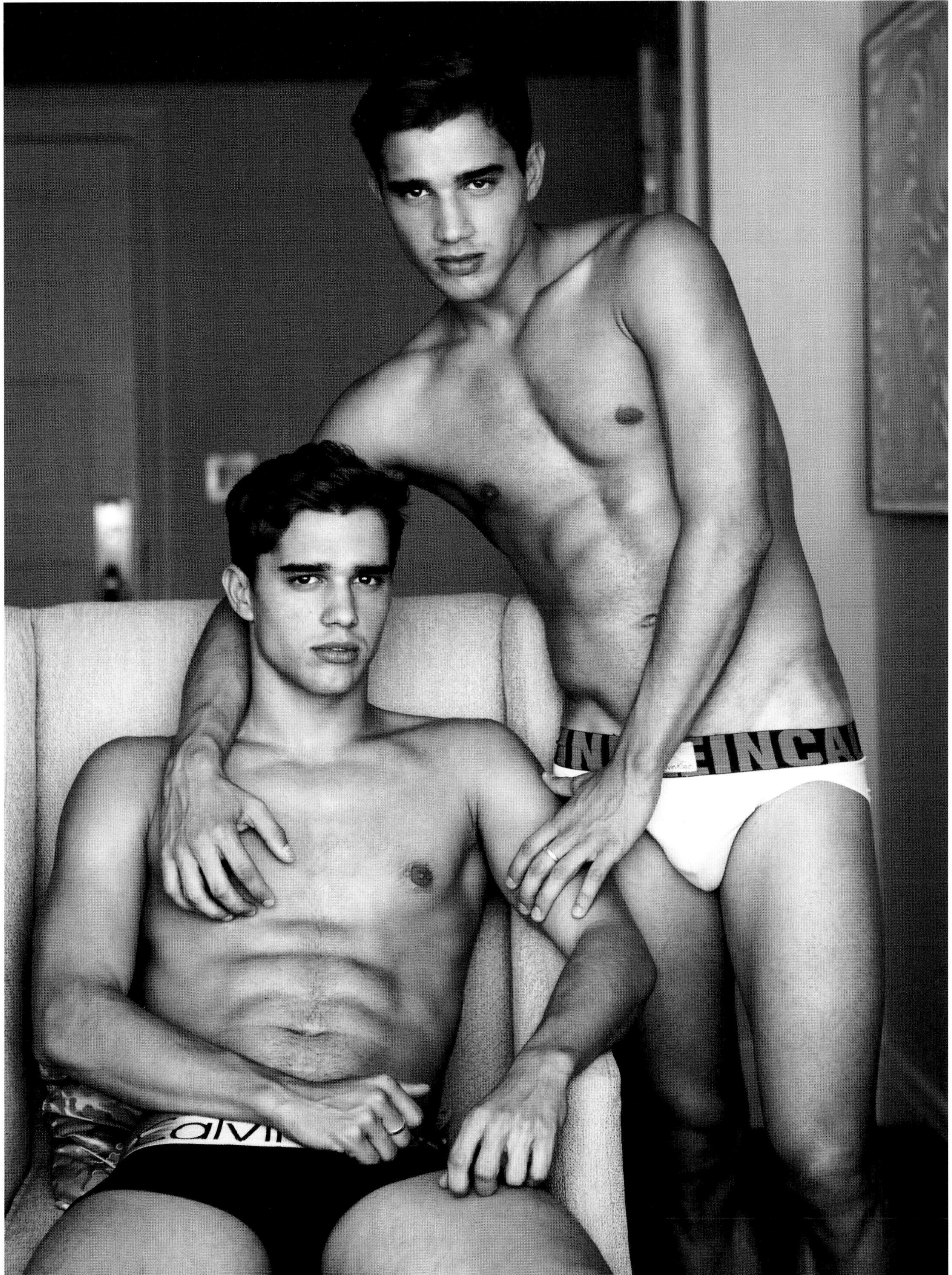

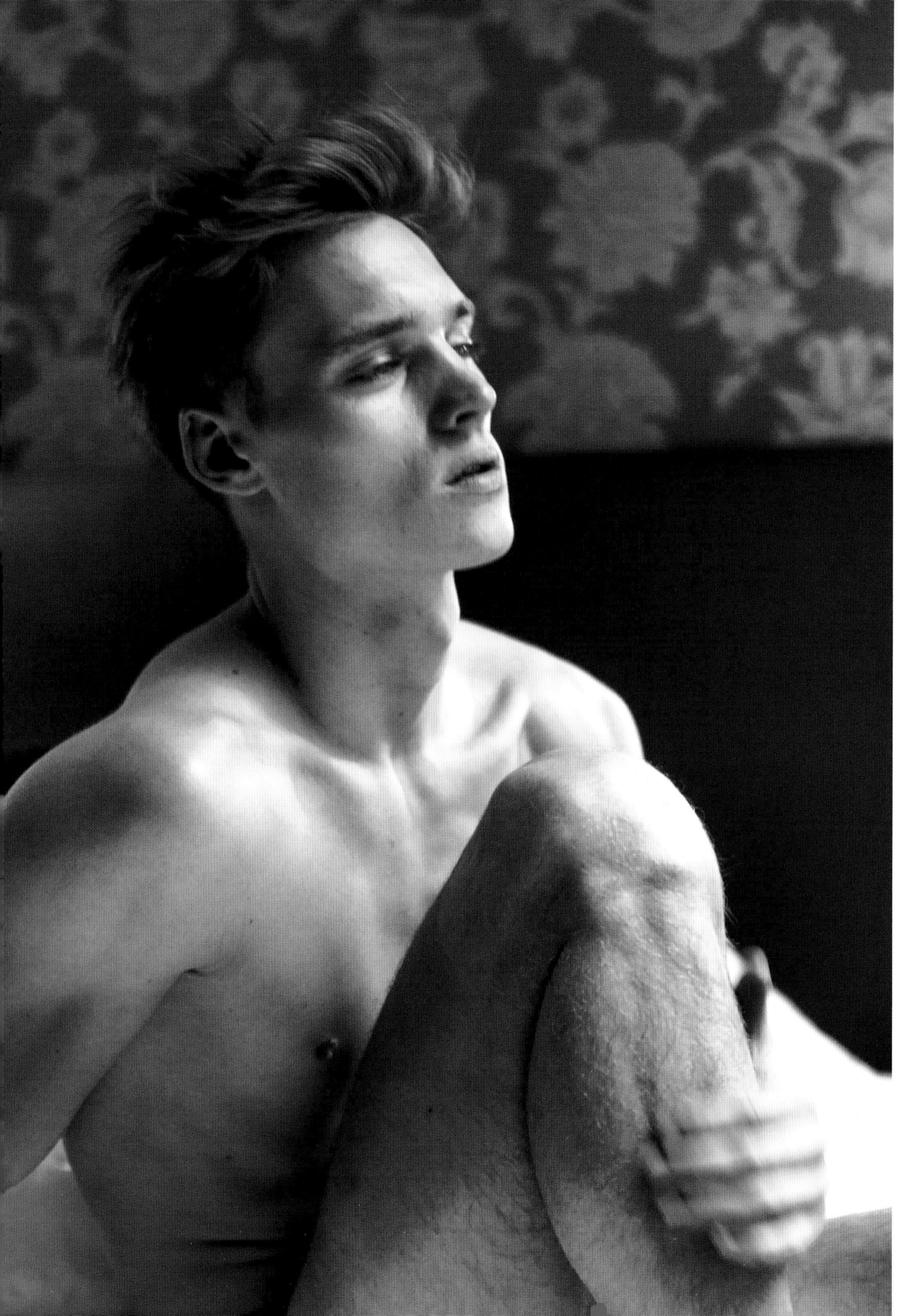

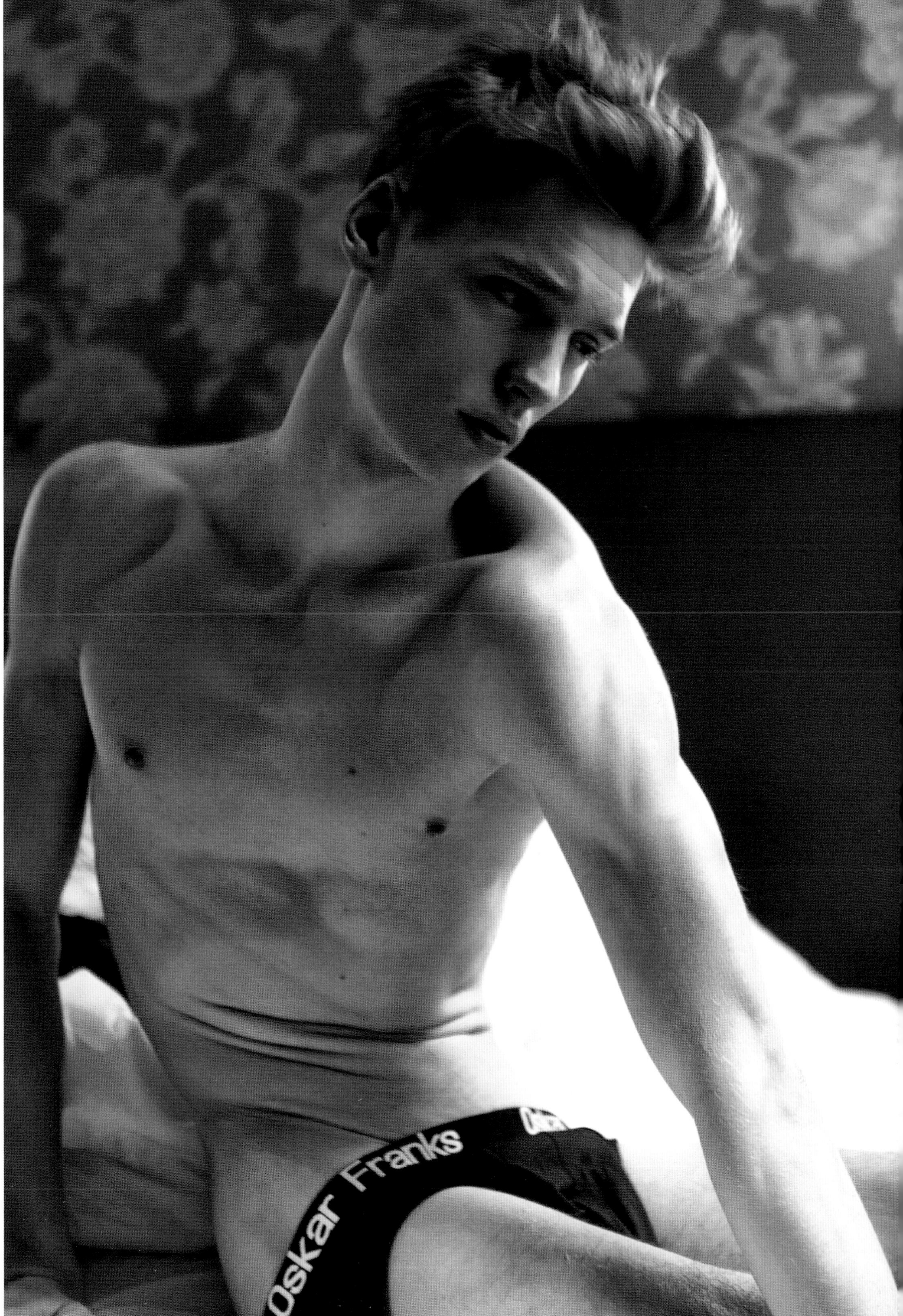
Oskar Franks

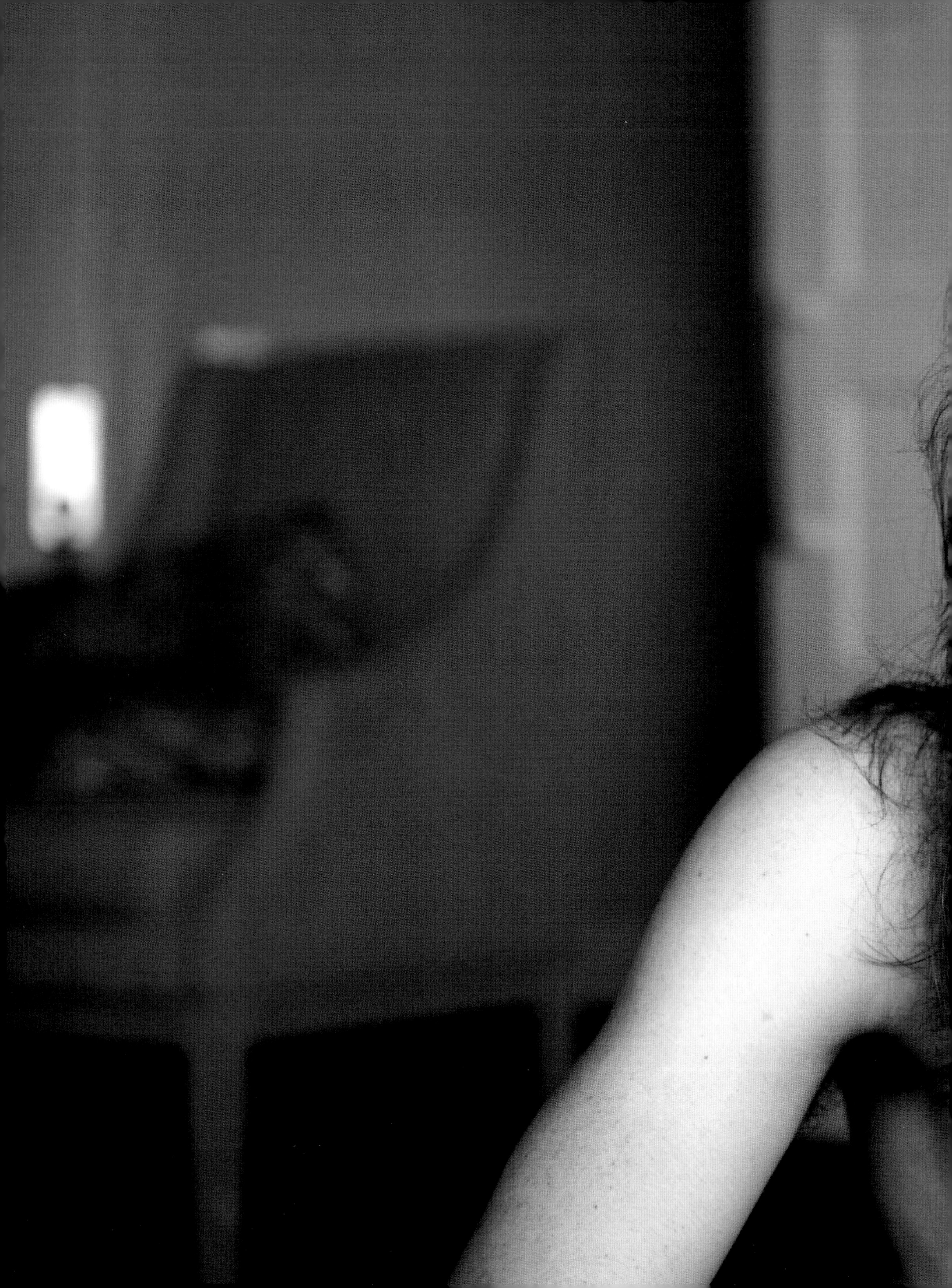

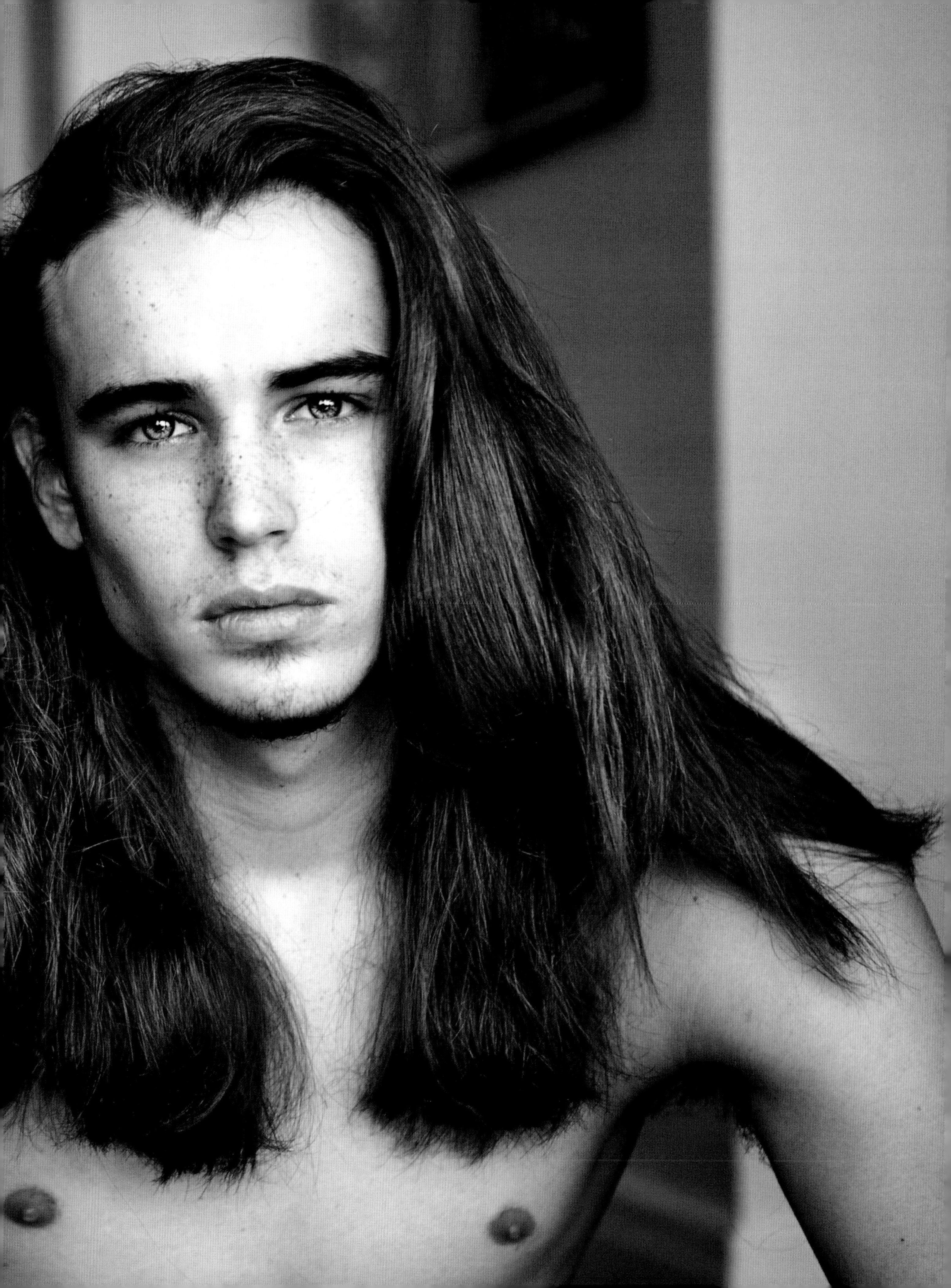

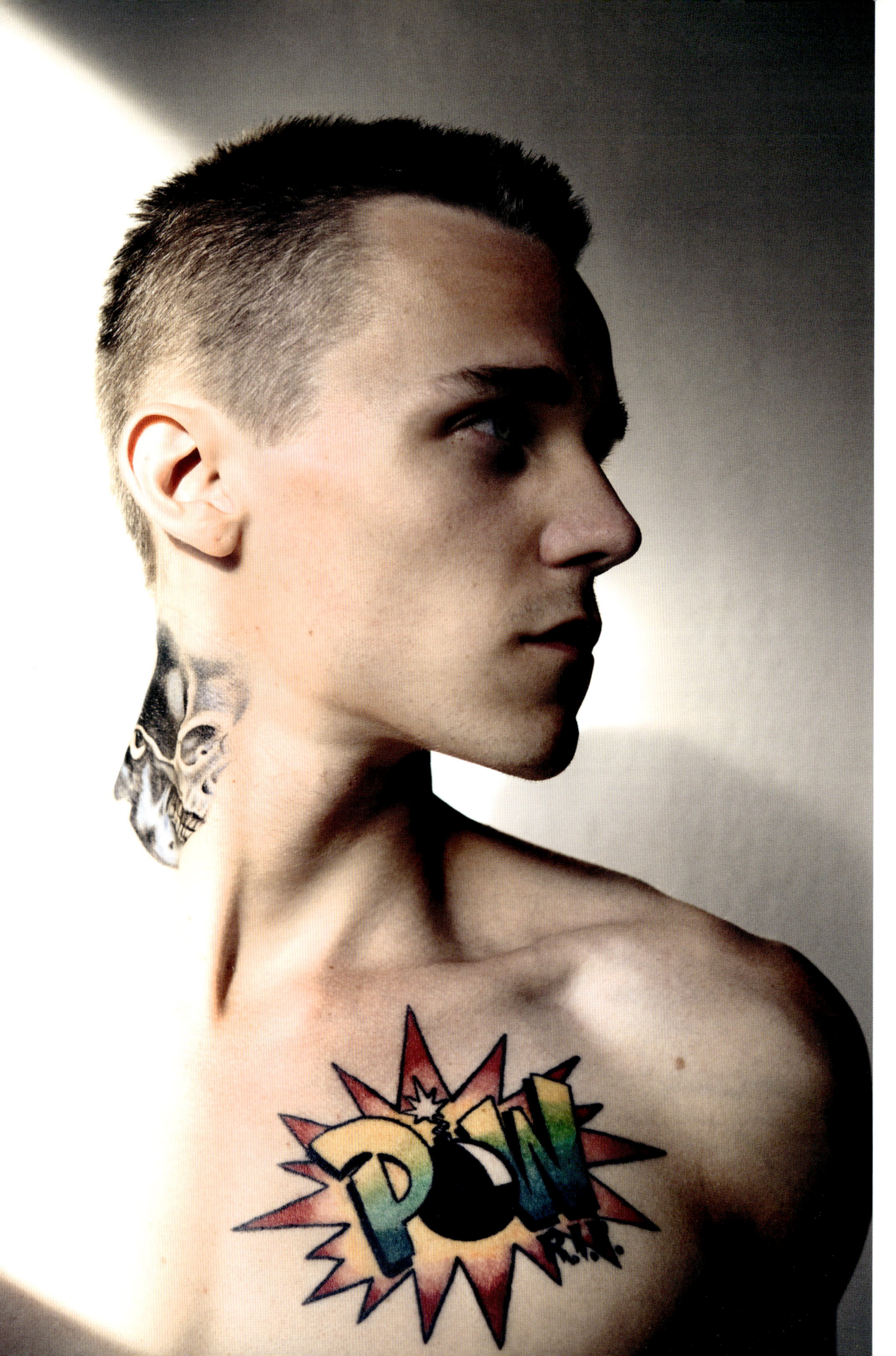

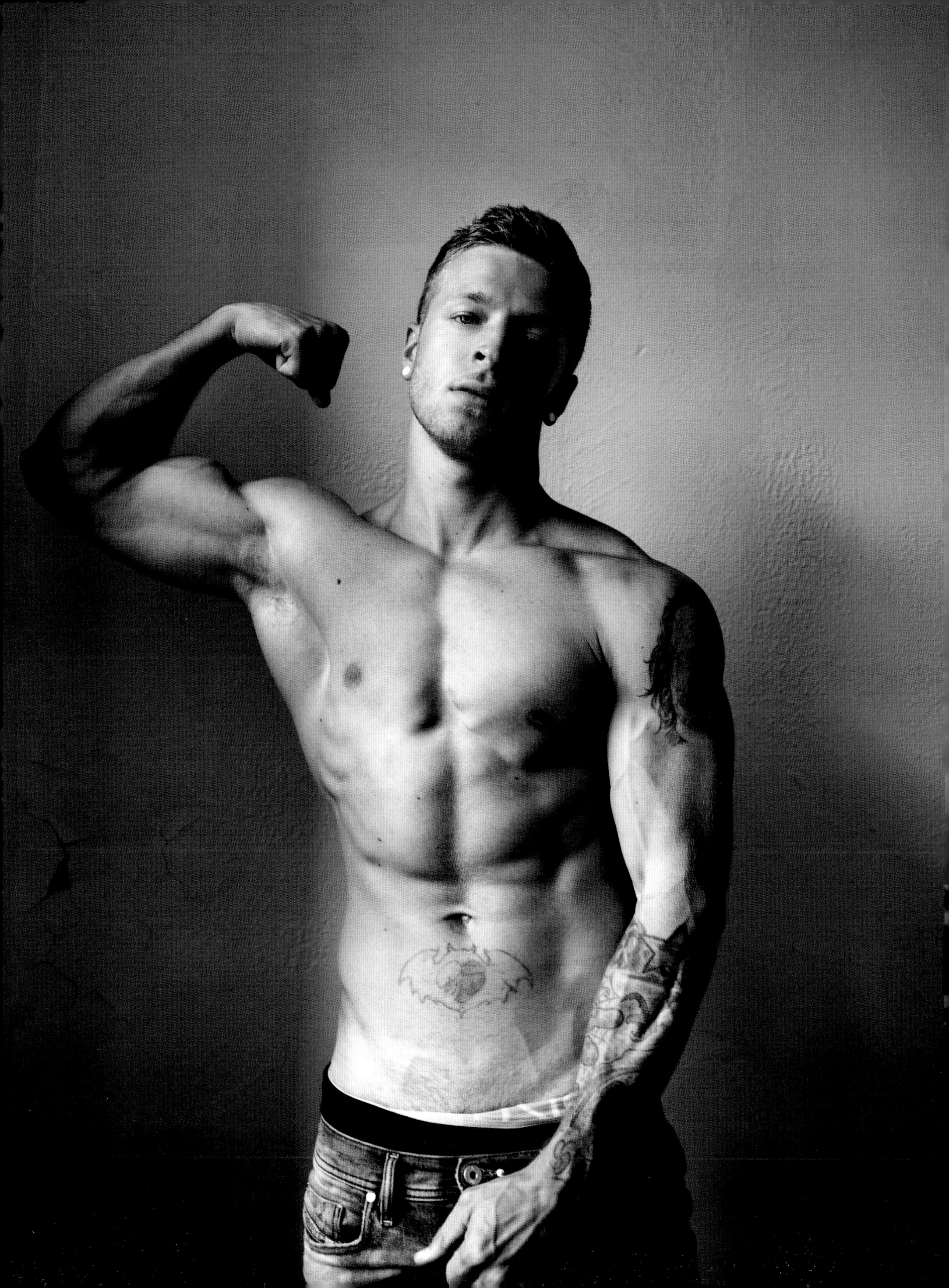

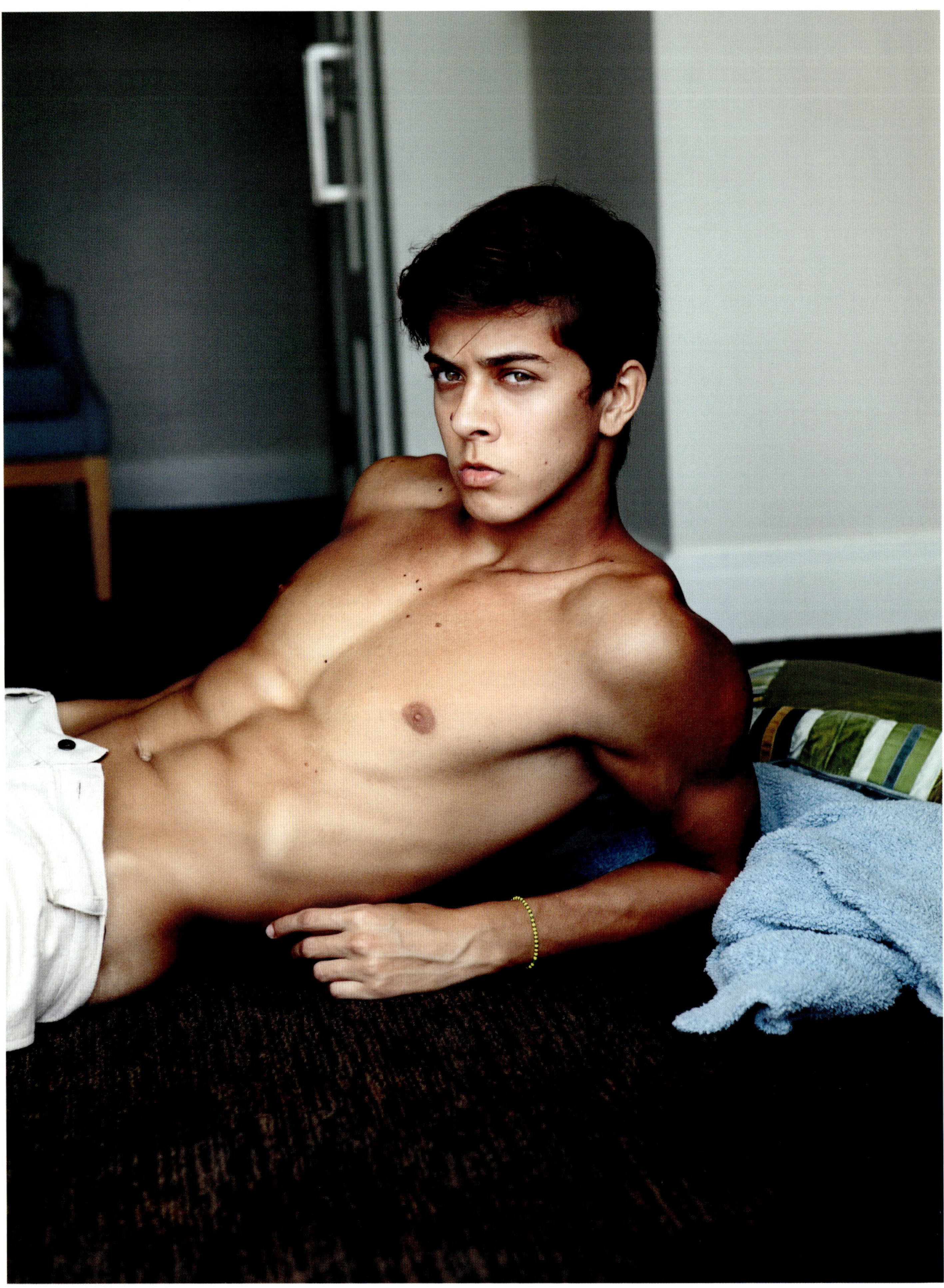

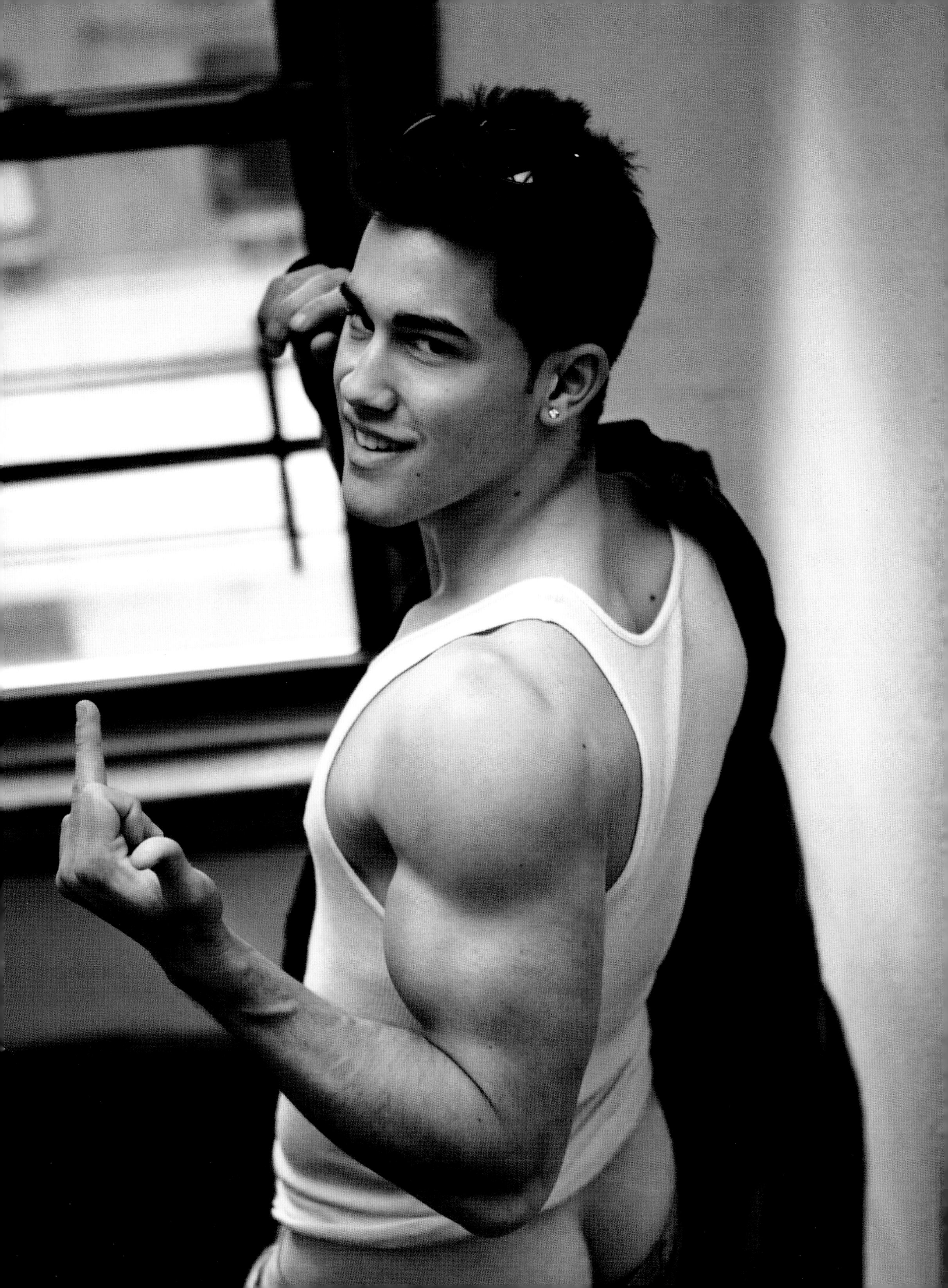

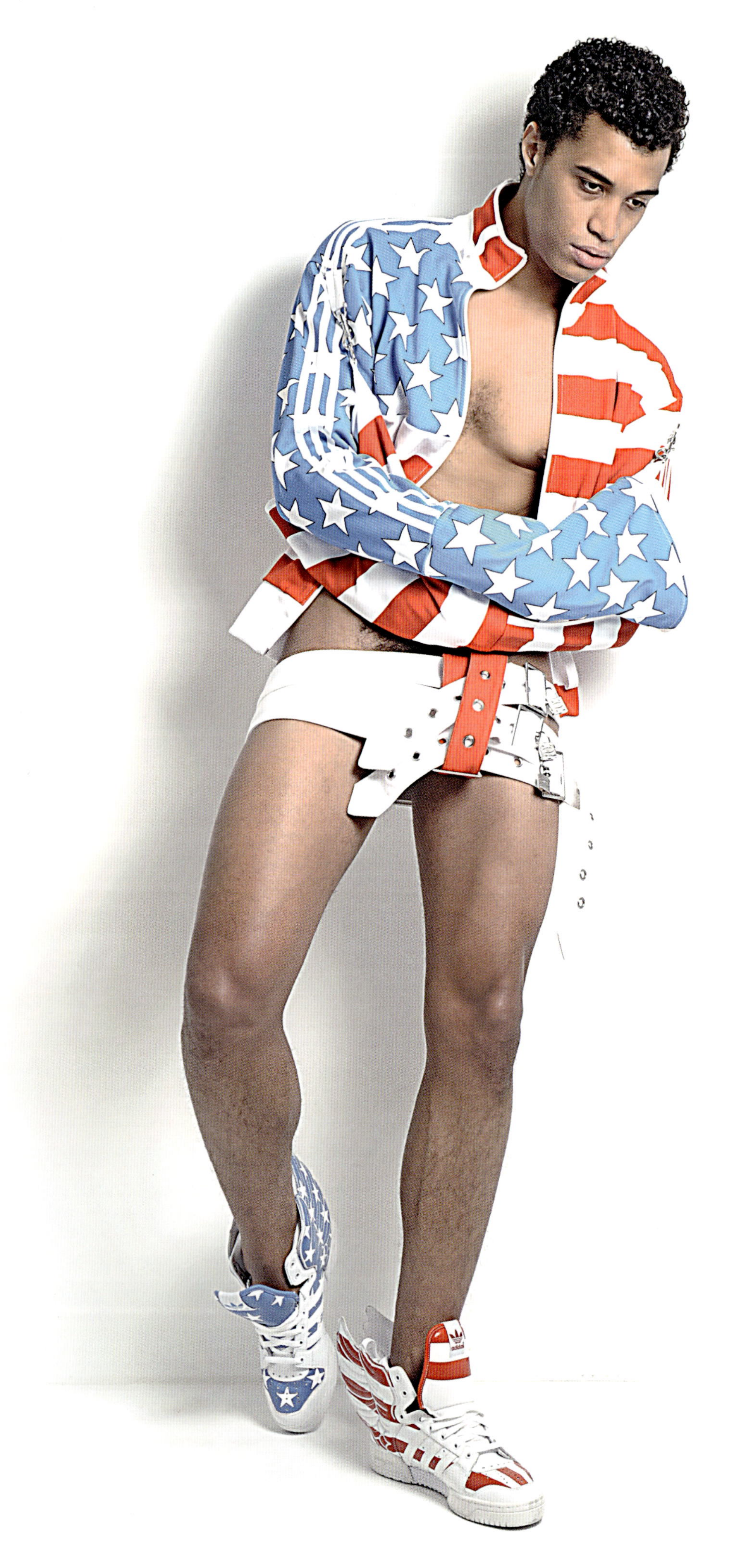

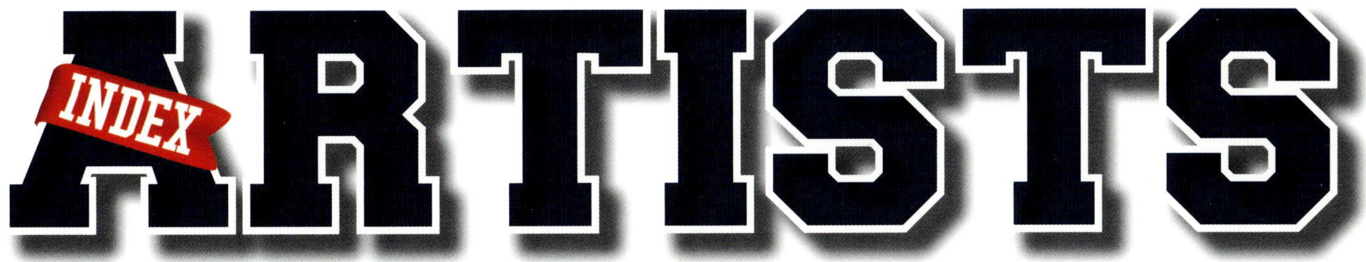

ARTISTS INDEX

Michael ANDREW
Germany
www.michaelandrew.net

Sandro BROSS
Switzerland
www.sandrobross.ch

Bartlomiej CHABALOWSKI
Poland
www.chabalowski.com

Jay DIERS
USA
www.jaededartstudios.com

Ian FRASER
UK
www.1stclassmale.co.uk

Cameron FROST
USA
www.cameronfrost.com

Jerome HAFFNER
France
www.jeromehaffner.com

Kevin D. HOOVER
USA
www.kiddmedia.com

Ethan JAMES
USA
www.ethanjamesphotography.com

Mark LYNCH
USA
mark@marklynch.us

Patrick METTRAUX
Switzerland
www.patrickmettraux.com

Byron MOTLEY
USA
www.byronmotley.com

Ed OLEN
USA
www.edolenphotography.com

Ohm PHANPHIROJ
USA, Asia, Australia
www.ohmphotography.com

Paul REITZ
USA
www.paulreitzphoto.com

Anton Z. RISAN
UK
www.atelier-az.org

Arno ROCA
Indonesia
www.arnoroca.com

JP SANTAMARIA
Spain
www.juanpablosantamaria.com

SBASTIEN
Spain
www.sbastien.com
Models: Mario Cardete (Barcelona)
Xavi Castan (Francina Models)

Allan SPIERS
USA
www.allanspiers.com

TeeJott
Germany
www.teejottmodels.wordpress.com

Chris TEEL
USA
www.christeel.ca

Justin VIOLINI
USA
www.justinviolini.com

© 2013 Bruno Gmünder Verlag GmbH
Kleiststraße 23-26, D-10787 Berlin
Phone: +49 30 61 50 03-0
Fax: +49 30 61 50 03-20
info@brunogmuender.com

Editor-in-Chief: Mischa Gawronski
Art Director: Steffen Kawelke
Editorial Coordination: Simeon Morales
Final Layout: Robert Schulze
Pre Press & Print Management: Zwei G Consult

Cover by Michael Andrew
Image titel page by Bartlomiej Chabalowski
Image intro page by Paul Reitz
Image artist page by Sandro Bross
Back cover image by Michael Andrew,
Sandro Bross, Ethan James and Paul Reitz

Printed in South Korea

ISBN: 978-3-86787-500-4

Check out all of our books:
www.brunogmuender.com